Also by Donald Johanson

JOURNEY FROM THE DAWN: LIFE WITH THE WORLD'S FIRST FAMILY
(with Kevin O'Farrell)

LUCY: THE BEGINNINGS OF HUMANKIND (with Maitland A. Edey)

LUCY'S CHILD: THE DISCOVERY OF A HUMAN ANCESTOR
(with James Shreeve)

BLUEPRINTS: SOLVING THE MYSTERY OF EVOLUTION
(with Maitland A. Edey)

ANCESTORS

ANCESTORS

In Search of Human Origins

DONALD JOHANSON,
LENORA JOHANSON,
AND
BLAKE EDGAR

VILLARD BOOKS
New York   1994

Villard Books is a registered trademark of Random House, Inc.

NOVA® is a registered trademark of the WGBH Educational Foundation.

Grateful acknowledgment is made to Jay Matternes for permission to
reproduce "Shanidar 1, Neandertal Reconstruction Painting" by Jay Matternes.
Copyright © 1981 by Jay Matternes. Reprinted by permission.

Library of Congress cataloging-in-publication information is available.
ISBN: 0-679-42060-6

Book Design by Signet M. Design, Inc.
Book Layout by Barbara M. Marks/Barbara Marks Graphic Design
Illustrations by Ian Everard
Maps by Carolyn Fish

Manufactured in the United States of America on acid-free paper

2   3   4   5   6   7   8   9

FIRST EDITION

*To my parents,
Donald and Joan, who
inspired my journey of
curiosity, and to Melissa,
who walks alongside.*
—B. E.

*To the Afar people,
whose friendship and
participation in our
research has greatly
enhanced the knowledge
of our origins.*
—D. C. J.

*To Bob and Helen,
for your unending faith
and support, even though
you never knew quite
what to expect.*
—L. C. J.

ACKNOWLEDGMENTS

FOR ASSISTANCE WITH THE HADAR RESEARCH Project, we thank Ethiopia's Ministry of Culture and Sports Affairs, the Center for Research and Conservation of Cultural Heritage, the National Museum of Ethiopia, and the Ministry of Mines. Special thanks go to Dr. Kassaye Begashaw, Mr. Jara Haile Mariam, Constantinos Tesfa Tsion, Mr. Tadessa Terfa, and Dr. Berhane Asfaw.

Our close friendship with the Afar people continues to play a vital role in our work at Hadar. We are indebted to the Afar Liberation Front, Sultan Ali Mira, Malo Seko, and Habib Bolku for their assistance. Recreational Equipment Incorporated (REI) provided generous discounts on camping equipment, and Apple Computer kindly supplied the team with Powerbooks. For funding our fieldwork we are indebted to the National Science Foundation, the National Geographic Society, and the L.S.B. Leakey Foundation.

Many people gave generously of their time and knowledge in appearing on camera, granting interviews, and in reviewing portions of the manuscript. We wish to thank: Ofer Bar-Yosef, Tim Becker, Lewis Binford, Robert Blumenschine, C. K. Brain, Al Deino, F. Clark Howell, Rhys Jones, William H. Kimbel, James Kitching, Misia

Landau, Michel Lorblanchet, C. Owen Lovejoy, Ann
MacLarnon, Henry McHenry, Michel Menu, Bill Neidjie,
Yoel Rak, Paul Renne, Kathy Schick, Sileshi Semaw, Pat
Shipman, Nigel Spooner, Chris Stringer, Alan Thorne,
Nick Toth, Alan Walker, Robert C. Walter, and Tim
White.

Advisers for on-location filming included: Norbert
Aujoulat, Paul Bahn, Robert Bégouën, Scott Cane, Jean
Clottes, Hilary Deacon, André Debenath, Herb Friedl,
Maurice Miller, Jean-Philippe Rigaud, Francis Thackeray,
Hugo van Lawick, Robert Ware, and the staff of the Well
Baby Nursery at Alta Bates Hospital in Berkeley.

The Hadar Research Project has been extremely successful because of the extraordinary dedication of every
participant. We particularly wish to thank Bob Walter and
Bill Kimbel, co-leaders with DCJ of the Hadar Research
Project, friends and colleagues whose skills, knowledge,
and dedication provided the foundation for the success of
the 1990–1993 field seasons. We are also indebted to
Michael Black and Michael Tesfaye for their energy,
enthusiasm, and good humor in their efforts to coordinate
camp logistics.

We extend our appreciation to colleagues James
Aronson, Tadiwos Asebwork, Alemayehu Asfaw, Zelalem
Assefa, Ray Bernor, Gerald Eck, Craig Feibel, Mulugeta
Feseha, Tekele Hagos, Jack Harris, Erella Hovers, Nanci
Kahn, Yoel Rak, Paul Renne, Sileshi Semaw, Solomon
Teshoma, Carl Vondra, Tamrat Wodajo, and Tesfaye
Yemane for their contributions to the scientific accom-
plishments of the project. We are particularly grateful to
our Addis-based crew and to our Afar friends, without
whose generous spirit and hard work our research could
not have been undertaken: Omar Abdulla, Doud

Abrahim, Dato Adan, Alemu Admassow, Edris Ahmed, Dato Ahmedu, Maumin Alehandu, Mulugeta Ayalew, Ahmed Bedaru, Abrahim Digra, Wubishet Fantu, Mohammed Gofre, Ese Hamedu, Hamedu Humet, Alayu Kassa, Meles Kassa, Getachew Kifle, Alemayehu Kneko, Hamedu Meter, Dato Michael, Abdu Mohammed, Mohammed Omar, Malo Seko, Getachew Senbato, Humud Waleno, Ali Yesuf, Alemayehu Zerihun, and Assaye Zerihun. Alan and Stella Broomhead provided welcome help in Addis.

At WGBH-TV, we wish to thank Paula S. Apsell, Evan Hadingham, Lauren Seeley Aguirre, William Grant, and Dick Bartlett. At Green Umbrella Ltd., our thanks go to Peter Jones, Michael Gunton, and Emma Fenton. For special effects, we thank 422 Video Graphics and Lyons Model Effects.

We appreciate the support and efforts of Don Cutler at Bookmark and Diane Reverand, our editor, and Alex Kuczynski and Amanda Murray at Villard Books. Victoria Nelson contributed her editorial expertise and thoughtful advice to the final manuscript. Ian Everard and Carolyn Fish, respectively, created the wonderful illustrations and maps.

We are particularly grateful to the Institute of Human Origins' Board of Directors for their support and encouragement throughout this project. Tom Hill, chairman of the board, was particularly helpful, and David H. Koch, treasurer, provided crucial financial support for the television series. Finally, the entire staff of the Institute of Human Origins, particularly Nanci Kahn, Eric Meikle, Al Miller, Pam Moody, and Larissa Smith, deserve special thanks.

FILM SERIES CREDITS

Series producer: Peter Jones
Producer/director: Michael Gunton (program one),
Lenora Carey Johanson (program two),
Lauren Seeley Aguirre (program three)
Production coordinator: Emma Fenton

Cameramen: Brian McDairmant, Richard Ganniclift,
Michael Fox, Alex McPhee, Mossi Armon, Ian Savage,
Tim Metzger, Mickey Freeman

Camera assistants: Duncan McCallum, Mark Zagar,
Mike Robinson, Eyal Zehavi, Hilary Morgan

Sound recordists: Fraser Barber, Chris Izzard,
John Osborne, Israel David, Saul Rouda

Electricians: Terry Hunt, Art Freyer

Actress: Ailsa Berk

NOVA
Science editor: Evan Hadingham
Film editor: Dick Bartlett
Associate producer: Lauren Seeley Aguirre
Executive editor: William Grant
Executive producer: Paula S. Apsell

CONTENTS

ANCESTORS

CHAPTER ONE

Prologue to a Mystery:

Return to Hadar

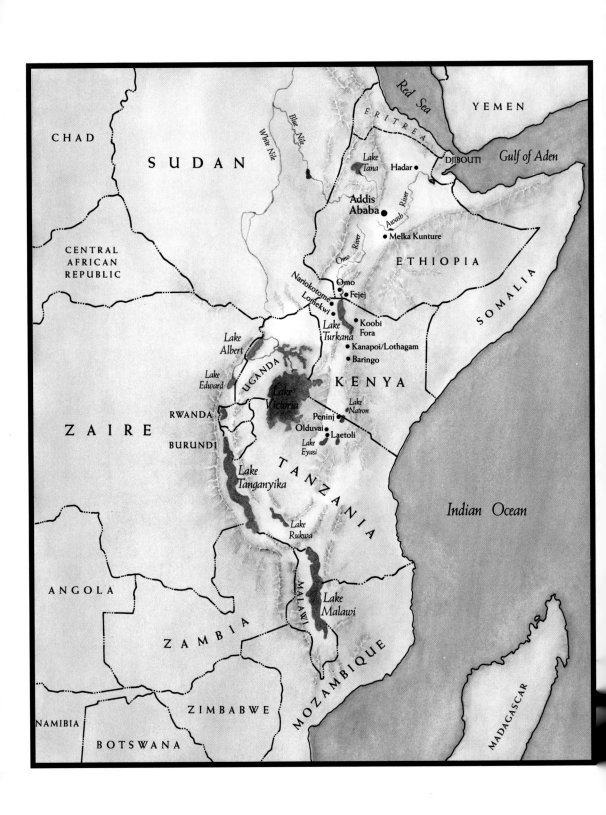

I HAVE TWO STORIES TO TELL. BOTH ARE COM-
plex, interconnected dramas whose full scope can only be
hinted at in these pages. The bigger of the two is, quite
simply, the 4-million-year epic of human evolution.
Behind this vast narrative is the adventure of the investigators over the last 150 years who have helped stitch its
various pieces together. As one of the many players dedicated to interpreting the saga of human origins, I want to
begin by taking you on a journey across the world and
back in time to the place I know best, where my own
story and what we know so far about the first episode of
the human story converge.

That place is a remote spot called Hadar, in northern
Ethiopia, at the top of Africa's Great Rift Valley. Located
in the Afar Depression, a funnel-shaped region due west
of the Horn of Africa, Hadar is a cornucopia of fossil animal remains. Two of the massive tectonic plates that form
the Earth's crust—the African and Arabian—meet here
and wage an ongoing geologic tug of war. The slow
grinding and shifting of the plates for the
past 30 million years formed the Afar
Depression and an even more magnificent
feature: the Great Rift Valley, a scar that
reaches one eighth of the way around
the globe, from Israel to Mozambique,
in a generally southerly direction. The
plates grind constantly, now and then
causing earthquakes and eruptions. The

*Donald Johanson discovered
this complete lower arm bone, or
ulna, at Hadar in 1992.*
IAN EVERARD

*Map of East Africa with
prehistoric sites.* CAROLYN FISH

bright volcanic ash that covers the ground at Hadar has prompted the Afar people of this region to call it the "place of the white river." This sometimes gradual, sometimes violent tectonic action also forces long-buried fossils to the Earth's surface, where they are exposed to erosion by wind and water.

Going back to Hadar means many things to me. Personally, it means returning to the field and my research, the primary location I've been excavating since 1973. At a deeper level it means going to the source, the root—where the bones of our oldest known ancestors lie. But my last journey to Hadar was one I had not expected to make.

In January 1992, my longtime associate Bill Kimbel, director of paleoanthropology at the Institute of Human Origins, went to Ethiopia intending to study some of the fossils stored at the laboratory of the National Museum in Addis Ababa. The Institute had helped to establish this lab and to train the Ethiopian researchers who worked there. Shortly after Bill arrived in Addis, he was told that Hadar might be accessible for fieldwork. The news delighted Bill, who like me has learned to leap at any opportunity to get into the field.

The government of President Mengistu Haile Mariam, an army colonel who came to power after the violent 1974 coup that toppled the forty-four-year reign of Emperor Haile Selassie, was never able to control the remote northern part of the country, where heavily armed rebel groups and rival tribes created a volatile atmosphere of antagonism toward each other and toward the central government. Furthermore, in 1982, the government declared a moratorium on all foreign research into prehistory. For the next eight years I could only wonder how many fossils were washing away with each year's rains

At the remote site of Hadar in northern Ethiopia, wind and rain gradually expose the fossilized bones of human ancestors that lived more than 3 million years ago. Fossils that revolutionized theories of human evolution have been found at Hadar since the 1970s, and in 1992 a team from the Institute of Human Origins returned to make further discoveries. D. C. JOHANSON

while the government revised its antiquities regulations. The Ministry of Culture and Sports Affairs also wished to update its storage and research facilities so that fossils no longer had to leave the country. In the past I had been burdened with the responsibility of safely transporting irreplaceable Ethiopian fossils to the United States for further study, and I sympathized with the Ethiopian government's concern to keep the fossils where they belong.

In 1990, I was allowed back to Hadar with an Institute team for two months. The long and frustrating hiatus had ended, but reacquainting ourselves with the terrain was time-consuming and we had to retrain our eyes to spot the fossils. Our eventual discovery of the partial fossil remains of fifteen humanlike creatures, or hominids—

At this barren-looking spot in 1974, Donald Johanson discovered Lucy, a 3.2-million-year-old hominid skeleton. Finding hominid fossils eroding from the ground involves looking in likely places and being in the right place at the right time.
D. C. JOHANSON

including some with new anatomical details—speaks for the richness of Hadar as a place to pursue the human past; we have never failed to find significant fossils there.

Following that successful season, we made plans to mount another expedition in the fall of 1991. When President Mengistu fled Ethiopia in May of that year as rebel forces converged on the capital, our plans were again stalled. Bill had arrived the following January, while the political situation remained tense. Now, when he heard the news that we might soon return to Hadar, Bill knew a few obstacles still remained. He would need to get official permission from both the government in Addis and the Afar Liberation Front, the group that controlled the region around Hadar. While securing government permission, Bill drove north to the village of Dubti for a visit with Afar officials. He explained our research goals and offered assurances that we would have Afar guides with us at all times. The discussions lasted several hours, but Bill, an able negotiator, came away with the permission he sought.

We all knew the good news by fax within twenty-four hours. I was in South Africa with a film crew shooting footage for the three television programs that would make up *In Search of Human Origins*. The startling bulletin from Bill meant that with a little judicious scheduling I could bring a television crew to Hadar for the first time. The crew could only come toward the end of the season, which itself would last a mere five weeks. I would be, as always, under tremendous pressure to produce. Would we find anything significant—or anything at all—in that small window of time?

On February 12, 1992, Charles Darwin's birthday, I stopped in Nairobi, Kenya, on my way to Ethiopia to rest for a few days. After an uneasy night's sleep, I wrote in my palm-sized field notebook, "I'm very concerned about what's in store for us in Ethiopia." I always feel anxious at the beginning of a field expedition, and this hastily arranged season made me particularly nervous. I had never come to Hadar at this time of year before, and I had been warned to expect heavy rains and even flash floods that might strand us for days in the camp overlooking the Awash River.

One of the prime advantages of belonging to an independent research organization like the Institute of Human Origins is the flexibility of its members to regroup quickly, unhindered by traditional teaching responsibilities. Though some of our colleagues could not break away from previous commitments to join us in the field without warning, a group of seven journeyed from several directions to Addis after a frantic scramble to obtain visas and pack equipment in Berkeley. The days are long gone when it's fruitful to look for fossils alone, and that fact led me in 1981 to found the IHO as a center where scientists from the different disciplines could combine efforts to make and interpret new discoveries. Accordingly, the 1992 group represented three of the disciplines that must collaborate in the field to achieve some understanding of our origins: paleoanthropology, archeology, and geology.

The IHO team, led by Bill Kimbel, myself, and Bob Walter, converged at the Ethiopia Hotel in Addis and met our Ethiopian scientific colleagues from the National Museum who would join us in the field. In a storage garage behind the museum's paleoanthropology laboratory, we found our four vehicles and field equipment, all a bit dusty but ready for the expedition ahead.

Before leaving Addis, we made sure we had all the food we would need for the first half of the season, when one of the vehicles would return and stock up again. Hadar has no convenience stores; if we forget yeast, we go without bread. We made sure we had essentials such as salt and sugar as well as fresh produce, peanut butter, honey, and cases of Kool-Aid. We squeezed those supplies into the trailers towed by our two Land Cruisers, alongside the equipment retrieved from our storage garage in Addis: tents, sheets of plywood and stakes for camp tables, linoleum to lay a firm floor beneath the tents, drums of gasoline, empty metal drums for water, and a water pump.

The journey from Addis to Hadar, about 375 miles, took us three days. I rode in the lead car, one of the Land Cruisers. The senior member of the Hadar vehicular team, a 1968 Land-Rover workhorse that we call the Blue Goose, brought up the rear. We headed north along the main paved highway that links the capital with the port of Aseb on the Gulf of Aden, planning to drive to Awash Station the first day, spend the night, and then travel about 150 miles to Odaitu. Then we would cross the Awash River and head northwest on a gravel road toward the western escarpment of the Rift Valley and Hadar.

We spent the first night on the road at a decaying hotel in the town of Awash Station. Before dawn we were back in the vehicles and heading to Odaitu, where we came upon an independence celebration for the Tigrean People's Liberation Front, one of the groups that had fought Colonel Mengistu's government for years. Bursts of red and blue tracer bullets streaked across the night sky and bright flares exploded overhead as crowds of shadowy figures milled in the darkness. It looked as if we had stumbled upon a skirmish. We pressed on in the dark, moving quickly if somewhat uneasily for the next forty-five minutes until we reached a plodding line of trucks that we joined for the next leg of the journey.

By midday we reached our destination for the day, Odaitu, a truck stop and repair facility, where we split off from the big pack of trucks. Bill Kimbel and geologist Bob Walter took one of the vehicles to a nearby village and paid a call on Ali Mira, the sultan of the Afar. Bill had been unable to see Ali Mira on his visit the previous month but wanted to thank the sultan personally for giving us the opportunity to enter his territory again. Meanwhile I went with Mike Black, who runs the IHO paleoanthropology lab, to meet with Mohammed Hundi, the regional head of the Afar Liberation Front. As we sat on a dirt floor and drank cups of dark, strong coffee, Mohammed gave our work his blessing. It pleased him, he told me through an interpreter, that people around the world recognize the importance of the Afar region in their distant ancestry. "It is an Afar tradition that all people are one," Mohammed said. "The color of skin is only a superficial difference."

During the three-day journey to Hadar, the team stops for coffee at a traditional coffee shop, or buna bet. *This woman roasts and grinds her own beans and uses her fire to boil water inside the long-necked pot.* D. C. JOHANSON

We left Odaitu early on the third morning. The smooth tarmac soon gave way to loose gravel, signaling the final leg of the trip. Instead of going straight to camp, however, we had to drive nearly two hours north of Hadar to pick up our Afar guides and guards in the village of Elowaha. These men happen to be keen fossil hunters as well; an Afar can spot a hominid tooth from standing height with the sun in his eyes.

•   •   •

A stoic group of Afar herdsmen stood waiting as we pulled into Elowaha. They wore colorful striped and checkered cloths around their waists, ammunition belts across their shoulders. Each of them carried a Kalashnikov rifle. One man I was particularly pleased to see in that crowd was Dato Ahmedu, a respected elder of his clan and a member of my field team for twenty years. A broad smile crossed Dato's weathered face as he caught my eye.

Dato Ahmedu is a veteran fossil finder and a clan elder of the Afar people who live around Hadar. While he was herding his goats at Hadar, Dato discovered a hominid lower jawbone before the research team returned in 1992. Dato's find led to a flurry of fossil discoveries during the first week of the expedition. IAN EVERARD

"Salaam Alekium," I greeted Dato. "Peace be with you."

"Alekium Salaam," he replied.

We shook hands and completed the formal greeting by kissing each other's hand three times.

In the midst of the chaos—children playing underfoot, trucks hurtling through the village, herds of goat and sheep kicking up dust clouds—we exchanged greet-

Young Abdu proudly displays his prize possession, a Kalashnikov rifle. One of the Afar guards who accompanied the fossil hunters to Hadar in 1992, Abdu appointed himself Donald Johanson's personal bodyguard.

D. C. JOHANSON

ings in three languages—English for us, Afar for the local residents, and Amharic for our Ethiopian colleagues from Addis Ababa. When words failed, we turned to hand gestures. No interpreters were needed to express our happiness at being so close to Hadar again.

Out of the multilingual mix I heard one of the Ethiopian government representatives tell me, "Dato thinks he has already found a hominid for you."

"That's wonderful. Let's leave soon so we can reach Hadar before dark."

Dato's expression turned serious. He was anxious about returning to Hadar now. He and the other Afar had once lived near Hadar, but they had moved because of an ongoing rivalry with a neighboring tribe. "We cannot guarantee there will not be trouble," Dato said, "but Hadar is our territory, and we will do our best to protect you."

We repaired to the rear of the local bar to discuss how much protection we might need. We made a conspicuous group: the Institute team, the government representatives, twenty Afar, and an associate of the sultan. A braying donkey tethered nearby punctuated our discussion. Knowing we were heading into a remote and volatile frontier, we agreed to take five men with us, four Afar and a Tigrean, Meles Kassa, another veteran of many field seasons. A fifteen-year-old Afar named Abdu, looking far too young to be carrying a rifle, decided he would be my personal bodyguard. Even though it was late afternoon when we finished, the team voted to resume the journey immediately and reach Hadar before nightfall.

From Elowaha we headed south with our new passengers and a wicker basket carrying chickens purchased at a local market. When we came to a flat, featureless gravel plateau, we drove as fast as we could while avoiding the small gullies that ate into its surface. An hour later we came to a steep drop-off at the edge of the plateau. Before

The final leg of the journey to Hadar from Addis Ababa takes the team's vehicles across rugged terrain and through a maze of gullies strewn with boulders.

D. C. JOHANSON

us a landscape of knobby hills jutted from the ground like the knuckles of a clenched fist. A series of dry river drainages sliced through the maze of volcanic deposits that held a rich assortment of fossils.

The vehicles wound down into the deposits one at a time and began the final hour's drive to camp. We entered one of the largest drainages, the two hundred-foot-wide Kada Hadar, and headed straight for the Awash River. Having made this trip so many times, we already knew which gullies were wide enough for a Land-Rover to pass through and which had enough clearance for us to drive around the boulders that might block our progress.

Soon we saw a fading glimmer of sunlight reflecting off the Awash River, the only source of water in this parched land. We were back in Hadar. Our camp remains in the same location I have favored since 1974. The landscape looks the same, except the beach where we once

The Hadar team's camp on a bluff by the Awash River includes an open-air dining tent, personal tents, a shower, and the Lucy Club field laboratory.
D. C. JOHANSON

This grass-walled hut on the edge of camp is the Lucy Club, a mini-laboratory where the scientists escape the afternoon sun at Hadar to study the latest discoveries.
D. C. JOHANSON

Fresh water for the team comes from the Awash River. In the background, Mike Black fills plastic drums with pumped river water. A compound called alum is added to settle silt and clay on the bottom of the drum. At left, Mike Tesfaye fills a second storage drum with clarified water before adding a purifier. D. C. JOHANSON

went for river swims has washed away. Lightweight nylon dome tents have replaced the heavy green canvas ones we used in the early expeditions. Tent after tent popped up on the bluff in the gathering twilight as our cook and his assistant set up the outdoor kitchen. The Afar serenaded us with a song of welcome about the small "city" we had brought from America to the banks of the Awash and the friendships we had made.

The field season was set to begin the following morning, on February 23. Though we still had trailerfuls of equipment to unpack, half a dozen of us could not restrain ourselves from using the remaining daylight to take a short drive and see what Dato had found in our absence. Dato directed us to the place where he had recently brought his herd looking for sparse patches of pasture—a dry riverbed called the Bouroukie Drainage. Even though we had driven past it countless times on the way to other sites, this place had never lured us. We knew the sediments here were younger than those in which we had found hominid fossils before, and in our experience the younger sediments at Hadar had never been fruitful. With such a short season ahead of us, we planned to focus

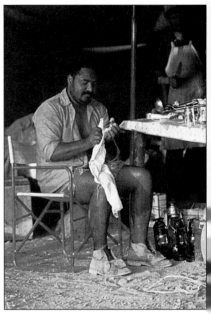

on areas where we were certain to find fossils, including some sites discovered as recently as 1990. We might have bypassed the Bouroukie Drainage yet again if Dato had not happened to lead his herd there.

Dato brought us to a spot in the gully where he had laid a ring of stones to mark the bone he had discovered. It was a hominid fossil, the left half of a lower jaw containing four teeth.

"You couldn't have given us a more fitting gift of welcome, Dato," I said. "This is fantastic—a hominid mandible."

"Look at the size of these molars!" Bill Kimbel exclaimed.

Geologists Bob Walter and Mike Tesfaye surveyed the site of Dato's find, trying to locate it within the larger picture of Hadar's geology. Crouching down for a closer look,

Morning in camp begins with hot tea or a cup of dark, rich Ethiopian coffee. Wild coffee has its origin in the highlands of Ethiopia, but it is in the volcanic maze of gullies beside the Awash River where the human line may have had its origin. D. C. JOHANSON

Getachew, the cook's assistant, dries dishes at the Hadar camp kitchen. D. C. JOHANSON

Geologists Bob Walter and Mike Tesfaye examine a layer of volcanic ash. Such ash layers serve not only as visible markers that help the scientists orient themselves among the vast fossil beds of Hadar, but also provide the raw material that allows geologists to date a site and place an age on a fossil found nearby.

D. C. JOHANSON

This hominid lower jawbone, or mandible, was discovered by Dato Ahmedu when he passed through Hadar with his goats. The fossil turned up in an area of Hadar that had never been explored before because it was thought to lack fossils. This jawbone turned out to be the first in a series of discoveries during an unusually short fossil hunt in 1992.

D. C. JOHANSON

Bob recognized this layer of volcanic ash from its color and texture; he had previously dated it to 2.9 million years ago. The jawbone had eroded from a spot about fifty feet below this layer, so it was probably 3 million years old, which made it 200,000 years younger than Lucy, the partial hominid skeleton I had discovered at Hadar in 1974.

Geologist Paul Renne sculpts a pedestal of ancient sediment. He will measure the direction of the Earth's magnetic field recorded in this sediment as a way to date the fossil-bearing levels at Hadar. This technique, called paleomagnetism, relies on the fact that the magnetic field has changed direction over time, and each change is captured in rocks of the same age.
D. C. JOHANSON

Until now, Lucy had been the youngest hominid discovered at the site. Lucy was an instant success. After 3.2 million years resting under Hadar's dry soil, she ignited the public's imagination in a rather amazing way. As the only representative of her species, Lucy became an ancestral ambassador of sorts. Everyone wanted to meet her, and she introduced me to more people than I ever expected to meet in my life. She is probably the best-known fossil ancestor ever found; people who don't recognize my name smile and nod when I mention Lucy's, as if I had mentioned an old acquaintance. She has even entered popular culture, immortalized in cartoons and on a postage stamp. In Ethiopia, where she is known in Amharic as *Dinquinesh,* or "wonderful thing," Lucy is a source of tremendous national pride. On the way to Hadar I sometimes make a short detour to the small village of Mile, where a hand-painted portrait of Lucy stands beside a building. Whenever I return to Mile, children welcome me as her father.

These days, though, when people ask me what I've been doing, I'm apt to say, "I'm still dating Lucy," because improvements in our dating techniques have allowed us to zero in on her age. We believe that Lucy lived 3.2 million years ago. Of the 250 hominid fossils we found at Hadar between 1973 and 1975 that led to the naming of a new species, *Australopithecus afarensis*, the earliest bones are from 3.4 million years ago. Dato's discovery—if it was 3 million years old—had allowed us to double our estimates as to the length of time that hominids lived at Hadar. To be absolutely certain, Bob would have to date samples of the sediment at the Institute laboratory in Berkeley, using "Flash Gordon," our argon-ion laser. He peered through his hand lens at some sand grains nestled in his palm and said that they looked large enough and pure enough to obtain a date from them.

The six of us spread out and scanned the ground for more fossils. After twenty minutes, Zelalem Assefa, a representative of Ethiopia's Ministry of Culture, called me

A hand-painted portrait of Lucy is displayed beside a building in Mile. D. C. JOHANSON

over to where he was standing. Zelalem's eyes were fixed on the sand at his feet. He had spotted a second hominid fossil, the right side of a lower jaw. It lay only 150 feet from Dato's discovery and was eroding from the same layer of sand.

Bob scanned a geologic map of Hadar on which he had marked rock outcrops and dozens of fossil sites. "We're almost off the edge of my map," he said. "There's not another hominid within a kilometer of here."

Whenever we find a hominid fossil, the site and each bone specimen is assigned a reference number. These mandibles promptly became A.L. 437–1 and A.L. 437–2, identifying them as the first and second bones from the four hundred and thirty-seventh Afar locality to yield fossils.

The fossil-hunting team assembles for breakfast under the canvas fly sheet and discusses the day's agenda. Donald Johanson sits at far right, next to co-leader Bill Kimbel. D. C. JOHANSON

After breakfast, the team begins work beneath a blistering sun. Some will walk for miles in search of new fossils. Others will head for the site of a previous hominid discovery and screen dirt through a wire sieve to search for more bone fragments. D. C. JOHANSON

Here was a case of real serendipity, since we had planned to focus on the younger sediments in this region. Now Dato's discovery encouraged our explorations to fill in what had always been a glaring fossil gap. We returned to camp buoyed by our unexpected good fortune even though we were exhausted from the hard trip. It was already too dark to set up the tables and canvas flysheet for our dining tent, so we sat on the ground and ate a hastily prepared spaghetti dinner, all the while slapping at the merciless camel flies that bit our legs.

On our second full day in camp, I awoke at my usual time in the field, around 5:30 A.M. The four-man kitchen crew had already been up for an hour; seductive smells of freshly baked bread and dark, strong Ethiopian coffee filled the air. By 6:30, the rest of the team appeared for a breakfast of toast and hot oatmeal. We had spent the previous day unpacking our gear and getting our water pump ready to bring water from the river. Now we were ready for the fossil hunt to begin in earnest, and our breakfast conversation focused on the day's work.

Mike Black and Bill Kimbel would lead the screening crew to the site of Dato's and Zelalem's discoveries. Before we decide whether to mount a full-scale excavation, the screening crew scrutinizes the surface sediment at each hominid site for more bones. The routine goes something like this: A pair of

Mike Black manages the paleoanthropology laboratory at the Institute of Human Origins and takes charge of the screening operations in the field at Hadar. D. C. JOHANSON

Geologist Bob Walter, shown with archeologist Sileshi Semaw, keeps track of nearly a million years of history preserved in the rock layers at Hadar. He recognized an ash layer near the initial 1992 fossil discoveries and informed the team that these finds were 200,000 years younger than any previous hominids found at the site.
D. C. JOHANSON

workers pile loose sediment into a sieve with a fine mesh screen and shake the sieve back and forth, sifting dirt through the bottom and leaving larger objects in the screen. The rubble left over is picked through in case any teeth or bone fragments have been caught. It's hot, dusty work—a bit like panning for gold without water.

Bob Walter and Mike Tesfaye planned to start at the new fossil site and walk along the Bouroukie Drainage to collect rock samples from the same sediment level where the new fossils had been found; Bob would take the samples back to the Institute laboratory for definite dating. Bob invited me to join him exploring an area he had been to the day before. We set off at 7:30 and hadn't gone far before Bob pointed out a large white object sticking up from the top of a cliff. It looked like it could be a bone or perhaps just a weathered, sun-bleached tree trunk.

Scrambling up the sandstone cap at the top of the slope for a better look, I could see that what Bob had spotted was an incredibly well-preserved elephant jaw. Other animal bones had eroded directly out of the surface of this gentle slope. Stooped in my fossil-hunting posture, knees bent and arms folded behind my back, I began pacing the area carefully. Before long, I saw some hand bones and the hip end of a femur. I picked up the thighbone and decided

After a hominid fossil is found, the surface sediment gets shaken through a screen to catch any tiny bone fragments that have been missed. The hot, dusty work is like panning for gold without water. D. C. JOHANSON

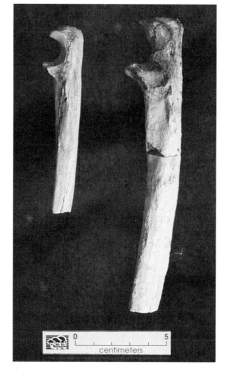

Buoyed by the team's discovery of two hominid lower jaws before camp had been set, Donald Johanson spent the third morning of the 1992 field season exploring the new territory at Hadar. He soon found himself staring at one end of a hominid arm bone, an ulna, that had been stopped by a clump of grass from washing into a ravine. The wrench-shaped end of this bone forms the elbow joint. D. C. JOHANSON

The first ulna fragment that Johanson found joined with a second fragment found later on the surface. Further excavation revealed the rest of the bone. Here the first two pieces of the new find, on the right, are shown next to the same bone from Lucy, the diminutive hominid skeleton found at Hadar in 1974. These two fossils demonstrate the wide range of body size that occurs in these hominids. D. C. JOHANSON

after a brief examination that it came from a medium-sized carnivore. I started to explore a small gully that branched from the main drainage. After an hour had passed, I realized that Bob and Mike might be wondering what had happened to me, and I set off to find them.

I looked down once more and found myself staring straight at the wrench-shaped upper end of an arm bone, or ulna, which everyone calls the "funny bone" of the elbow. I blinked and knelt by the bone, which had been stopped, fortuitously, by a clump of grass from washing down the gully. The bone was large, but I was still confident it came from a hominid, perhaps only because it was the same bit of anatomy that first caught my eye on the November morning in 1974, leading me to Lucy. I wanted to continue searching for more of this skeleton, but I decided to find Bill Kimbel and ask him to leave the screening crew and assist me. I marked the spot by sticking my rock hammer on a knoll above the fossil.

Bill and I walked back to the gully and hiked upslope. I showed him the bone. "There's something weird about it," he said. "A bone that big must be from a carnivore."

"I know it's big, Kimbel. It's twice the size of Lucy's ulna, but that's a hominid."

"I say carnivore."

"Let's see what Yoel thinks."

We went looking for Yoel Rak, an Israeli paleoanthropologist who had interrupted his anatomy lectures at Tel Aviv University to join us in the field. Yoel had looked furiously for hominid fossils at Hadar in 1990 but came up empty-handed. He said he couldn't leave this year without finding a hominid, and as an expert on the australo-pithecine face, what he *really* wanted was a skull, which had so far eluded us.

We found Yoel at Zelalem's hominid site. I offered him the ulna. "This is hominid, all right," he said, examining the fragment. Yoel, Bill, Zelalem, and I returned to the ulna site and began to look upslope from where I had found the fragment, in case any other bones lay on the surface. I found a bone from the palm of the hand, a second metacarpal, looking more like a fresh twentieth-century bone than one that had been buried for 3 million years. Soon Zelalem spotted a similar bone from the third finger. Farther uphill I picked up a fragment from the upper arm.

"Here's another piece of the arm," I called to the others.

This occipital bone forms the back of a skull, and the cross-shaped ridges mark the location of veins that drain blood from the brain. The fossil was found by Ethiopian government representative Zelalem Assefa and prompted Yoel Rak to lecture the other team members about how to search for skull fragments. D. C. JOHANSON

An expert on the faces of australopithecines, paleoanthropologist Yoel Rak could spare just a week in the field at Hadar in 1992. He hoped to find a hominid skull, something no one had achieved at Hadar. D. C. JOHANSON

centimeters

These are the pieces from an adult male Australopithecus afarensis *skull discovered by Yoel Rak. At top is the lower jaw. The bones remain stored at the National Museum in Addis Ababa, where they will be cleaned and reconstructed.* W. H. KIMBEL

Perhaps because Yoel was with me, I began mentally picturing skull fragments—smooth, flat, slightly dished pieces of bone. Then I blew away some soft sand in front of me and saw the edges of a pair of eye sockets. "Oh my God," I shouted. "Here's part of the skull. We've got glabella!" Glabella, one of the reference points used for skull measurements, is the most forward projecting part of the forehead, just above the bony ridge over the eye sockets.

Bill and our friend Tim White, of the University of California at Berkeley, had painstakingly constructed a Hadar hominid skull using fossil fragments from several individuals found in earlier expeditions and filling in the gaps where they lacked the actual bone by deduction. They had done it, however, without having this part of the forehead; this fragment would add an important new piece to the puzzle.

The fossil had not been exposed for long. Its broken edges showed no sign of wind or water damage; delicate, paper-thin bits of bone from the nasal sinus still clung to the back. "There should be a lot more bone out on the surface," I said to Bill. "These breaks are incredibly fresh."

"Either the skull's still in there or it's washed away," he answered.

"But if it washed away, you'd think there would be a flake somewhere. There'd be *something*. Even if this fragment came off a long time ago, maybe the rest . . ."

". . . just hasn't moved," Bill completed my thought.

I had a vivid picture of a skull buried beneath my feet.

Around noon Bob Walter and Mike Tesfaye returned from their sediment-collecting trip up the drainage. Our excitement drew them like a magnet. I showed Bob the hominid bones and challenged him to figure out where on the slope we might find the rest of the skeleton. We stayed at the site for another half hour while Bob and Mike looked around. These new bones had eroded from the same band of sediment beneath the ash layer that Bob recognized at the site of Dato's and Zelalem's discoveries, so they too were much younger than Lucy. We found a tooth root and another piece of the ulna that attached to the first fragment and then postponed any further searching; after the screening crew finished at the mandible site, they would come here, and we didn't want to damage or dislodge any bones by walking over the site. Before we left, we photographed the site, marked the location of each bone with a metal pin wrapped with red tape, and collected the fossils.

Every paleoanthropologist who has ever hunted fos-

Unperturbed by curious spectators, Bill Kimbel prepares to place a marker on the spot where he has removed a hominid fossil, part of the male skull found by Yoel Rak. D. C. JOHANSON

Yoel Rak scans the surface of a slope for more skull fragments, while Mohammed Gofre stands guard. Each nail wrapped with red tape marks the exact spot where a piece of hominid bone has already been found and collected.
D. C. JOHANSON

sils in Africa fantasizes about an ideal discovery. Yoel wanted a skull. I wanted a male *afarensis* skeleton, a companion for Lucy, so that we could finally learn just how much the males and females differed. I could scarcely believe that we had discovered at least part of one. As my own worst critic in the field, however, after returning to camp I swapped my field boots for sneakers and grabbed my copy of *Fraser's Anatomy.* With the fossils in front of me, I consulted the illustrations and reassured myself that we had indeed found a hominid.

On the third day of the expedition, Zelalem found his second fossil not far from the site of my discovery. It was an occipital bone, a piece from the back of the skull. As we discussed this discovery at lunch, Bill brought out a

cast of the same bone from a different Hadar specimen and compared it to Zelalem's new one. The cast came from a large male, one of thirteen individuals found at the so-called First Family site in 1975; it was older and bigger than the new find but looked essentially the same. Separated by 200,000 years, these fossils were almost identical—making a good case for little evolutionary change in this hominid species. From fossils found at a site south of Hadar, the Middle Awash, we know that *Australopithecus afarensis* existed as far back as 3.8 million years ago, so it seems to have lived for almost a million years, remaining remarkably similar for all that time.

Inspired by Zelalem's skull fragment, Yoel Rak gave us a pep talk about how to find a skull. He pointed out a characteristic *afarensis* feature on this bone: the compound crest where neck muscles once attached. Then he showed everyone the inner surface of the bone, which contains

A trio of fossil hunters gets an early start on the day's exploring, when the light is best for spotting bone and the temperature is below blazing. D. C. JOHANSON

grooves for veins that drain blood from the brain. With many of our team accustomed to spotting only jaw and teeth fossils—they preserve more readily than most bones—I hoped that his lecture would alert everyone to search for skull fragments.

The day after Yoel's lunchtime lecture, I drove with Bob Walter to a younger, more distant site where Bob had a sticky geological problem to solve. The site, known as Gona, has hundreds of stone tools—flaked pebbles and cobbles of lava—that may be the oldest example of human technology, some 2.5 million years old. The ash layers at Gona, however, do not give reliable dates, and Bob has been struggling since 1975 to determine the age of these artifacts. Two of our team members, Rutgers University archeologist Jack Harris and Sileshi Semaw, an Ethiopian graduate student, were excavating at Gona, and I wanted to observe their work and photograph the site. Bob and I stayed for several hours before turning back.

As our Land-Rover drove into camp, I heard

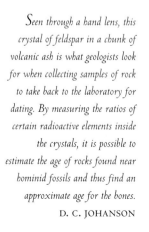

Seen through a hand lens, this crystal of feldspar in a chunk of volcanic ash is what geologists look for when collecting samples of rock to take back to the laboratory for dating. By measuring the ratios of certain radioactive elements inside the crystals, it is possible to estimate the age of rocks found near hominid fossils and thus find an approximate age for the bones.
D. C. JOHANSON

Beethoven's Ninth Symphony blasting from the dining tent. In 1990, Yoel had initiated a tradition of playing that symphony on his portable stereo after each hominid discovery. Bob and I jumped out of the vehicle as Bill Kimbel emerged from the tent. "The hits keep coming," he drawled.

"Another hominid?" I asked incredulously.

From the far side of the tent Yoel beamed at me. "I found a skull," he said simply.

Yoel had been exploring a new gully that morning. As

This typical stone tool from Gona belongs to the Oldowan industry, named for the famous site of Olduvai Gorge in Tanzania.
IAN EVERARD

Archeologist Sileshi Semaw examines some of the artifacts that he excavated from the site of Gona, which may be among the world's oldest stone tools.
D. C. JOHANSON

he scanned the ground his gaze fixed, almost in disbelief, on what was unmistakably a fragment of occipital bone. He marched triumphantly uphill, holding the forked staff given him by one of the Afar. Next he found a chunk of the upper jaw with teeth intact. After that came a loose canine, scattered pieces from the sides of the cranium, and the face.

Yoel showed Bill and me the spot where he had found the first skull fragment. Starting at the bottom of the slope, we walked uphill, looking for the exact location where the skull had initially eroded from the ground. By

Bill Kimbel ponders a hominid fossil in the shade of the Lucy Club. Every new fossil has its own Specimen Record Sheet to record the date and place it was discovered, the specimen number, and a description of the bone and the site's geology. D. C. JOHANSON

walking uphill, we were less likely to bury any bone fragments under sliding sand. Bill was the first to find more bone—a fragment of the right side of the lower jaw. A group of Afar who had followed us to the site stood behind Bill and Yoel, talking excitedly among themselves. One fired his rifle into the air by way of celebration.

"Looks like we've got a chimp here," Yoel joked, remarking on the facial bones he had just picked up. They projected sharply forward, one of the apelike features in *afarensis*. Then he showed us an impressively large cheekbone. "Never in my wildest dreams did I think I would see one like this."

"This guy was a monster," Bill said flatly. "Here's another piece of the cranium. Unbelievable."

The last hour of daylight disappeared and we returned to camp, jubilant, for tea, a shower, and a fabulous dinner. The team was on a high I hadn't seen at Hadar since the heady days of the mid-1970s. We had made spectacular discoveries then, but during the first week of the 1992 expedition we unearthed fossils at an unprecedented pace. My anxiety was replaced with jubilation.

The sovereign rule of fossil collecting, however, is to always expect the unexpected; a trend that holds one day or one season may never again be repeated. As it turned out, most of what we would discover in our 1992 season we found that first week. This is the archetypal field experience, the true camp "routine"—a strange mix of

Paleoanthropologist Bill Kimbel uses a dental pick to remove part of a hominid lower jaw from the ground. This was another piece of a male skeleton found at the same site that yielded an arm bone, two hand bones, and a skull fragment before the team ran out of time to continue searching.
D. C. JOHANSON

tedium and excitement that has remained the same over the past century even as scientific techniques have progressed beyond recognition.

While the events of a field season may be counted on to be reliably unreliable, good interpretation of that season's harvest of fossils depends heavily not only on accuracy and meticulousness in the field but on sound analysis and dating techniques that are growing more sophisticated almost literally by the hour. Ethiopian paleoanthropologist Berhane Asfaw, Tim White of Berkeley, Gen Suwa of the University of Tokyo, and a team of Ethiopian geologists and archeologists recently began a mapping survey of sites in the northern and southern Ethiopian sectors of the Rift Valley. First they analyzed photographs from NASA's

The nomadic Afar people herd their goats through the Hadar landscape unconcerned with the IHO team heading back to camp. D. C. JOHANSON

orbiting Landsat satellites and from the *Challenger* space shuttle to locate likely fossil-bearing deposits by remote sensing. Then they walked the ground themselves, uncovering many new hominid fossil sites within the context of greater enhanced geological knowledge about the area.

This sort of survey work may not share the dubious glamour of digging up bones, but it's equally important. In its first few years, the survey team discovered three dozen new fossil sites, some bearing hominid bones and hordes of stone tools. No doubt these new sites, such as Fejej and Konso-Gardula, both at the southern end of the Ethiopian Rift, will soon be making news as other anthropologists return there. Because of advances like these, the current decade may well prove to be another golden age for African paleoanthropology, richer than even the 1970s were.

All the fossils from our hasty 1992 season are now safely stored at the National Museum in Addis Ababa, waiting to be cleaned, reconstructed, and molded for casting. All the 1992 Hadar hominids are about 3 million years old; the oldest Hadar hominids come from sediments that are 3.4 million years old. Add on the fossils from Laetoli, a site in Tanzania, most of which date to 3.4 and 3.5 million years ago, and you have a half million years of documented *Australopithecus afarensis* evolution. Including the Middle Awash site south of Hadar, where hominid fossils are 3.8 or 3.9 million years old, that adds up to almost a million years with *afarensis* around, evolving very little, from what we could tell after our first look at the new fossils.

What of this first ancestral species? Over this considerable span of time the fossil remains of *Australopithecus afarensis* reveal a unique but constant mosaic of features: from the neck up, chimpanzee; from the waist down,

At night, the Afar guards serve as the eyes and ears of the camp, ready to detour lions, bandits, or rival tribesmen. D. C. JOHANSON

human. For all their apeness, Lucy and her kind did share
the first human evolutionary marker: They walked. They
kept on walking, beautifully adapted to their African
environment, for another million years.

But if *Australopithecus afarensis* looked and moved much
the same at 3 million years ago as it had a million years
earlier, when should we expect to find the first signs of
our own genus, *Homo*? When do the rest of the main
markers—the evolutionary *events*, as we call them—begin
to appear in these hominids, or members of the family
Hominidae, signaling the movement toward "human"? I
used to say in lectures that *Homo* appeared somewhere
between 2 and 3 million years ago, but now I think we
can narrow the time range, to between 2.5 and 3 million
years ago. By then, two separate and distinct evolutionary
paths had emerged. One became a dead end; the other
led to *Homo*.

Humans are the only hominids alive today, and we
are, to put it mildly, a highly self-conscious, introspective
species. We live in the present but look constantly to the
future and the past. We want to understand our beginnings, how we came to be who and what we are. To this
end, paleoanthropologists and archeologists are prehistory detectives piecing together a complicated puzzle. The
story of our past is loaded with clues, some already found
and many yet to be discovered. We have archeological
sites where past events must be painstakingly reconstructed from scraps of evidence. We have an array of increasingly sophisticated analytical techniques at our disposal,
although first and foremost, we depend on our own powers of deduction and analysis.

Most important, we ask questions during the analytical process. Why did Lucy's species break with primate

tradition and stand up? What was the evolutionary advantage in doing so? How did she and the hominid species that followed get their food? Why did some hominid species die and others survive? When, where, and why did modern humans evolve? What role, if any, did the notorious Neandertals play in human evolution? What turns out to be the most characteristically "human" of all these turning points?

Some people have the impression that paleoanthropologists need only to find one more piece of skull or fill in one or two more dates in a geological sequence and then we will have neatly solved the problem of the "missing link" and can all go home to dinner. Unfortunately, that's not the case. There are many gaps in our record of the human past and a tremendous amount of work remains to be done. For every question answered, ten more spring up in its place. Above all, the study of human origins is a mystery that inspires our most profound intellectual curiosity.

Let's look now, one by one, at the distinctive evolutionary events on the road to *Homo sapiens*—and the men and women who have reconstructed the story of our species from scant and often enigmatic evidence. Join me in the double tale of that unfolding mystery.

CHAPTER TWO

The Ape That Stood Up:

Australopithecus afarensis

WHENEVER I GIVE A PUBLIC LECTURE, SOME-
one in the audience is sure to ask, "Well, Professor, exactly when did we get up off all fours? And why did we
bother to?"

I don't know the answer to either of those questions,
even though for decades paleoanthropologists have pon-
dered the possible reasons behind our ancestors' curious
decision to begin walking—instead of climbing, swinging,
cantering, or crawling—as well as the time when this first
major human evolutionary turning point may have taken
place. Bipedalism, habitual two-legged locomotion, is an
activity that distinguishes humans from all other primates.
Lucy was not human just because she could walk. By virtue
of this ability, however, she retained the one trait of
humanness that can be traced further back in time than any
other. We use bipedalism as the main criterion for deciding
which fossils we include as
hominids instead of apes.

Along with its role as
the first crucial innovation
that separated our ances-
tors, the hominids, from
more distant ape ancestors,
bipedalism carries with it
another distinction: It is one of
the oddest behaviors found in nature.
Yet two-legged walking must have provided some essential evolutionary

*The earliest evidence that has
been found for two-legged walking,
or bipedalism, in human ancestors
is this 3.8-million-year-old
end of a femur, the thighbone.
Paleoanthropologist Tim White
discovered the fossil in 1981 at the
site of Maka in Ethiopia.*
IAN EVERARD

advantage or it would never have developed or endured. Was it a key part of the first hominid survival strategy, paving the way for the appearance of modern humans a few million years down the road of evolution? Piecing together some provisional answers to that question takes us back to Africa—and once again to Hadar.

My first Hadar hominid find, in 1973, was a knee joint. On the face of it, this was not as dramatic a discovery as the skulls and skeletons to come, and it was of little use in identifying a hominid species. But this humble knee joint was important for two very good reasons. It confirmed my hunch that there were hominid fossils at Hadar. And it ushered me into one of the hottest controversies in paleoanthropology.

Before I began exploring Hadar, my only field experience in Africa had been at the Omo site in southern Ethiopia, where F. Clark Howell, my graduate adviser at the University of Chicago, was co-leader of a team of American, French, and Kenyan scientists. The excavations at the Omo, in sediments between 1 and 4 million

Tim White, left, and J. Desmond Clark, at the Maka site in Ethiopia. Clark is holding the partial hominid femur that White discovered. IAN EVERARD

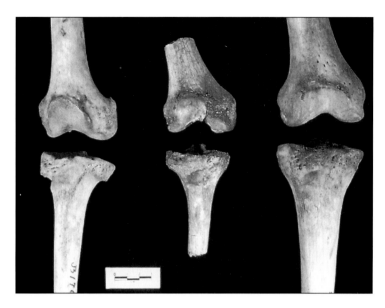

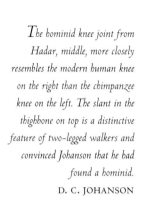

The hominid knee joint from Hadar, middle, more closely resembles the modern human knee on the right than the chimpanzee knee on the left. The slant in the thighbone on top is a distinctive feature of two-legged walkers and convinced Johanson that he had found a hominid.
D. C. JOHANSON

years old, set worthy standards in international coopera-tion (instead of competition) and meticulous excavation for subsequent fieldwork in East Africa. The Omo remains a valuable yardstick for figuring out the ages of sediments at other East African sites. Yet despite the wealth of animal fossils found there, the Omo has yielded only fragmentary hominid fossils.

Richard Leakey led the Kenyan team during the first Omo expedition, in 1967. Toward the end of that field season, he went to Nairobi on business. During the return flight to the Omo, a chance thunderstorm changed the course of the flight—and Richard's career—when the pilot diverted the small plane from the west side of north-ern Kenya's Lake Turkana to the east side. Here Richard spotted a landscape of layered volcanic sediments similar to the Omo that had never been explored for fossils. A few days later, he borrowed a helicopter from the Omo team and returned to test his hunch. Virtually the moment he touched down and climbed out the pilot's side, Richard began finding fossils and stone tools. He promptly dropped out of the Omo expedition and began his own fossil hunt along this lakeshore at the site of Koobi Fora. By the time I first got to the Omo in 1970, Richard's team at Koobi Fora was already making spectacular hominid discoveries.

I came to Africa hoping for a similar break. My first two summers working at the Omo gave me valuable field experience, but I was eager to finish my doctoral degree and strike out on my own. Richard Leakey had taken a risk to explore new territory. Why shouldn't I? Opportunity beckoned in an unlikely setting—a Parisian cocktail party. I had stopped in Paris on my way home from the Omo in 1971 to study chimpanzee skulls in a museum for my dissertation. At this party, through my French colleagues from the Omo team, I met Maurice Taieb, a geologist writing his dissertation on the geology of northern Ethiopia. He captivated me with stories about places where the ground was littered with fossils. The names he recited—Awash River Valley, Afar Depression—meant nothing, but I knew that this region, like the Omo and Koobi Fora, was part of the fertile Great Rift Valley. When he asked me to join him in the field to examine these fossils, I said yes, even though I had no degree, no job, and no money.

In April 1972, before I returned to the Omo for a third year, I met Maurice in Addis Ababa. We scrounged some camping equipment and he took me to some of the areas where he had worked. We were accompanied by a knowledgeable Afar guide, who brought us to a spot by the Awash River that he called Hadar. I was overwhelmed by the array of mammal fossils lying scattered over the ground—the bones of antelopes, baboons, elephants, and pigs. Some of the species I recognized from my work at the Omo. If we just took the time to look, I was convinced hominids would turn up at Hadar. We had only three days to spend at Hadar on that first visit, and we left without finding a hominid. But we were determined to mount a full-scale expedition and return the next year.

In October 1973, we arrived at Hadar with nine other French and American scientists, prepared for a two-month stay. By this time I had left Chicago and taken a job teaching anthropology at Case Western Reserve University, in Cleveland. With these credentials, I had managed to get some funding for my first expedition as a co-leader. I knew, though, that I had to prove myself by finding some hominids or the money would dry up. The first month passed in a flash. We found many fossils, no hominids.

Late one afternoon I was scouring the ground for fossils in my paleoanthropologist's slouch—which has been likened to typical hominid posture—and was at the point

Donald Johanson and Bill Kimbel examine the spot at Hadar where a hominid upper arm bone was discovered in 1990. This particular fossil is quite large and covered with muscle-anchoring ridges. IAN EVERARD

of giving up for the day when I noticed a bone sticking up in the sand. I kicked idly at it, thinking it was that most mundane of Hadar relics, a hippo rib. The bone came loose and I recognized that flat triangular surface that topped the tapered shaft like a pedestal. This was no rib; it was the top of a right shinbone, or tibia. And it came from a primate, not a hippo—most likely a monkey, I thought, judging from the small size. I picked it up, jotted a description of the site in my notebook. A second bone lay on the ground a few yards away. I went over to take a look. It was a femur, the lower part of a thighbone—and it was similar in color and size to the shinbone. I had in my hands both halves of a fossil knee joint from the right leg of the same animal.

I placed the bones together as they would have looked in life. I held the tibia, the bottom of the joint, in my right hand and the femur in my left. Only a bit of the femur shaft had been preserved, but I could see that the bone angled downward from my left to my right, ending in a pair of bony knobs that connected it to the tibia, which had a straight shaft. Something looked strange. I knew that a monkey's leg bones form a straight line in the body across the knee joint, so I turned the femur until the shaft was vertical and tried to fit it with the other bone. That looked even more unnatural. When I stopped picturing a monkey's leg bones and began picturing a human leg, it dawned on me that this must be a hominid fossil. A human thighbone extends downward and inward from the hip joint, forming a distinct angle with the straight shinbone. This arrangement places the knee beneath our center of mass and provides support for our standing on two legs. If the fossil in my hands made the same angle at the knee joint, then this animal had stood—and walked—like a human.

My first reaction was glee: My risky decision to search an unknown area for fossils had paid off. I had proven that hominids once lived at Hadar. I called to my colleague from Cleveland, Tom Gray, who was exploring nearby. I showed him the shinbone and, just as I had, Tom identified it as a monkey's. When I added the top of the knee joint, Tom came to the identical revised conclusion: hominid. I hastily wrapped both bones inside a bandanna, stuffed them into my shoulder bag, and hurried back to camp. Tom's validation was reassuring, but I found myself longing to get the opinion of a real expert on this part of the body. I needed to show the fossil to C. Owen Lovejoy.

I had known and admired Owen, a professor at Kent State University, since my graduate school days at the University of Chicago. When it comes to postcranial anatomy—that is, how everything below the neck fits together—there's no one better. Moreover, he had already published scientific papers comparing the modern human knee with the few known fossil samples from australopithecines in South Africa. At the close of the Hadar expedition, I carried the knee joint—packed in a cotton-lined box and stowed next to my feet—on the plane back to Cleveland, where Owen had agreed to meet me. One question that nagged at me during the trip was the age of the knee joint. Though we had no confirmed dates yet from the rocks at Hadar, by comparing other mammal fossils from Hadar, especially pig teeth, with those that had been found at the Omo, Tom Gray and I suspected that the knee joint could be between 3 and 4 million years old.

The plane landed on an icy runway in Cleveland. Looking out at the dreary winter landscape, I wished I were back under the baking sun at Hadar. At the baggage carousel I heard Owen's deep voice announce without preamble, "Over here, Don. Where's the knee?"

During the drive to Kent, I told Owen how I had spotted the knee eroding from a brown clay layer. He wanted to know the age of the sediment. At least 3 million years old, I told him. We both knew that this fossil could be the earliest evidence of bipedalism ever found.

We pulled into the driveway of his house. I opened the cardboard box that contained the fossils and placed each bone on the living room floor. Owen picked up both halves of the joint, first the femur and then the tibia. He peered at them in a trance of concentration. After a long silence, he looked up. "These bones belong to a biped," he said emphatically.

Owen wanted to compare the Hadar fossil with some human and ape joints. Since he didn't have any spare knee bones lying around the house, it was our good fortune that the Cleveland Museum of Natural History housed the Hamann-Todd collection of more than three thousand human skeletons, as well as some chimpanzee skeletons. In the next few weeks Owen made several visits to the museum.

On one of those expeditions we took the knee joint to Kingsbury Heiple, an orthopedic surgeon Owen knew. Handling the bones matter-of-factly, as if they were from one of his patients in need of a prosthetic knee and not irreplaceable fossils, Heiple placed them on a metal examining table and took a long, hard look. His conclusion: The only difference between this fossil combination and a human knee was the fossil's small size.

As the largest human joint, Heiple told us, the knee is not just a simple hinge like the elbow. It's a complex mechanism, harder to duplicate and replace than hips or any other human joint. Three bones come together here: the femur, the tibia, and the circular kneecap, or patella, which I had not found at Hadar. In addition, a delicate arrangement of injury-prone tendons and ligaments surrounds the bones. Of course, these parts had not been preserved with the fossil, but the surviving bones suggested that the hominid knee may have been just as complex as our own.

Judging from Heiple's information, Owen and I decided that upright walking might have been the only way the Hadar hominids moved about. Over the next few weeks we compared the knee joint with as many chimpanzee and human bones as we had time to study. It was a great learning experience for me, a tooth expert, to sit alongside a master like Owen and observe the way he sys-

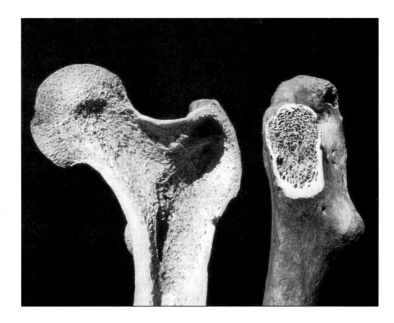

Two views of a modern human femur, the thighbone, reveal the inner structure of the bone's neck, which connects the shaft to the round end that attaches at the hip joint. On the left, a cutaway shows that the dense outer layer of bone is thinner along the top of the neck than at the bottom. This is another feature of upright walking that also occurs in the earliest fossil evidence for this form of locomotion. On the right, a cross-section shows the pattern of dense bone as well as the shock-absorbing spongy bone that fills the femur neck. OWEN LOVEJOY

tematically compared and contrasted every detail of the ancient fossil with the modern bones. Although the fossil was about the same size as the chimpanzee knees we examined, it had a distinctly different shape.

Some of the differences were obvious ones I had noticed when I found the bones. The two bony bumps, or condyles, on the end of the femur had a long, fairly flat edge where they rested on top of the shinbone. That is a human trait, but in a quadruped like the chimpanzee the condyles are shorter and rounder. When I first tried to put the fossil bones together at Hadar, I had also noticed the angle of the femur shaft and how it differed from the straight line made by monkey and ape leg bones. As bipeds, we have widely spaced hips and narrowly spaced knees to keep us balanced as we walk. In contrast, a chimpanzee, in its four-legged posture, has a center of mass far in front of the hind limbs. When the chimpanzee stands, it teeters and must walk by throwing its weight from side to side because it lacks both the wide hips to hold up the upper body and the arrangement of former climbing muscles bipeds have adapted to support the hipbones during walking.

As an expert on the bones below the neck, Owen has had to learn a lot about how physical forces influence the shape of bones—a science called biomechanics. He could appreciate nuances of the knee joint that escaped my eyes at first. For instance, Owen pointed out a lip of bone on the outer edge of the femur that helps hold the kneecap in place. A human's knee has this same feature; a chimpanzee's does not. "Limbs are gross, sloppy things," Owen complained. "You slap together a skeleton with some muscles and it works."

Owen knows better than anyone that it's more complex than that, of course. He has devoted much careful thought to how a biped's bones respond to the forces imposed by its strange form of locomotion. Two other fossils that I found at Hadar in 1973 after the knee-joint discovery gave him plenty to ponder in this matter. These were fragments of the femur's upper end, which forms half of the ball-and-socket hip joint. The narrow bridge between the bone's thick shaft and the ball that fits into the hip socket, the femur neck, bears the brunt of a biped's upper-body weight. It's a part of the body that continues to plague people today; most of the "broken hip" injuries that afflict more than 280,000 Americans each year actually occur in the neck of the femur, which lies next to the hip joint.

The fossil femur was conveniently broken so that Owen could show me a cross-section of the neck, where a thin layer of dense outer bone surrounded a cavity of spongy bone. Spongy bone looks like fine filaments woven together in every direction. The ends of human limbs are packed with this shock-absorbing type of bone, so the human skeleton appears bigger and puffier, like a sponge tossed into a bucket of water. We sawed through the neck of a chimpanzee femur and Owen pointed out the differences. Instead of the paper-thin layer of outer bone, there was a thick layer of dense bone around a smaller cavity containing less spongy bone. The chimp also had a tapered bony ridge running along the top of the neck, which in cross-section gave the bone a teardrop shape.

This extra ridge of bone reinforces the femur neck in the same way that an I beam supports a building. A chimpanzee climbing in a tree subjects its femur to bending stress—caused by tension on the top of the neck and compression on the bottom. If the bone cannot withstand

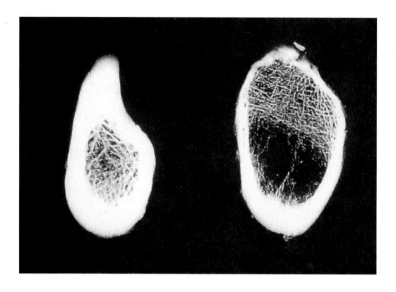

X-rays show dramatic differences between the femur necks of a chimpanzee, on the left, and a modern human. The chimpanzee has a thick layer of dense bone that forms a bony ridge at the top. This design withstands the physical forces that a chimp encounters while climbing trees. The human design, with more spongy bone inside and a thick outer layer at the bottom, withstands the forces of two-legged walking. The Hadar fossils are almost identical to the human pattern. OWEN LOVEJOY

this stress, it will break. The dense ring of outer bone can absorb the force from compression but not from tension, so the neck needs the extra bone on top, where tension occurs.

Human and hominid femurs aren't built this way. Their substantially longer necks would be even more vulnerable than a chimp's to the dangers of fracture while climbing. And unlike the uniformly thick outer bone layer of the chimpanzee femurs, they have a layer of dense outer bone that is thin at the top and thick at the bottom. Finally, both the hominid and human femur necks contain more spongy bone than those of chimpanzees.

Each of the small differences I was looking at, Owen explained, is a dramatic testament to the fact that walking generates entirely different forces than climbing does. Here was physical proof of the radical redesign a biped's body must undergo to accommodate the change from four legs to two. Longer femur necks let the former quadruped's leg muscles stabilize the hip while one leg swings forward in midstep. As soon as one leg lifts off the ground, the muscles fire and press the femur's neck into the hip socket. This action relieves the tension caused by weight bearing down on the top of the neck and focuses stress along the bottom of the neck, where the bone is thicker. In the same way, the spongy bone inside the neck absorbs shock at the point in each step when lifting one leg places a force equal to three times the body weight on the standing leg.

If we *Homo sapiens* suddenly decided to go back to the trees, these muscles could not return to the former way of functioning that relieved stress on the femur. Eventually, it would fracture from all the tension tugging at the bone. And from the evidence lying before us, it seems the Hadar hominids would have had the same problem, too.

"That's all?" Owen asked wistfully after we had examined the limb fossils from the 1973 expedition. "You didn't find anything else?"

"Owen, this is a fossil match made in heaven," I cried. "Your specialty is bipedalism and I found you a knee joint. What more do you want?"

"A skeleton," he answered promptly. "I want a pelvis to go with that knee."

•   •   •

Eleven months later, in November 1974, I was back at Hadar, again co-leading a French-American team of scientists with Maurice Taieb. I had a new job, as curator of physical anthropology at the Cleveland Museum of Natural History, and thanks to Owen Lovejoy's refusal to settle for a simple knee joint, a new impetus to find more fossils.

I spent the morning of November 30 scanning the ground for fossils with my associate Tom Gray. To be perfectly truthful, I was avoiding the busywork in camp that had built up after several visitors had come to Hadar, including Richard Leakey and his mother, Mary. There were fossils to label, letters to write, but I felt the urge to explore. At midday, under a murderous sun and in temperatures topping 100 degrees, we reluctantly headed back toward camp. Along the way I glanced over my right shoulder. Light glinted off a bone. I knelt down for a closer look. This time I knew at once I was looking at a hominid elbow. I had to convince Tom, whose first reaction was that it was a monkey's. But that wasn't hard to do. Everywhere we looked on the slope around us we saw more bones lying on the surface. Here was the hominid skeleton Owen wanted.

It's almost ancient history now, and I have told the story more times than I can remember, but the find launched a celebration in camp that lasted into the next morning. We must have been a curious sight to the nomads in the desert, our work tent aglow with butane lamps and the music of "Lucy in the Sky with Diamonds" blasting from a cassette player. Inspired by the song, we affectionately named the partial skeleton Lucy.

In January 1975 the soon-to-be world-famous Lucy and I set off together from Ethiopia for Cleveland. Each fragment of her precious skeleton was wrapped in toilet paper and stored in a bulging carry-on suitcase. From 32,000 feet in the air, I stared down at the Great Lakes and tried to fathom the fact that the scrawny primate whose remains were tucked under my feet had evolved into a species capable of constructing the Boeing technology that carried me home. Word of Lucy's arrival drew Owen like a magnet to my lab in Cleveland. He burst into my office a few days after I got back. "All right, hotshot," he demanded. "Where's the skeleton?"

Carefully removing the bones from their nest in a

While hunting for fossils at Hadar in 1974, Donald Johanson discovered the remarkably complete, 3.2-million-year-old skeleton that came to be called Lucy. She is one of the most famous hominid fossils ever found. INSTITUTE OF HUMAN ORIGINS

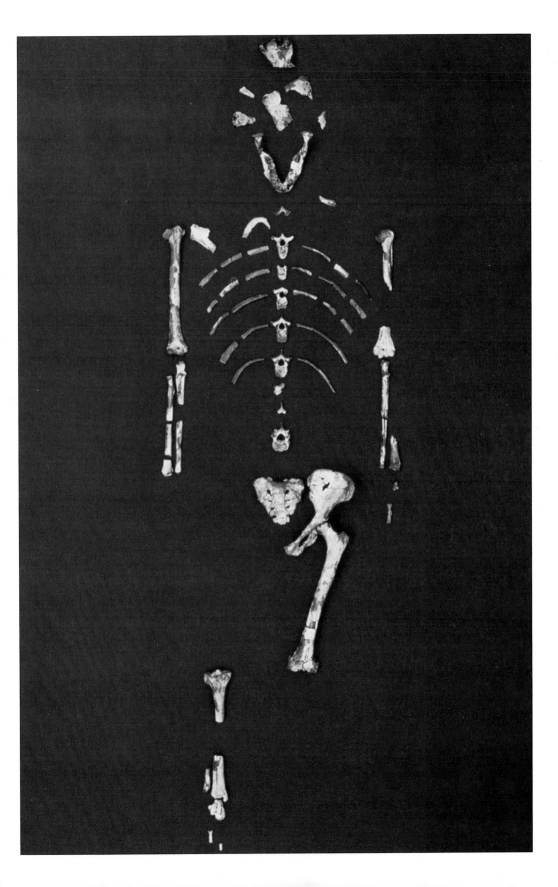

foam-lined tray inside my office safe, I placed each fragment on the padded lab table. Owen's eyes widened as I
arranged the arms, the ribs and vertebrae, the lower jaw
and skull fragments, the leg bones and, finally, part of the
pelvis. "It's so small," I said when all the bones lay before
us. "Do you think it's a female?"

He leaned back in his chair. "It's a safe bet this is a
female."

"You don't think it's a dwarf, do you?"

"Nah, the skeleton doesn't show any pathology. And
what's more," Owen pointed to the leg bones, "these are
about the same size as the knee joint from last year. I'll bet
you the females were small and the males were large." His
eyes glinted. "Just to be sure, though, you'd better go back
there and find a collection of bones. You know, a family."

Owen's challenge was inspiring, but I knew it was
unrealistic in the extreme to expect to find a whole group
of hominids. The gods thought otherwise. I returned to
Hadar in 1975 and once again was out looking for
hominids when I heard that Mike Bush, our camp medical
doctor, had found some bones. I rushed over to the site.
Hominid premolars poked up from a block of rock. At the
urging of *National Geographic* photographer David Brill, we
postponed the search for more bones until early the next
morning, when the light would be better for taking photographs. That decision allowed David to document the
unparalleled fossil-finding spree that began the following
day. Eventually, we discovered bones from at least thirteen
hominids, which we dubbed collectively the First Family.

The bones from the 1975 expedition were a bonanza
for Owen's investigations into bipedalism. Fewer than 10
percent of the nonskull bones or fragments in the australopithecine fossil record tell us anything about how

these animals moved around, and many of these bones come from that single site at Hadar. The fossils drew excited researchers from all over to the lab at Cleveland, and intensive anatomical analysis began. Owen and other anatomists were able to compare bones from many parts of the body among a wide range of individuals. From this work came our announcement in 1978 that the Hadar hominids were part of the new species *Australopithecus afarensis* and, four years later, the publication of detailed fossil descriptions in a 720-page volume of the *American Journal of Physical Anthropology*.

At some point during this frenzy of activity Owen undertook the task of putting Lucy's pelvis back together. This group of bones that separates our upper and lower bodies looks distinctly different in bipeds and quadrupeds, so Owen knew that it contained critical clues about how Lucy moved around. One important part of Lucy's pelvis, the sacrum, was intact. This is a triangular

Lucy has become more famous than her discoverer. In Ethiopia, she appears on a postage stamp and has magazines and cafés named after her.
©1989 BY NICK DOWNES

"Not the Lucy?"

bone made up of five fused vertebrae at the base of the spine; it holds both halves of the pelvis together in the middle of the back. The other piece Owen had to work with was the left side of the pelvis: the innominate, or "no-name," bone, which is really three bones fused together into the hip-joint socket. These are a large, fan-shaped bone, called the ilium, and two smaller bones, known as the ischium and the pubis.

Lucy's left innominate had been bent out of shape and broken into about forty pieces while it was embedded in the ground. Owen X-rayed the fossil and discovered that the back of Lucy's pelvis, where the sacrum connects with the innominate, had smashed against a rock or another bone during burial, shattering and twisting the ilium. He then spent six months carefully outlining and numbering each fragment of ilium, casting each piece of the fossil in plaster, smoothing out the edges, and then reassembling them in a three-dimensional jigsaw puzzle. Every fragment had to line up with adjoining pieces from both the front and the back side of the bone to convince Owen that he had overcome any distortion that occurred after the bone was damaged. Once Owen had restored the left side of the pelvis, he sculpted a mirror image of the right side in plaster and placed Lucy's sacrum in between to complete his masterpiece. Now it was possible to see how Lucy's pelvis looked in life.

When I first saw Owen's restoration, I knew at once that all the time and hard work had been worth the effort. Just as we had done before with the knee joint, we could now compare this perfectly symmetrical pelvis with human and chimp bones. Basically, a human pelvis is shorter, deeper, and wider than a chimpanzee's. It is bowl-shaped because each ilium has rotated toward the middle of the body and flares outward at the edges, a shape that supports the weight of our upright upper bodies. In contrast, each ilium in a chimpanzee pelvis lies flat beside the spine and sticks out to the side like a wing, creating a long, shallow pelvis.

Lucy's pelvis bears a striking resemblance to a human one. When Owen brings a human pelvis, a chimp pelvis, and a cast of Lucy's pelvis into an elementary-school classroom, the children have no trouble deciding which two look alike. Lucy's pelvis has a bowl shape like a human pelvis, but it is not as deep. Each ilium flares outward, even more than in humans, then curls forward. The same goes for the sacrum. A chimp sacrum looks like a wedge of cheese, while a human sacrum looks more like a piece of pie. Humans have a wider sacrum than any other living primate, to help set the hip joints apart; but Lucy's sacrum, for its size, is even wider. This may indicate that the sacrum had to narrow throughout human evolution while another of our adaptive landmarks, larger brains,

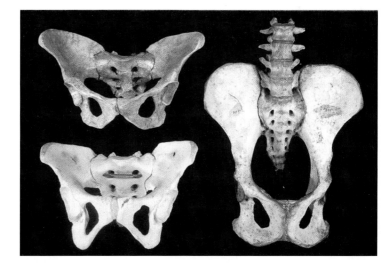

Lucy's pelvis, top left, which Owen Lovejoy painstakingly restored, shares the bowl-like shape of a human pelvis, bottom left, and can easily be distinguished from a chimpanzee pelvis. The fan-shaped bone on each side of Lucy's pelvis, the ilium, curves outward and forward as in modern humans to support the upper body during walking.
OWEN LOVEJOY

evolved. Lucy's wider sacrum and shallower pelvis gave her a smaller, kidney-shaped birth canal, compared to that of modern human females. She didn't need a large one because her newborn infant's brain wouldn't have been any larger than a chimpanzee infant's brain. As humans evolved, however, the birth canal had to become rounder to pass a big-brained baby.

• • •

By the early 1980s, Owen and I felt that we had put together compelling evidence that *Australopithecus afarensis* was as well designed for bipedalism as we are, if not even better. We had the knee joint and partial femurs from the first Hadar expedition, we had Lucy's pelvis, and we had additional limb bones from the First Family site.

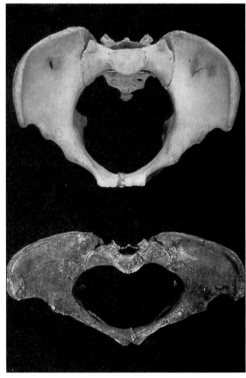

We even had a set of footprints. Owen called the famous footprint trail discovered in 1978 by Mary Leakey's team at Laetoli, Tanzania, the "perfect cementing evidence" for bipedalism. In a trail of ash that has been dated to 3.5 million years ago, the tracks of two hominids were captured for a distance of nearly eighty feet, lasting impressions that give us a direct glimpse of how they got around.

In an overhead view of a human pelvis, top, and Lucy's pelvis, the relative size and shape of the birth canal can be seen. Humans have a nearly circular birth canal, whereas Lucy's wide, shallow pelvis forms a smaller, kidney-shaped birth canal. The shape of the human pelvis changed to accommodate the larger brain that evolved in the descendants of Lucy's species. DAVID BRILL

I believe that *afarensis* made the footprints—first, because *afarensis* fossils have been found at Laetoli, and second, because a composite foot, made from fossil bones belonging to *Homo* from nearby Olduvai Gorge combined with Hadar toe bones, has been shown to fit the Laetoli prints. When a chimpanzee walks on two legs, it leaves a print with the big toe splayed away from the rest of the foot. The Laetoli prints resemble modern human footprints, with the big toe in line with the other toes. Pulling the big toe into line with the rest of the foot creates another human feature that is present in the footprints: an arch. This is just the sort of energy-absorbing feature we would expect in an animal that spent most of its time standing and walking.

I thought this was plenty of evidence to close the case on bipedalism. Other researchers didn't. Some of our colleagues at the State University of New York at Stony Brook—Jack Stern, Randall Susman, and Bill Jungers— argued in a series of scientific papers that the Hadar hominids retained some primitive anatomical features, such as curved finger and toe bones, implying that the hominids were still regular tree climbers who left the ground to forage, sleep, or escape predators. Although they accepted the evidence that *afarensis* walked on two legs while on the ground, the Stony Brook scientists insisted that the *afarensis* gait was less like a modern human walk and more like the bent-hip, bent-kneed locomotion of a bipedal chimpanzee. Owen, meanwhile, insisted that the curved fingers and toes and other apelike features were merely evolutionary leftovers from a tree-climbing past that were insignificant in light of the anatomical changes that had already occurred in the pelvis, knee, and foot.

Debate erupts punctually over every discovery or theory in paleoanthropology. That's a sign of a healthy science when the debate centers around arguable data. Because we had so much new material to discuss, it seemed fitting for the Institute of Human Origins to organize a scientific conference on "The Evolution of Human Locomotion." The meeting took place in Berkeley over two spring days in 1983, and more than a dozen scientists attended, including Owen and the Stony Brook team.

An astonishing trail of hominid footprints was discovered by Mary Leakey's team at Laetoli, Tanzania, in 1978. The prints were preserved in volcanic ash that erupted 3.5 million years ago and are among the oldest evidence for upright walking, or bipedalism. RON CLARKE

Australopithecus afarensis most likely made the Laetoli footprints, which contain such features of a modern human foot as a big toe that is in line with the other toes and an arch. In contrast, a four-legged ape leaves a print with the big toe splayed sideways and lacking an arch. RON CLARKE

Paleoanthropologist Ron Clarke helped excavate the Laetoli footprint trail in 1979. By the end of the excavation, more than seventy footprints covering a distance of eighty feet had been discovered. PETER JONES

From left to right: Owen Lovejoy, Randall Susman, William Jungers, Jack Stern. Jungers, Susman, and Stern have argued that the Hadar hominids were climbing trees either to procure food or escape predators. They also suggest, contrary to Owen Lovejoy, that the two-legged gait of afarensis *was not as well developed as in modern* humans. DAVID SMELTZER

With a mix of public talks and closed-door sessions, where scientists argued over casts of bones and footprints, the meeting provided an energizing exchange of ideas that one participant later called "an orgy of shop talk." Like bookies at a racetrack, the scientists took odds on which theory was correct; Jack Stern gave 10 to 1 odds that the Hadar hominids climbed trees, while Bruce Latimer, a student of Owen's who now holds my old job at the Cleveland Museum of Natural History, offered 9.5 to 1 that they stayed on the ground.

Part of the Stony Brook group's contention that *afarensis* was not an efficient biped relied on measurements taken from a cast of Lucy's unrestored pelvis. They did not take into account the damage and distortion that occurred while the bones were buried, and an artificial joint had formed between the sacrum and the ilium that misled the team to conclude that Lucy's pelvis looked more chimplike because the ilium did not curve forward as it did in humans.

Using casts of Lucy's pelvis made before and after his restoration, Owen demonstrated that connecting the sacrum to the false joint in the unreconstructed pelvis pulls the pubis—the bone at the front of the pelvis—two inches to the side of the body's midline, an incorrect position. After he had restored the pelvis, Owen realized that the joint between the ilium and the sacrum had twisted 90 degrees. Correcting for this damage, he could attach the sacrum to the real joint in the ilium, which swung the pubis back to its proper position in the middle of the body and also brought the ilium into its natural position, which resembles a human pelvis. Having studied the original fossil, Owen had the advantage on this point.

Further disagreement arose over the arm and leg bones. Lucy is the only specimen from Hadar for which we have both the upper arm bone, or humerus, and thighbone, so this debate focused on her. Lucy has a short femur, shorter than a human's, for her size. The Stony Brook group suggested that a short thighbone suited Lucy in the trees but was inefficient for walking. There's no reason a good biped couldn't have a short femur, Owen countered. For one thing, a shorter bone would be less prone to injury. Consider the most successful and least injured running backs in football, he said. They tend to be the players with big trunks and short, stocky thighs.

As for the upper arm, Lucy's is long compared to a modern human's but not compared to any ape's. Bill Jungers of Stony Brook compared the lengths of Lucy's humerus and femur and found that their ratio was 84, much closer to the human mean figure of 72 than to that of the nearest ape, a chimpanzee, at 110, and that of the most acrobatic ape, a gibbon, at 130. Apes that spend more time in the trees have longer arms, but the *afarensis* arm seems to have gotten shorter and already had several traits that Owen said would make the hominid a poor climber. Because *afarensis* already has so many anatomical adaptations from the waist down for walking, the arms should be especially designed for climbing if this hominid still depended on the trees.

What about those long, curved fingers and toes? It's true that these bones in *afarensis* are curved like those of other tree-climbing primates, and Jack Stern compared them to those of pygmy chimpanzees. Compared to total body size, however, the *afarensis* fingers and toes are shorter than those of all other hominoids—the group that includes hominids, living apes, and their ancestors—except humans. After studying the foot bones from Hadar, Bruce Latimer determined that *afarensis* could lift its toes like a human but could not curl them forward to the heel, something any good tree-climbing ape could do. If Lucy had worn shoes, they would have creased across the top as her toe bones lifted in midstep.

Bruce also compared the few heel bones found at Hadar with chimp and human heels. A human heel is four times the size of a gorilla heel and twice that of a chimpanzee, because it contains lots of spongy bone to absorb the shock of walking. Besides being smaller than a human heel, a chimp heel has a thicker coating of bone around the outside. The *afarensis* heel has only a thin outer bone layer like a human heel and is partly inflated with spongy bone. The shape and size of the heels from Hadar suggests that the hominids already had a similar design, another clue that they were efficient, full-time walkers.

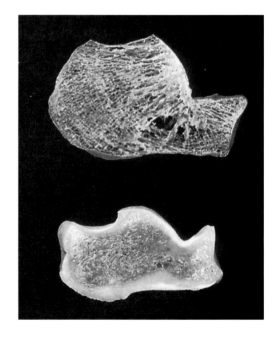

A human heel bone, top, is bigger than an ape heel bone because it is full of shock-absorbing spongy bone, which aids two-legged walking. The hominid heel bones from Hadar also are expanded in size due to extra spongy bone, another piece of evidence that these hominids spent most of their time on the ground rather than in trees. BRUCE LATIMER

Perhaps not surprisingly, each side in the debate went away from that 1983 locomotion conference more convinced than ever that it was right. Each side continued to publish articles advancing its interpretations. Owen, however, gradually retreated from the fray and turned to other interests, such as figuring out an equation to calculate the degree of size difference due to sex in human skeletons and learning about how bones begin to develop in an embryo. He passed up the last major meeting on hominid locomotion, a conference in Paris in 1988, where Bruce Latimer carried the banner of bipedalism. At that meeting Susman and Stern criticized Owen and Bruce for dwelling on what they call "magic traits," such as the femur neck or the expanded heel, as certain evidence for bipedalism. But as Owen said to me after I coaxed him into presenting his case one more time for NOVA, "Traits cease to be magic when you compile a list of them and the list described the skeleton at hand."

With so much left to discover in paleoanthropology, I'm tempted to say that this issue of early bipedalism should be considered resolved and we should move on to topics that sorely lack data. At the back of my mind, though, I know it will linger, in part because of a fossil found at Hadar in 1990. The bone in question is the top of an upper arm, the humerus, and it's probably the largest one we have. (After the discovery, I wrote in my notebook, "This looks like the Schwarzenegger of them all.") The bone has pronounced ridges where powerful muscles—the pectoralis and latissimus dorsi, favorite muscles of modern-day body builders—once attached. These muscles pull back the shoulder, so the ridges on the fossil indicate that the hominids exercised their upper bodies.

Although we don't have the entire humerus—gnaw

marks on the end indicate that a hyena beat us to it—if we estimate its length, it appears to be a short bone, and the ridges may have developed because the muscles had less room for attachment. Another explanation, however, is that this hominid may have pulled itself into the trees that covered Hadar a few million years ago. Although we can still climb trees today, most people don't do it regularly, and I think the Hadar hominids had already passed the point where climbing was a frequent activity. They may have sought out special trees to gather fruit, but I doubt they obtained much of their food by climbing. They were saddled with hind limbs that only worked well on flat ground, and their arched flat feet and squat pelvis no longer allowed them the freedom to leap from limb to limb.

It's easy to imagine that if our ancestors had not stood up we might never have evolved—after all, the quadru-

The Land-Rover marks the spot where an unusual hominid upper arm bone was found in 1990. This photograph was taken from Kenia Koma, the highest point at Hadar, and shows the rugged terrain of the fossil-laden sediments.   D. C. JOHANSON

This upper arm bone, or humerus, found at Hadar in 1990 may renew debate about whether the hominids climbed in trees. The fossil is from a particularly large individual and has ridges where powerful shoulder muscles once attached, causing Donald Johanson to refer to its owner as the Schwarzenegger of the population. D. C. JOHANSON

pedal apes have remained apes, while the hominids became human. But we mustn't fall into the trap of believing that once our ancestors made the switch to two legs, our own evolution was inevitable. As we will see, other bipedal hominids evolved and went extinct before modern humans ever appeared.

But still the second question remains: Why walk at all? When *Australopithecus afarensis* stood up and walked, we were left with a 3-million-year legacy of sore backs, broken hips, dislocated knees, and fallen arches. Humans are the only animals that suffer from hip fractures in bones weakened by osteoporosis, which stem from our unusual compulsion to move about on two legs.

If bipedalism doesn't offer immediate physical advantages, maybe the answer to its evolution and persistence is some social advantage. The main goals in the evolutionary game are to eat, stay fit, stay alive, and reproduce. Somehow, the two-footed players in our family tree had an edge in one or more of these goals. The edge wasn't speed, because most four-legged animals move faster than humans. It wasn't efficiency, because moving on two legs uses no more nor less energy than moving on four legs. Bipeds also reduce their access to the trees, a rich source of food. So what could it be?

Owen started thinking seriously about why bipedalism evolved while he was teaching undergraduate courses in human evolution. The existing ideas about the origin of upright walking were full of holes and lacked supporting data. Many hypotheses for bipedalism can be boiled down to one-word explanations—tools, fire, efficiency—to account for this bizarre behavior. The early hominids probably did use some form of tools that have not been preserved, but chimpanzees and other quadrupeds can be perfectly good tool users, too. Since crafted stone tools occur much later in human evolution, I don't see how tools could be the initial driving force behind bipedalism.

Owen sought a broader explanation that would incorporate as much of the available hard evidence as possible, plus some speculation about sex and other behaviors that, unfortunately, do not fossilize. In constructing his hypothesis for why bipedalism evolved—an explanation so elaborate I can only do justice to a few key points here—Owen stuck to biological and evolutionary rules that hold for any mammal, invoking no special traits for hominids. "You've got to make something as weird as a human being using only the rules that apply to beavers," Owen told me during a recent visit to IHO. "That's the trick."

In 1981, Owen published his hypothesis, a social model for bipedalism's beginnings, in the journal *Science*. Since then there has been no dearth of critics stepping forward to shoot down his ideas, calling them wrong or untestable or both. For my money, though, no one has offered a more compelling or comprehensive alternative.

Owen Lovejoy has proposed that bipedalism evolved as part of a social strategy that allowed male hominids to provision their single mates and offspring with high-energy, high-protein foods that the males obtained and carried back to their territories in their free hands. Here is a reconstruction of Australopithecus afarensis *gathering fruit in a forest.*
D. C. JOHANSON

"In a certain sense, it's a really strange model," Owen admitted. "But so are humans."

Humans are strange for several reasons. We have a huge brain, part of our evolutionary heritage of the past 2 million years or so, and this brain is an important sex organ that governs most of learned sexual behavior. We also have what are called secondary sexual characteristics—features such as facial hair, body hair, and enlarged breasts—that Owen considers to be our evolutionary inheritance from Lucy's species, just as her curved fingers and toes come from previous arboreal ancestors.

What's odd about human secondary sexual characteristics is that both males and females of our species have these body decorations. In the animal world, the males of many species have some kind of adornment—think of the vibrant tail plumes of peacocks—when they compete for the affections of females. The fact that human males and females are equally, if differently, adorned suggests that both sexes choose their mates. Another unusual feature of humans is that the birth of our offspring is spaced more closely together compared to birth patterns in other primates, even though we take a long time to mature and have a longer life span.

Owen took these oddities under consideration and combined them with anatomical evidence from the Hadar fossils. Like a prosecuting attorney, he put together what circumstantial evidence he had and devised a hypothesis to explain a past event. Owen's scenario opens in an East African forest more than 4 million years ago. The same tectonic forces that formed the Rift Valley have caused mountains to rise and have created cooler climates that gradually shrank the humid forests. Fast-breeding monkeys managed to survive and moved into the expanding grasslands. Meanwhile, the apes clung to scattered patches of forest and began their slow decline into near extinction that continues today. As for the hominids, they were already bipedal and had evolved a breeding strategy that enabled them to raise more offspring to adulthood and com-pete in a new, expanding envi-ronment: the savanna.

Judging from the several males and females whose remains were found at the First Family site, *Australopithecus afarensis* was probably a social animal. Within a larger group, males and females formed monogamous mating pairs and put equal energy into raising offspring. Imposing monogamy upon a large social group is the most novel—and to some critics, unacceptable—aspect of Owen's hypothetical hominid breeding strategy.

How would being bipedal make members of a species better breeders and parents? It comes back to choice of

Bipedalism evolved while hominids still lived in a forested habitat, but as African forests continued to shrink a few million years ago, our ancestors eventually moved into more open, savanna environments near waterholes and lakeshores.
D. C. JOHANSON

mates. In Owen's model, both sexes choose a mate because each has something to offer: The female offers the male a guarantee that his genes pass into the next generation, and the male offers the female a reliable source of food and shared parenting duties. In many monogamous bird, rodent, and carnivore species, males provide food for their mates, so Owen considered the possibility that a bipedal male hominid could "court" and keep a female by foraging for a few food items that he carried back to her in his free hands. The male could save perhaps half of his mate's time that would otherwise be spent searching for food and could now be devoted toward raising young.

A male hominid wouldn't need to carry armfuls of bananas to keep his mate happy. The blunt cusps on the fossil teeth indicate that *afarensis* was an omnivore with a broad diet that probably included insects, worms, eggs, tubers, fruits, lizards, and other foods that were both nutritious and easy to transport. "I was on a plane once," Owen recalled, "and the passenger next to me ate three packages of honey-roasted nuts, each containing ten grams of fat. That made me realize early hominids only needed to collect a few high-fat items to make a difference in their diet." The chimpanzees studied by Jane Goodall, for example, spend half their time searching for insects, which make up only 4 percent of their diet but pack a lot of protein.

If a male hominid is going to go to the trouble of providing food for a female and her offspring, he wants some certainty that he sired the offspring. Owen speculated that the hominids were monogamous and maintained their pair bond from the fact that human females have lost all visible signals of mating availability. Female apes swell around the rump and sex organs during the brief time when they are receptive to mating, but humans have concealed ovulation and can mate at almost any time without advertising the fact. In a joke that eluded the editors, Owen attributed the assertion in his *Science* article that "human females are continually sexually receptive" to "D. C. Johanson, personal communication," as though I was the scientific source for this bit of information; maybe that's why I was nicknamed "the Don Juan of paleoanthropology" by one of my colleagues in a recent book. Besides hiding most signs of ovulation, finally, human females have enlarged breasts. If female hominids had a similar feature, it may have evolved to mimic the condition of providing milk to an infant and thus being unable to breed.

Admittedly, there is not a lot of hard evidence for the sort of breeding strategy I have described, but the canine teeth of the Hadar hominids provided Owen with an important piece of evidence. Chimpanzees have pointed, clawlike canines, with the male's much larger than the female's, whereas modern humans have flatter, spatula-shaped canines that differ little in size between the sexes. In *afarensis* the pattern is peculiar. The fossils show dramatic differences in overall body size—a circumstance I attribute to differences between males and females—but the conical canines in both large and small jaws are about the same size. Stranger still, the canines have large roots that bulge from the jawbone—a typical ape characteristic—but the teeth themselves are small, closer to human size.

From the presence of a tiny crown perched on top of an enormous root, Owen concluded that the hominid canine had shrunk for some reason—a social reason, he presumed. If the change involved diet, then the whole tooth should get smaller rather than just the crown. Instead, evolution had operated only on the visible part of the tooth. Male chimpanzees use their fanglike upper canines as formidable weapons and in threat displays against other males, but the male hominids apparently had no need for dental daggers. Owen thinks that the male *afarensis* canine shrunk to the smaller size of the female's tooth because the males did not have to fend off rivals for their mates. They fought less, cooperated more, and eventually evolved a cooperative network of their kin to share information on the location of choice food in the vicinity of where they lived.

Cooperation increased the odds of males finding food and keeping mates, but certain individuals were better at it than others. Evolution occurs because not everyone succeeds at reproduction and survival. Yet in this network of cooperating, socially interacting hominids, Owen surmised, lay the seeds of a later human evolutionary event—the dramatic growth in brain size that marks the emergence of *Homo*. Thus bipedalism could well have been an important catalyst in a novel hominid breeding and survival strategy that incorporated parenting skills, tool use, and other behavior that encouraged brain growth.

Because a big brain needs elaborate programming, at some point hominids must have delayed the maturation of their young after birth just like modern humans do. Delaying the maturation of young decreases the number of offspring that parents can have. By involving males as food providers, however, hominids doubled their parenting energy and increased the odds that each of their fewer offspring survived.

At a recent public lecture at the Institute of Human Origins, Owen presented his scenario for the evolution of bipedalism much as I have told it here. Afterward, a few colleagues we had invited took turns raising questions and concerns about Owen's model. The first was Henry McHenry, a paleoanthropologist at the University of California at Davis, who studies the limb bones of early hominids. He criticized Owen's model on the grounds that the Hadar hominids have a range in body size between the sexes far greater than in any living monogamous primate. Gibbons, the smallest of the apes, are monogamous, and males and females are the same size, but Henry's measurements from Hadar hind limb joints suggest that male hominids were 50 percent larger than the females. On a size range scale of living apes, that places *afarensis* between chimpanzees and gorillas, neither of which are monogamous.

Monogamous primates tend to be territorial, Henry went on. They live in small groups, not the sort of social arrangement envisioned for *afarensis*. As for male hominids providing food to their supposedly single mates, Henry said that such behavior is unknown among other monogamous primates. Among the hunting and gathering !Kung people of the Kalahari, women obtain more calories' worth of food than men and walk thousands of miles while carrying children. Since only one fifth of contemporary human societies prohibit polygamy, he added, we

Part of the fossil evidence for Owen Lovejoy's idea about the origin of bipedalism is the lack of size differences in upper canines between male and female Hadar hominids despite obvious differences in body size. This may be due to reduced fighting among male hominids, who did not need to compete for mates using large, formidable canines. At far left is a chimpanzee upper canine, compared with a modern human upper canine on the right and a fossil upper canine from Hadar in the middle. The fossil has a thick root but a surprisingly small crown. D. C. JOHANSON

would have to say that monogamy occurs infrequently among the descendants of *afarensis*!

Henry and his Davis colleague Peter Rodman have proposed their own explanation for the origin of bipedalism. Their model is based on energy efficiency and, like Owen's, presumes that bipedalism arose in a rapidly changing African environment marked by islands of forest in a rising sea of grass. The core of their argument is that the hominids still depended on the shrinking forests for food and became specialized bipeds because that form of locomotion offered a more energy-efficient way to move on the ground between widely spaced forests, where food could be found. They reached the conclusion that bipedalism was more energy-efficient than the four-footed alternative from observations of the amount of energy expended by a quadrupedal chimpanzee as it moved along the ground.

Another speaker, Katharine Milton, a Berkeley primatologist who studies the diets of South American monkeys, criticized Owen's interpretation of the fossil canines from Hadar. Citing her studies of the rare woolly spider monkey of Brazil, she argued that the small canines in *afarensis* males could not be used as evidence for monogamy and reduced aggression.

Male and female woolly spider monkeys, she told us, have a similar body size, and the canines in both sexes are only a little larger than the incisors. The small canines could be linked to the monkey's diet of coarse leaves or to its far-from-monogamous mating behavior. A half dozen or more males may mate with the same female on the same day, Katharine said, and the males don't stick around to help raise their offspring. The promiscuous males have small teeth but huge testes—probably the largest testes of any primate for its size—because the males compete with each other not with their teeth but with their sperm, trying to mate with a female as many times as possible to increase the odds of fathering her offspring. Given the unusual case of the woolly spider monkey, according to Katharine, the size of fossil canines cannot predict what the sex life of a particular primate was like.

Owen returned to the podium and responded to the comments. He dismissed his critics' primate and human behavior analogies as irrelevant to early hominids. There is no evidence for or against the sort of sperm competition found in the woolly spider monkey occurring in hominids, Owen said, but because modern humans have relatively small testes, it's safer to assume that our ancestors did as well. Modern human mating practices also shed little light on the past because our learned social behavior has evolved and changed dramatically in a few million years.

As for the energy-efficiency model, Owen reminded the audience that bipedalism is neither efficient nor inefficient as a means of locomotion. By studying a young chimpanzee with a higher metabolic rate than an adult, Peter Rodman and Henry McHenry concluded that chimpanzees expend too much energy as quadrupeds, but Owen suggested that the result might not be so clear-cut if an adult chimpanzee had been studied. Chimpanzees spend a lot of time on the ground. If bipedalism could save them so much energy, why didn't they make the switch to two legs? If, as Owen contends, there is no difference in energy efficiency between moving on two legs or four, then we must look elsewhere for the evolutionary stimulus that caused the hominids to stand.

Owen has always encouraged his critics to devise alternative scenarios for bipedalism that account for as much of the imperfect evidence as his model. He's still waiting. Recently, I asked him what new evidence he would want to support his own model. His eyes glinted in the way I knew so well. "More of the same," he said. "Something like the First Family—just more of them."

I don't doubt that Owen's model contains flaws, but its elegance lies in its insistence that hominids evolved bipedalism and a big brain from a unique mix of otherwise ordinary aspects of their biology. Bipedalism reminds us of the strange blend of compromise and contingency that we find throughout human evolution. Our ancestors stopped climbing and learned to walk, but they couldn't chase down prey or run from predators. Instead, they found themselves standing upright in an empty savanna with two free limbs, no place to hide, and a brand-new set of survival problems. A brave new world indeed—and how on Earth were they going to stay alive in it?

CHAPTER THREE

Scavenger Hunt:

Homo habilis

Before they had fire, our ancestors must have been terrified by nightfall. I learned this first-hand one evening in Castleton, South Africa, when the largest lioness from an unusually active hunting pride stalked our film group. As I watched in frozen disbelief, she made a decision about whether or not to jump up on the hood of the Land-Rover where I sat with several other members of the crew. Fortunately, she turned away. It was a close call, and the experience left us literally shaking with fear. Until we had been stripped of our technological armor and put in that position ourselves, we had simply never felt the sheer physical helplessness of the human surrounded by animal predators.

It was also a humbling experience for anyone tempted to exaggerate the accomplishments of *Homo sapiens* over the modest technology of our early forebears. During that excruciatingly long moment, without a windshield on the vehicle or a gun in my hand, I was considerably more helpless than a hominid of a few million years ago would have been. He would have had the wits, the reflexes, and the physical agility to be high up in the branches of a nearby acacia tree while I sat paralyzed with fear.

This brings me once again to the survival dilemma faced by *Australopithecus afarensis* at the end of the last chapter. To get to the answer to their problem—which was to be the next major plot twist in the unfolding human story—we must fast-forward the evolutionary tape a full million years. Now, at 2 million years b.p. (before the present), we are still in Africa, but we have moved south to Olduvai Gorge, the famous East African site in northern Tanzania. Here the fossil record reveals two almost simultaneous evolutionary adaptations that arose from the quest for survival in a changing environment: a dramatic increase in the size of hominid brains and the sudden appearance of the first technology, stone tools.

As prosecuting attorneys of the past—to keep to Owen Lovejoy's analogy—paleoanthropologists will never be able to prove conclusively to the jury the exact connection between these two developments from the fragmentary evidence available. Still, it seems fair to speculate that a growing reliance on tools could have been both a cause of and a stimulus to expanding brain size. Together, tools and bigger brains formed a feedback loop that made an important impact on the subsequent development of our species.

There's been intense debate, however, on just what survival strategy these smarter hominids adopted and the

Archeologist Rob Blumenschine sits by a campfire at Castleton in South Africa. The first hominids who stepped out onto the savanna lacked fire, but the ability to make and control fire became a critical part of our evolution in the past million years. D. C. JOHANSON

The shore of Lake Manyara in northern Tanzania resembles the type of environment that existed at Olduvai Gorge when hominids lived there nearly two million years ago. D. C. JOHANSON

role their tools played in carrying it out. Now that they were walking upright in a mixed savanna-forest environment, how did our ancestors put their expanding wits and rudimentary technology to use? Were they—to put the current controversy in a nutshell—noble hunters, or were they wily scavengers?

Scavenging is not a particularly glamorous occupation. The notion of a group of hominids feeding furtively on a stinking week-old carcass stalked, killed, and gutted by some bolder animal does not present us with a charming image of our ancestors. How much more appealing to imagine them striding off courageously to spear their prey than to picture them humbly waiting until their master the lion has finished his own supper before they slink out of hiding to dine on the remains! Hunting was undoubtedly an important dimension in human development, but where and when and to what extent it entered the picture is the subject of a controversy that continues to rage.

To open up this complex question, let's look to the archeological evidence—for now, moving from Hadar to Olduvai, we are adding to paleoanthropology the discipline of archeology, the study of material remains other than the hominids' own bones. The oldest known stone-tool technology, the crude chopper tools of quartz and lava found at several African sites, is called the Oldowan industry, a name derived from Olduvai. In a sense, then, archeology begins at Olduvai.

A dusty, kidney-jarring ride on the gravel road that crosses northern Tanzania brings us to Olduvai Gorge, not far from the wildlife wonders of Ngorongoro Crater

On the plateau above Ngorongoro Crater, Donald Johanson shows a group of young Maasai warriors where they are on a map. The famous prehistoric site of Olduvai Gorge lies in the distant background.
LENORA JOHANSON

and the Serengeti. Even to an untrained eye, the differences between Olduvai and Hadar are immediately striking. At Hadar, bones eroding out from the sediments are well preserved and often intact. At Olduvai, the bones are smashed to smithereens and stone tools lie everywhere. That visual evidence alone suggests the hominids at Olduvai 2 million years ago behaved in a fundamentally different way from those at Hadar about a million years earlier. Once stone tools appear, hominids begin to leave a significant signature of their activities.

But *what* activities, exactly? The presence of tools seems, on the face of it, solid and incontrovertible evidence. These earliest known stone tools are immediately recognizable as having been modified by hand. They have flakes dislodged at acute angles and bear "bulbs of percussion" generated by the force of a hammerstone blow. Yet the earliest African archeological sites, as we will see, remain enigmatic places. The trail of clues amounts to no more than just these flakes of stone,

*Olduvai Gorge is a **Y**-shaped gash in northern Tanzania near the Serengeti. This is where Louis and Mary Leakey worked for decades, excavating thousands of stone tools and the fossils of two hominid species.* D. C. JOHANSON

rough-edged cobbles, and broken animal bones. That's really all we have to reconstruct the lifestyles of our ancestors: bits of bone and stone utensils of unknown function. An equivalent act of inference would be trying to guess the total diet and daily behavior of a modern group of people from a single site yielding a battered fork, knife, chicken-wing bone, and the tooth-wear marks on a mandible found in association with these bits and pieces. Imagine all that's missing in this evidence, and you'll have some idea of the mistakes we are likely to make in re-creating the hominid past. The wildly different interpretations that investigators draw from scanty and ambiguous evidence are a constant recurring theme in the modern investigations of this chapter in the human mystery.

The late Louis Leakey and his wife, Mary, pioneered excavations at Olduvai Gorge. In 1964, Louis was one of the anthropologists who named the hominid species Homo habilis *from fossil discoveries made at Olduvai.* IAN EVERARD

Olduvai is a household name among hominid sites and a place of pilgrimage for paleoanthropologists principally because of the decades of devoted survey and excavation conducted by Louis and Mary Leakey, their children, and colleagues. Louis Leakey found his first stone tool at Olduvai in 1931, but he and Mary did not begin actively excavating the gorge for another twenty years. One momentous day in 1959, as she was walking her dalmatians, Mary Leakey noticed a skull eroding from a slope at a site, dubbed FLK, that was to become probably the most thoroughly studied of all hominid archeological sites. In his personal field notes, Louis first suggested that this spectacular skull might be squeezed into the human ancestry (he even toyed with naming it *Titanohomo mirabilis*), but later he realized that the brain-

This plaque marks the spot where Mary Leakey found the "Zinjanthropus" skull at Olduvai Gorge in 1959. This same site later became an archeological battleground with scientists using the same broken bones and tools found there to argue that early hominids hunted or scavenged for meat. D. C. JOHANSON

case was too small, the teeth too large, and the face too strange for it to belong to *Homo*. He settled instead on the name *Zinjanthropus boisei*, nicknamed Zinj. The Zinj skull proved to be 1.75 million years old, and it made Olduvai famous. I was a high school student when Zinj was found, and—just as it did for many other paleoanthropologists of my generation—reading about that discovery fired my own passion to find fossil ancestors.

We now know that this specimen and others like it from East Africa belong to a specialized subset of the genus *Australopithecus*. It wasn't until the following year that Olduvai confirmed Leakey's long-standing convictions by yielding a bona fide early *Homo*. Not far from the location of that first skull his son Jonathan found some skull fragments and part of a mandible from a hominid that was strikingly different from Zinj. Later, hominid hand and foot bones turned up at the same site and two fragmentary skulls were found elsewhere. The brain capacity of these fossils, averaging 650 cubic centimeters, was larger than that of any australopithecine (whose brain capacity was, very roughly, 380 to 530 cc, as compared to our own 1400 cc).

The Leakeys had found the maker of the tools that were scattered so promiscuously at Olduvai. In 1964, Louis and his colleagues announced a new species of hominid, *Homo habilis*, with a species epithet from the Latin for "able, handy, mentally skillful, vigorous." In an article published in the British science journal *Nature*, the authors stated, "While it is possible that *Zinjanthropus* and *Homo habilis* both made stone tools, it is probable that the latter was the more advanced tool maker and that the *Zinjanthropus* skull represents an intruder (or a victim) on a *Homo habilis* living site."

As is the case with the naming of any new species in this field, the announcement was met with mixed reviews. Despite the presence of stone tools at Olduvai, some prominent paleoanthropologists thought that the fossils attributed to the new species of *Homo* could fall within the genus *Australopithecus*. Nearly three decades after its debut, *Homo habilis* has until recently been generally accepted as a valid species, in part because of skulls found during the 1970s by Richard Leakey's team at Koobi Fora, in northern Kenya.

The reality of early human evolution may have been more complex, however, and it's worth briefly listing the caveats about this putative first species of genus *Homo*. Remember that a genus is no more than a theoretical construct, usually defined as a group of species more closely related to each other than to any other species. Just what distinguishes the members of genus *Homo* besides the loose description "bipedal primate with an increasingly large brain" is still under debate.

Whereas the first critics of *habilis*, then, thought that the new species was not distinct enough from *Australopithecus*, a growing number of scholars now argue that the fossils lumped together as habilis display too much anatomical variation to belong to a single species. The same kind of objections, of course, were raised about the fossils from Hadar. Though some of my closest colleagues, including Bill Kimbel and F. Clark Howell, agree that *Homo habilis* really should be divided into two species, I'm not yet convinced that this is the case.

My colleague Ian Tattersall, of the American Museum of Natural History in New York, has called *Homo habilis* "a wastebasket taxon, little more than a convenient receptacle for a motley assortment" of skulls and other bones. As he points out, assigning the Olduvai fossils "to *Homo*, no less than the specific epithet *habilis*, depended on little more than the presumption of tool manufacture (together, perhaps, with some fractional enlargement in brain size)."

Other paleoanthropologists, unwilling to use only the name *habilis* but unsure of what other name to use, have adopted the colloquial "habilines" as a label for the early *Homo* fossils. One of the main advocates of splitting this species in two is Bernard Wood, of the University of Liverpool, who has concluded after exhaustive studies that Olduvai does harbor a single species, which he calls *habilis*. However, he also argues that Richard Leakey's Koobi Fora site contains two other coexisting species of *Homo*, only one of which, known as *Homo ergaster*, could have been our ancestor.

Yet Olduvai still holds the spotlight on the earliest representatives of our own genus and the tools they used. Louis Leakey was an enthusiast in his trailblazing *Homo habilis* discoveries. Sometimes that enthusiasm colored his interpretations of the Olduvai finds, such as his suggestion that the stone spheres, called spheroids, that were ubiquitous at Olduvai had been used by horseless

hominid gauchos as a kind of hunting *bola* to bring down game on their Paleolithic pampas. Louis also suggested that early hominids may have used stone tools to scavenge. When he made this statement in the 1960s he was alone with that assessment, and even he viewed scavenging as an intermediate behavior, a transition phase between plant-food foraging and full-fledged hunting.

Why was it unusual at that time for an investigator even to suggest scavenging as a hominid survival strategy? Because prevailing thinking ran along quite different lines. The year 1966, in the middle of a tumultuous decade, had witnessed a watershed scientific meeting, a gathering of anthropologists under the title "Man the Hunter." Out of that meeting emerged a rigid scientific hypothesis that would prove both enormously influential and remarkably

Antelope and acacia trees are familiar sites in an East African dawn. This scene is at Lake Ndutu in Serengeti National Park. LENORA JOHANSON impervious to assault for the next two decades. Using case studies of modern human hunter-gatherers, particularly the !Kung of the Kalahari, and living primates, the conference helped reconstruct a vision of hominid evolution that placed an enormous emphasis on hunting as the central hominid behavior. Because our ancestors were hunters, the story went, they developed cognitive skills reflected in the growing size of their brains and formed complex societies that included division of labor, sharing of food, maybe even language. Hunting, in short, paved the way for the rest of human evolution.

Although the archeological evidence from hominid sites had little initially to do with constructing the "Man the Hunter" hypothesis, the result of this conference was to give the idea such prominence in theories of human evolution that investigators began seeking evidence for hunting in every piece of bone and stone at early sites. If hunting was an ancient and important aspect of human behavior, as was now uncritically assumed, then the presence of stones and bones together at an archeological site provided proof that early hominids hunted.

One archeologist who spoke at that meeting was Lewis Binford, who before long would tear through the archeological community like a whirlwind, smashing holes in theories, ripping interpretations from their flimsy moorings of data, and casting a cloud of healthy skepticism over the entire field. "When you dig up a stone tool, you are not digging up human behavior but something that had dynamic behavior behind it," Lew told me as we chatted outside the Institute of Human Origins. "It isn't hard to find gross analogies between the past and the present in human behavior. What's tricky is justifying an interpretation of the archeological record based only on analogy, without understanding why it was the way it was in the modern case."

Lew had made the same point back in 1966, telling those gathered to celebrate "Man the Hunter" that the past cannot be interpreted solely through the eyes and activities of living humans and primates. Our only real way of looking into the past is through a window of inference, so the accuracy of the picture we create depends on how well we infer from the evidence. He demanded that his colleagues justify their interpretations without reverting to circular attempts that skirted the testing of assumptions.

Now a professor at Southern Methodist University in Texas, Lew Binford continues to play devil's advocate. Though the archeological community did not take kindly at first to Hurricane Lew, he has convinced most of his colleagues of the need to back up interpretation with solid data. A bearded, barrel-chested man with a wry sense of humor, Lew rails against the pleasing pictures that presented our hominid ancestors as, to use his phrase, "Granddad or Uncle Wilbur."

The modern image of hominids as happy campers goes something like this, according to Lew: "Here's Grandma picking berries with granddaughter on her shoulder. Grandma's presumably transmitting culture and knowledge. Here's Daddy walking into camp, bringing home a pig. Mother's got a child at the breast." What's wrong with this picture? It seems familiar precisely because it relies far more on the facts of the present than on those of the past. "This is a social organization that's already us," Lew said. "The only thing missing is the stock market."

Such notions about early hominids, along with extra fuel for the hunting hypothesis, were drawn largely from the archeological record at Olduvai. "There's nothing at

Archeologist Lew Binford pioneered the use of more critical, experimental methods to examine the bones and stones found at early hominid archeological sites. Binford has long argued that the famous site of FLK at Olduvai Gorge contains no evidence of hunting by hominids, but rather was a butchery area by the lakeshore where the hominids brought parts of scavenged carcasses. NANCI KAHN

Olduvai Gorge that will justify this image," asserted Lew, "but if you assume it, you can make Olduvai fit it." About the bone scatter at Olduvai he cautioned, "The hominids were a part of that, but just because I find stone tools and four feet away I find a *Deinotherium* doesn't mean the hominids were killing *Deinotherium.*"

Lew's point is that the hominids may not have hunted the extinct ancestors of elephants at Olduvai. What's more, they may not have hunted at all. And now we come to the crux of the debate that has raged in African archeology for over a decade. Did our ancestors survive as hunters or as scavengers? Did they feed off the animal carcasses whose bones we find at their sites before or after the four-legged carnivores got to them?

Even if we set aside our need to view our ancestors through the filter of our own culture, another big interpretative obstacle blocks the way. The problem is simply that hominids weren't the only ones accumulating bones in savannas 2 million years ago. As even the most casual visitor to Africa knows, there are any number of predators out there—lions, leopards, hyenas—that regularly gut carcasses and break bones. So the presence of stone tools and broken bones by itself doesn't tell us enough about what the hominids ate and how they got their hands on it.

To fill in the picture a bit more, we need a thorough knowledge of all the players on the African landscape and what sorts of traces they left on the bones they discarded. We also need to know how the landscape has changed since the early hominids lived there and how that isolated patch of ground we call an excavated site fits into the larger landscape around it. Until we know these things, we will have lots of questions and no good answers about how early hominids lived, what they ate, and how they obtained their food.

Appreciating the variety of sites and settings in an area lies at the heart of landscape archeology, a term coined by Lew Binford for an analytical approach only recently applied to the African Paleolithic. The excavated archeological sites in open lakeshore environments such as Olduvai represent only tiny pieces of a very big picture, so interpretations drawn from those few pieces can be misleading. An accurate interpretation requires knowing what constitutes the natural background at an archeological site and what would accumulate if hominids had never set foot there.

Rob Blumenschine, one of a new generation of archeologists who rose to Binford's challenge, came to the field while the hunting hypothesis still influenced interpretations of hominid sites. Rob's mentor at the University of California at Berkeley was the late Glynn Isaac, who championed the "home base" notion that early hominids hunted or scavenged meat and brought it back to central camps, where the food was shared among family groups. Though the home-base hypothesis, a popular successor to the hunting hypothesis, was itself later debunked, Glynn also pioneered a larger natural-history perspective on the study of early hominids, urging that we look at them as whole organisms that interact intimately with their environment. Following Glynn's example, Rob Blumenschine has spent the last decade investigating the ecology of early hominid habitats.

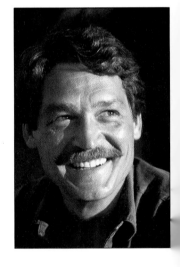

Rob Blumenschine was trained as an archeologist but traded his trowel for binoculars to study African carnivore behavior as a way of exploring early hominid behavior. D. C. JOHANSON

For insight into early hominid behavior, Rob traded in his archeologist's trowel for a naturalist's binoculars in 1983 and headed off to the savannas of the Serengeti to study modern carnivores. Stretching 15,000 square miles through Tanzania and Kenya, the Serengeti is one of the last places left on the planet that can seem to have remained unchanged for the past 2 million years. Because the savanna environments typical of East Africa today expanded around that critical 2 million-year juncture in human evolution, the modern landscape may contain clues as to how our ancestors lived and what dangers they encountered in similar settings. The Serengeti is also a living laboratory for ecologists, the best-studied woodland-savanna ecosystem in the world. Biologists flock there to witness the dynamics of life and death on the savanna. Classic carnivore behavior studies, such as

George Schaller's work with lions and Hans Kruuk's study of spotted hyenas, have been conducted in the Serengeti. These studies and the stunning films of wild dogs and other predators made by Hugo van Lawick have overturned some traditional ideas about carnivore behavior. We now know, for example, that lions often scavenge and that hyenas are formidable hunters. In the same way, Rob Blumenschine's work has contributed to a growing body of evidence that casts early hominids in a new light.

As research for his doctoral dissertation, Rob spent nearly a year in the Serengeti studying the eating habits of a range of carnivores, particularly lions and hyenas. He wanted to test the idea that early hominids might have subsisted by scavenging. Was food obtainable from a carcass, and was there enough to warrant the presumed risks of getting it? Could scavenging have been an effective strategy

Water holes like this one are the source of life in the Serengeti, the vast grassland that stretches from northern Tanzania into Kenya. The Serengeti still resembles the East Africa of 2 million years ago and its savannas are a living laboratory for studies of animal behavior. D. C. JOHANSON

that provided large payoffs in protein for the amount of time and energy expended? (During his fieldwork, let it be noted, Rob himself subsisted mainly on peanut butter spread on the Indian flat bread *chapati*, with the odd ostrich-egg omelette or impala stew thrown in for variety.)

Until recently, scavenging has enjoyed a reputation as the ugly duckling of survival strategies. In our modern eyes hunting has traditionally suggested productivity and purpose, while scavenging signifies shiftlessness, danger, and unreliability. It is certainly true that scavenging is an uncertain survival strategy, like patronizing a capricious restaurant that serves an ever-changing menu and often nothing at all. Yet once in a while, with no advance warning, you hit the jackpot—a seven-course *cordon bleu* dinner. There's no getting around it: Carcasses do provide substantial nutritional windfalls for scavengers. And so, quite possibly, they were a critical food resource for our ancestors, who probably still relied heavily on plants in their diet.

The rare African hunting dog travels in nomadic packs over a territory of hundreds of square miles. As its name suggests, the hunting dog is a fierce predator, and a pack can quickly tear its prey to pieces.
D. C. JOHANSON

Scavenging has its distinct advantages. Assuming you have a prior knowledge of promising locations, you can spot or even predict the presence of a carcass from simple cues like a tree filled with vultures or a hyena's distinctive cackle. Conceivably, then, scavenging took less time than hunting. Better yet, the hominids didn't have to waste their energy chasing down prey; their meal would have been brought down for them. Best of all, hominids would have put themselves in no more danger as scavengers than they would as herbivores munching grass or picking fruits. In contrast, hunting would have placed them at greater risk, since their freshly killed carcass would quickly attract vultures and more formidable foes hungry for meat.

One of the big arguments against hominid scavenging is that primates in similar habitats—such as chimpanzees and baboons—rarely scavenge. Even when they do, they don't go after carcasses much larger than their own bodies. Clearly, however, our ancestors were in a position to be doing something different to survive. To assume that hominids didn't scavenge because modern primates don't do it simply denies early hominids their adaptive uniqueness.

Rob's first task when he got to the Serengeti was to get his bearings, just as a scavenging hominid would have done. In the Seronera region of Serengeti National Park, he chose the most conspicuous features in the landscape, the massive outcrops of granite boulders, known as *kopjes*, and climbed to the top to survey his surroundings. There he watched for soaring vultures and other clues that might reveal the location of a carcass. It was the dry season in Seronera, and much of the vast herds of game—the wildebeest, zebra, and Thomson's gazelle—had migrated to the north in search of greener pastures. Rob learned to

Wildebeest migrate each year across the Serengeti in vast herds headed for greener pastures. These herbivores are a common prey of East African carnivores such as lions and hyenas, and hominids may have scavenged the carcasses of these and other herbivores to survive on the savanna.
LENORA JOHANSON

cultivate patience. Ten days into the study, he saw a vulture plummet to the ground. He leaped into his Land-Rover and drove to the site, where he found hyenas eagerly devouring the remains of a male impala. Little was left for Rob's inspection. Hyenas are the ultimate bone crushers of the African plain; they have incredibly powerful jaws and teeth, specially designed to exert great force as they close. If hominids had to have meat, Rob wondered as he surveyed these first pitiful remains, *would* there have been any leftovers at all for them? How could they ever compete with carnivores like hyenas, which could turn a carcass into little more than a puddle of blood in the twinkling of an eye?

In the months to come Rob observed many more animals attacked and devoured by predators. He had to be careful, just as our ancestors were, waiting for lions to leave a kill before sneaking up to examine the carcass, always staying within a short dash of the Land-Rover's open door in case a carnivore returned unexpectedly. After observing more than 250 feedings by lions, hyenas, cheetahs, jackals, and vultures, he noticed a similar consumption pattern. Carnivores adopt a strategy of instant gratification, eating as much as possible of what is easiest to eat. First to go is the flesh, starting from the rear end of the carcass and moving forward. The innards disappear almost at once, followed by the meat on the hind limbs and around the pelvis and some of the vertebrae. The feeding sequence continues along the spine to the ribs, the front limbs, and finally the head. After reaching the head, the carnivore returns to the rear end to begin extracting the marrow inside the limb bones.

This pattern allowed Rob to predict that if hominids came upon a carcass after another carnivore had begun to eat it, they would most probably be left with the limb bones, particularly the lower ends of front limbs. If the hominids were scavenging, the archeological sites should

The spotted hyena is the ultimate bone breaker on the African savanna. With its huge teeth and crushing jaws, it can easily devour a complete animal carcass in minutes. D. C. JOHANSON

show that they took what they could get. If they were hunting, on the other hand, the archeological sites should show clear signs that they had first access to the choice parts—namely, the meat-bearing bones such as femurs.

As he spent more time in the Serengeti, Rob began to question his initial assumptions that the hominids were after only meat and that they had sufficient access to it. The ancestors of *Homo habilis*, after all, had been omnivores. Maybe too much emphasis was being given to meat in the early hominid diet simply because it was assumed that they were hunters. Perhaps the hominids sought marrow, those nutritious morsels prepackaged inside the long bones often left behind at a carcass site—at least until the hyenas got there. Though the marrow of young animals is nonnutritious tissue that makes red blood cells, adult bone marrow is full of fat, grease, and calories. It's excellent fuel for a roving, small-bodied primate.

Rob also looked at how much and what sort of damage various carnivores inflict on carcass bones. Using a hammerstone like those found among the ancient Oldowan stone tools, he broke apart bones from impalas and other antelopes that had been shot to feed park guards and scattered the bones as they might be found on the surface of an archeological site. After carnivores had come to his simulated sites, he examined the bones and noted the extent of tooth marks they left behind. Overall, about 15 percent of the bones showed tooth marks and more than half of these occurred on the ends of limb bones.

Hyenas made the biggest impact on the bones at Rob's sites. Eighty percent of all the bones in a hyena-influenced assemblage had tooth marks. Rob also noticed that the hyenas consistently ignored shaft fragments from the middle of a limb in favor of the grease-filled ends of bones. He could use these figures as a litmus test for the bones found at archeological sites such as the famous FLK complex of sites at Olduvai, where the Zinj skull was found. If more than 15 percent had tooth marks and the bones also showed signs of having been broken by stone tools, then it was likely that hominids arrived on the scene to scavenge after other carnivores had eaten their fill—but before hyenas got to a carcass.

While Rob was working in the Serengeti in the 1980s, he first doubted whether hominids could have survived by scavenging in grasslands during the dry season. It was only as he began exploring riparian habitats, the strips of forest lining the banks of rivers, that the potential for hominid scavenging became clear. Rob observed that the carcasses of medium-sized herbivores left by lions lasted longer in riparian woodland than in open grassland. He also noticed that hyenas seemed skittish and fewer in number in riparian forests, perhaps wary of the lions with whom they have evolved a fascinating antagonistic relationship. That might explain why carcasses of lion kills persist in wooded areas. "You just look at the state of the bones and it's clear that hyenas play less of a role in destroying and dispersing skeletons than they do on the plains," Rob said. Hominids, then, had a chance to play more of a role in finding meat or marrow in riparian forests. Most of the early hominid sites were mosaics of forests and savanna, so hominids had access to such habitats.

One of Rob Blumenschine's students, John Cavallo, another ecological archeologist, has added substantially to the argument that hominids had ample opportunity for, and reward from, scavenging in riparian forests. Whereas Rob had mainly studied hyenas and lions, John Cavallo looked at the Serengeti leopards.

Leopards eat insects, snakes, birds, baboons, and small antelope, a considerably more diverse diet than any of the other large African cats. Leopards may focus on this smaller game as a way of avoiding competition with other carnivores. They are also solitary predators with specific territories. These territories may overlap, and a male's territory often includes the range of a few females. A leopard keeps the same territory for several years, and within that area it may select certain trees that it uses for storing the carcasses of its larger prey, such as Thomson's gazelle, Grant's gazelle, and impala.

This tree storing, John believes, is another way that leopards avoid competition. Clasping its neck in their jaws, they drag the body of their prey up into a tree for safekeeping. There they can feed on their kill alone, without fear of lions and hyenas interrupting the meal, though hyenas will often gather around the trunk of a tree where a leopard kill is stored. No other carnivore will climb a tree to claim a leopard kill, and vultures easily miss leopard kills obscured by a canopy of trees. A kill may remain stored in a tree for a few days as the leopard returns to it periodically to eat more. Tourists in East Africa today are lucky to catch a glimpse of a leopard during daylight, but they often have a ghastly glimpse of an abandoned leopard kill—the skin, skull, and lower limb bones of a gazelle dangling from a branch like a limp marionette.

John Cavallo found that he could predict places and trees where he would expect to find a leopard kill. If hominids also became familiar with a leopard's pattern of behavior, they had a fantastic opportunity to obtain a rich meal. John noticed that the consumption sequence for leopards eating prey paralleled what Rob had observed among other predators. First they eat the rump and fleshy

flanks, moving forward to the ribs, backbone, and guts, on to the face and throat, and ending with the flesh and marrow-filled ends of the front upper limb bones. But the kill isn't eaten all at once. A leopard will leave its kill hanging for anywhere from three to nine hours a day while it roams its territory. Thus, there was a window of time during which a hominid could have climbed the tree, lopped off body parts, or even nudged the entire carcass out of the tree to butcher it on the ground.

These kills may have provided hominids with a substantial amount of food, not just small animal carcasses. Rob's study concentrated on what was available on the ground only, so when John started looking in the trees, it dovetailed nicely with Rob's work. If hominids were able to get enough meat from tree-stored leopard kills, they might have relied on larger lion and hyena kills only for marrow morsels.

The relationship between leopards and baboons may shed light on how hominids behaved toward leopards. John noticed that in daylight a troop of baboons could displace a leopard from its kill and help themselves to meat. At night, however, a leopard could turn the tables by attacking a baboon as it slept in a tree. Leopards tend to kill adult male baboons, and adult males are the ones who tend to torment leopards by day.

How do we factor this back to our ancestor *Homo habilis*? Judging from the fossil record, the savanna carnivore community changed dramatically 2 million years ago. Several species of hyena became extinct, and the spotted and striped hyenas we see today appeared for the first time. By then, leopards had also become part of the carnivore picture. It's curious that such developments coincided roughly with the development of stone technology among

A leopard pulls the carcass of a Grant's gazelle into a tree for safe storage. Leopards leave their kills in trees for days and often abandon them for hours. Hominids may have scavenged abandoned leopard kills for meat and marrow.
GERALD CORSI

hominids. Just as hyenas, the hominids' main competitors for bone marrow, became less diverse, the leopard, a new carnivore that may have provided a steady source of food for hominids, suddenly appeared. We must also consider that 2 million years ago there were many more herbivore species grazing in the savanna than there are today. Did the hominids take advantage of these circumstances and devise a unique survival strategy?

In June 1992 I brought Rob Blumenschine to Castleton, a game ranch in the eastern Transvaal of South Africa, for a firsthand observation of his field techniques in an African setting different from the Serengeti. The habitat at Castleton is a dense woodland with rivers and water holes; hominids could well have lived in similar surroundings.

I had read articles about the hunting-versus-scavenging debate for years and was well aware of the arguments on both sides, but nothing prepared me for the impact of exploring the landscape with Rob, trying to obtain the perspective of *Homo habilis*. We had come to Castleton in

The thick bush country of Castleton, a private camp adjacent to Umfolozi Game Reserve in South Africa, could have been the type of landscape occupied by early hominids. Castleton was the site of an investigation into whether our ancestors survived by scavenging meat and bone marrow from carcasses. LENORA JOHANSON

the middle of a devastating drought. Some of the over-populated herbivore herds were being culled and the meat was distributed to local villages. One night Herb Friedl, our hunter guide, took an impala carcass and tied it to a bush not far from our camp. Then he turned on a tape of wild-animal sounds to lure hyenas.

We knew the hyenas would come. Every night we saw and heard them around camp, darting back and forth in the darkness, delivering their sinister giggle as they waited for the camp cooks to dump out the bones from our dinner. Right on schedule, five hyenas appeared out of nowhere. We watched them tear through the carcass in the back-to-front order Rob had observed so many times in the Serengeti. After we filmed the hyenas feeding, we frightened them away and retrieved the carcass.

The next morning, on the edge of a plain as large as a football field, Rob and I sat in a blind watching the same

impala carcass, now repositioned squarely in the middle
of the plain. After three hours of watching and waiting,
we saw a black-and-chestnut-colored bateleur eagle
descend upon the remains. The eagle clasped the impala
with its talons and began tearing flesh off the carcass with
its down-curved beak.

Suddenly, a group of white-headed vultures appeared.
The eagle flew off and the vultures covered the carcass,
squabbling and jostling for space. Within ten minutes the
vultures stripped off all the remaining flesh. A few
marabou storks flew down, wings creaking like rusty door
hinges, and joined the vultures. With their pink heads,
tufts of white neck feathers, and long black feathers trail-
ing down their backs, the storks looked like bald, beak-
nosed butlers waiting patiently for the proper moment to
serve the next course at a feast. Once again we were the
ones to stop the meal.

Rising out of our blind, Rob and I approached the carcass. Had we been hominids searching for food, the sight
of vultures circling and descending would have lured us
here. The birds flew off noisily as soon as they sensed us
coming. That meant our ancestors probably had little
trouble chasing this carnivore, at least, from a kill. We
found a devastated carcass. Skin sagged over empty space
that had once held flesh and entrails. A bare rib cage
poked up sadly to the sky.

I looked at it dubiously. "What's left on this thing to
eat?"

"There's a great meal here for the taking if you know
what to do," Rob cried with an enthusiasm I could not
share. "But you can't process a carcass of this size or larger
with your hands. You'll need stone tools to get to the
nutrients."

Marabou storks often chase vultures away from carcasses. They have long, sharp beaks for ripping off pieces of meat, which they swallow with a backward toss of the head. D. C. JOHANSON

Rob grabbed one of the bloody limb bones and laid it on a flat rock that would serve as an anvil. He took a battered piece of quartz out of his backpack to use as his hammerstone. The hammerstone is a bone breaker, one of the essential elements of the earliest tool kit. "A hominid would have had easy access to something for pounding bone," Rob said. "I just picked this up in a nearby river drainage."

A simple, unmodified stone cobble like this one could have been the first tool, allowing an opportunistic hominid to scavenge a carcass. Unlike the flakes and cores of the oldest recognizable tools, implements like these would leave no archeological traces. Flakes and cores show signs of obvious thought, planning, and craft, but they must have had some technological precursor. A river-rounded cobble of quartz or lava like the one Rob held may have set in motion a path and pace of evolution unprecedented at any time on Earth—the development of technology and culture.

Rob delivered a sharp blow to each end of the impala leg bone and then twisted it with his hands. The bone splintered into jagged, spiral fragments and an eight-inch rod of pink marrow slid out. "Not counting the viscera, the marrow bones are the major source of fat in a healthy animal," he said. "Lion and leopard kills usually have plenty of marrow left on them."

"How nutritious a meal does marrow make?" I asked.

Rob has calculated that a healthy, well-fed adult impala would yield 1,500 calories worth of marrow from the twelve major limb bones. The tibia, or shinbone, contains the most marrow. "It's a full meal, all right," he said. "It would probably provide about sixty percent of a hominid's daily caloric requirements, and it only takes about ten minutes to process."

"The first fast food?"

"A great food source, isn't it?" Rob said with a connoisseur's relish. "There's no other way you could get so many calories so fast out here."

I was powerfully struck by just how much marrow there was and how many nutrients it provided. These limb bones were the power bars of the past. All it took was a little ingenuity to open the package.

"How long would a carcass this size last on the savanna?" I asked.

"It depends on who gets to it first," Rob said. "Spoiling wouldn't have been a problem, because flesh can sit out for two or three days before it decays, and the marrow inside bones can stay fresh for up to ten days."

By anchoring a hypothesis in the ecological reality of places like the Serengeti, Rob has shown in his research that early hominids could have relied on scavenging for important sources of fat and protein. It doesn't prove that hominids scavenged, only that the opportunity existed. To carry through the courtroom analogy, we can say that this opportunity casts a reasonable doubt on the hunting hypothesis. We know that hunting did become an important human behavior at some point in our evolutionary history, but Rob's work shows that we cannot assume scavenging never was an important strategy for our ancestors.

In north-central Tanzania, not far from Olduvai Gorge, living humans are practicing all the survival strategies we've been looking at in this chapter. This is a group of hunter-gatherers called the Hadza. Hunting and scavenging are closely connected for the Hadza; each is part of a broader strategy for obtaining food. One recent study found that scavenging supplied a fifth of the medium and large mammals consumed by a group of Hadza.

Donald Johanson watches while Rob Blumenschine demonstrates that this apparently carnivore-ravaged impala carcass could have provided early hominids with plenty to eat. Though the impala's flesh is gone, simple stone tools substituting as hammers and knives could be used to butcher the remaining bones. Such opportunities may mean that our ancestors were scavengers long before they became hunters. LENORA JOHANSON

A nutritious meal lies inside an impala limb bone. With the bone resting on a rock anvil, Rob Blumenschine uses a second stone as a hammer to shatter the shaft. Then he twists the shaft with his hands, exposing the bone marrow. The high-protein marrow in all of this impala's limb bones would yield about 1,500 calories.

D. C. JOHANSON

A tiny flake struck from a chunk of quartz makes a handy slicing tool. Such flakes were probably the most important implements in the earliest known stone technology, the Oldowan, which appeared over 2 million years ago.

D. C. JOHANSON

At night, the Hadza listen carefully for the calls of lions and hyenas that might be feeding at a nearby kill. By day, the Hadza scan the sky for vultures. If they come upon a carcass, the Hadza immediately abandon any other activity. Often, before they can gain access to the meat, they must scare predators or other scavengers that have come sooner. Leopards and hyenas spook easily. Lions, however, tend to be tenacious. Sometimes only a volley of arrows drives them away from the kill.

The Hadza people are hunter-gatherers who live near Lake Eyasi in north central Tanzania. Their finely honed hunting skills date back many thousands of years, but the hominids of 2 million years ago most likely obtained their meat by scavenging rather than hunting. D. C. JOHANSON

It is a testament to the power of the hunting hypothesis that the Hadza's scavenging practices were only discovered after they had already been studied by anthropologists for two decades. Certainly, the Hadza are also accomplished hunters, exhibiting a range of skills that are fast disappearing in our modern age. Their activities appear to be rooted in the past, but how deeply? Increasingly, the archeological evidence suggests that habitual hunting did not begin until late in human evolution, perhaps not until after the appearance of modern humans.

There's one factor in the potential hominid scavenging niche that can't be tested today—not in Serengeti, Castleton, among the Hadza,

or anywhere else. It involves a once-intimidating group of carnivores that no longer exist—the sabertooth cats and their relative, *Dinofelis*, called a "false sabertooth." At the time when stone tools first appeared and hominids inhabited the savannas, at least three species of these unusual cats also lived in East Africa. Although no one knows whether they were agile climbers that may have stored kills as leopards do, the sabertooths had stocky bodies, built more for stealth than speed, and they probably lived in riparian habitats, where hominids would have found the most successful scavenging.

Sabertooths are so named for their incredibly elongated upper canines, which they use to slash lethal wounds in

A Hadza father and son wait patiently for a chance to hunt such big game as zebra, wildebeest, impala, giraffe, and buffalo. The Hadza succeed in killing a large animal only once every few weeks, so they also subsist by scavenging meat and gathering roots, fruit, and honey.   D. C. JOHANSON

When an animal comes within range, a Hadza hunter loads his bow with a metal-tipped arrow that has been dipped in poison. If the arrow strikes, the hunter will stalk the quarry while the poison takes effect.
D. C. JOHANSON

their prey. A sabertooth's upper and lower incisors are arranged in arcs that form a beak when the jaws are closed, a likely adaptation for tearing flesh from a carcass. Sabertooth cats clearly lack the bone-crushing capacity of hyena teeth and jaws, and the huge canines must have impeded a sabertooth's ability to remove flesh from a carcass. It seems likely that sabertooth cats were taking large chunks of flesh as quickly as possible, leaving all the bones, as well as some of the meat, behind. Sabertooth kills may well have offered substantial amounts of meat as well as marrow to hominid scavengers.

• • •

Every animal has a niche, a space it fills and a role it plays in an ecosystem. Given the diet of their ancestors, it's likely that *Homo* straddled the carnivore and herbivore niches. Niches can shift over time as various environmental factors change. Hominids may have developed a mixed ground- and tree-based scavenging niche that suited their diurnal habits, social nature, and technological abilities. Scavenging may have been a dry-season strategy for hominids, who relied more on plant foods in the wet season. Processing meat and marrow was not a nutritional necessity for hominids at first, but perhaps it became one over time.

When Rob came to Castleton, he was struck by how different it appeared from other areas where he had worked in Africa. As Rob pointed out, it was an especially tricky spot in which to scavenge because the forest was dense, and where there weren't trees, the ground was covered in heavy brush. In the Serengeti Rob could park his Land-Rover and scan a treeless plain for visual cues to carcasses such as carnivores on the ground or vultures overhead. This was harder to do at Castleton.

A scavenger faced with such obstacles, I realized, would require as much cunning and cleverness, if not more, than a hunter. The same skills that scavenging takes would also serve for hunting, but why couldn't the hominids have honed those skills as scavengers first? Scavenging has traditionally been portrayed not only as a risky and marginal means of subsistence but as intellectually unchallenging as well. Rob believes, however, that scavenging would have put an evolutionary premium on hominid intelligence.

For one thing, scavenging requires a certain amount of knowledge about animal behavior, a perception of where in the environment the eating opportunities are, and the skill to get into the bones without the benefit of powerful teeth and jaws. Hominids had to be able to detect and locate a carcass. They also had to know when not to interfere with other carnivores taking their turn at a carcass, a lesson I learned from the lioness we filmed.

Hominids may have made mental maps of the land-

Sabertooth cats occupied African savannas when our early ancestors did. Their long shearing canines could remove large chunks of flesh from a carcass, but these cats may have left behind meat and marrow that hominids scavenged.
IAN EVERARD

scape and used them to predict where likely food resources were. It's not a farfetched idea. Chimps know their territories well, so why wouldn't hominids be just as adept? I think that even though technology may have instigated some major steps in human evolution, one unfortunate consequence is that humans have lost our once-intimate connection with nature. As we struggle to comprehend our place in nature philosophically, we often get lost in it literally. It's hard to imagine just what sort of keen awareness of their surroundings our distant ancestors had.

"Primates do make mental maps, especially the fruit-eating primates, who depend on a resource that's very unpredictable in time and space," Rob told me as we hiked through the bush at Castleton. Giraffes quietly browsed on an acacia tree nearby. "They need to know the location of resources. The same species of fruiting tree can vary in when it bears fruit."

"So *afarensis* may have had similar maps of the fruiting trees in its forest environment?" I asked.

"Why not? This mental map-making ability would be a perfect preadaptation for scavenging in early *Homo*."

"I still think the hominids would have been vulnerable out here," I said, thinking of our lion encounter. "They needed to be extremely cautious."

Rob knew my feelings about bipedalism. "I know you don't want to admit it, but they *were* nimble. They were anatomically equipped to get up a tree quickly. They kept that ability right up to *Homo erectus*, when the evidence for arboreality disappears."

Chimpanzees in the forests of Taï National Park, in the Ivory Coast, he reminded me, have been observed carrying wooden billets on foraging trips to smash open panda nuts. The chimps also use stone hammers to crack the nutshells, and they save a good stone for future foraging trips. Hominids were probably at least equally resourceful with a food supply—carcasses—that held greater nutritional rewards.

But if even chimps use rudimentary tools, do our ancestors' modest implements really count as much of an advance in the evolutionary scheme of things? In response to assertions that *Homo habilis* had only the cognitive power of a chimpanzee, archeologists Nick Toth and Kathy Schick, of the Center for Research into the Anthropological Foundations of Technology (CRAFT) at Indiana University, decided to see if a chimpanzee could duplicate an early hominid's technological acumen. Nick and Kathy, like Rob Blumenschine, studied under Glynn Isaac at Berkeley and have joined the ranks of the new experimental archeologists.

Nick and Kathy didn't know if they could teach a chimp how to make stone tools, but they began with a premise that making even simple tools required a complex chain of decisions. They did know that Kanzi is a curious and clever chimp. He's actually a pygmy chimpanzee, or bonobo, a separate species from the common chimpanzee and one that has only recently become the focus of field studies in Central Africa. Kanzi lives at the Language Research Center in Atlanta, Georgia, where he is the star pupil of psychologists Susan Savage-Rumbaugh and Duane Rumbaugh. In 1981, they began an experiment to teach Kanzi's mother, Matata, to communicate with the researchers using a board covered with 256 geometric shapes, each representing a different noun or verb. Matata never caught on, but young Kanzi began to learn and use the symbols just by watching. By the time he was

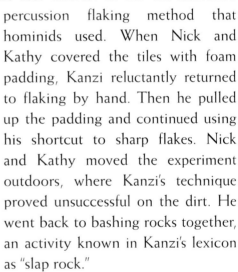

ten years old in 1991, Kanzi had a vocabulary of two hundred words.

To see if Kanzi could learn other skills, Nick, an expert on re-creating the earliest types of stone tools, began demonstrating stone-making techniques in front of him. Kanzi soon began banging rocks together. After nine months he was able to remove flakes and use them to obtain food.

Kanzi also demonstrated a precocious flair for innovation. Once he learned that he could spontaneously shatter rocks by throwing them onto the tile floor of his indoor enclosure, he lost interest in the old-fashioned percussion flaking method that hominids used. When Nick and Kathy covered the tiles with foam padding, Kanzi reluctantly returned to flaking by hand. Then he pulled up the padding and continued using his shortcut to sharp flakes. Nick and Kathy moved the experiment outdoors, where Kanzi's technique proved unsuccessful on the dirt. He went back to bashing rocks together, an activity known in Kanzi's lexicon as "slap rock."

Kanzi quickly developed an affinity for stone tools when he was put in situations where they came in handy, such as cutting a cord tied to the closed lid of a box containing such prizes as bananas, grapes, raisins, M & M's, and Popsicles. Kanzi takes anywhere from thirty seconds to

Kanzi, a bonobo, or pygmy chimpanzee, at the Language Research Center in Atlanta, has been the star pupil in a study designed to test an ape's aptitude for making and using stone tools. Although Kanzi quickly learned to strike off flakes and use them to cut a rope and open a box containing a food prize, his tools show less skill than is apparent in the earliest hominid tools.
ROSE A. SEVCIK, LANGUAGE RESEARCH CENTER

twenty minutes to cut through the rope cord. He seems to sense the sharpness of a flake with his tongue and then makes a unidirectional slashing motion, rather than sawing back and forth, with his right hand. When a flake becomes dull, he tends to persevere rather than discard it for a new, sharp flake.

It's noteworthy that Kanzi's tools do not match the Oldowan type of hominid tools in any way, according to Nick and Kathy. The cores are bashed and have steep-angled edges rather than the acute angles that characterize stone tools. Although Kanzi is learning to use the edge of the stone core rather than relentlessly bashing the middle, he still does not analyze the core as an unformed rock with a potential tool inside, the way a sculptor would picture a conceived form residing in a rough block of marble.

Though Kanzi's example shows us that apes have some capacity for making and using stone tools, it's unlikely that Kanzi will ever match the tool-making prowess of *Homo habilis.* So the next question to ask is: What did the hominids have that Kanzi apparently lacks? When did technology become uniquely human? And what new light does all this shed on Olduvai Gorge? Let's go back to Olduvai and look at the *Homo habilis* evidence using the wide-ranging perspective and the wealth of information this new school of archeological investigation has given us.

The initial interpretation of the FLK "living floor," where tools and animal bones but no *Homo habilis* fossils were found, was that hominids hunted game and butchered the carcasses here at a base camp. Hyena tooth marks and other signs of carnivore presence were taken as evidence that carnivores came later and scavenged the hominids' kills. Lew Binford turned this interpretation inside out. He argued that, yes, the hominids were processing meat from carcasses on the Zinj floor, by the ancient lakeshore, but the meat and bones came from carcasses that the hominids themselves had scavenged from carnivores and carried to this site.

While Rob Blumenschine was at Castleton, he showed me how to identify hominid stone-tool cut marks from carnivore tooth marks. Each leaves a highly distinctive signature on bone—stone tools a **V**-shaped groove, carnivore teeth a broader, **U**-shaped groove. Rob collected bones from the impala carcass scavenged by hyenas and butchered them with stone tools. He mixed up these bones with other impala bones collected from a lion kill and boiled them in a cast-iron pot over our campfire. When we examined them under a simple hand lens, it was easy to distinguish Rob's cut marks from the tooth marks and gnaw marks. In addition to the shape of the mark itself, the type of bone on which a mark occurs and its location on the bone help diagnose the agent that inflicted the damage. Cut marks, for instance, tend to cluster around joints and the ends of meaty limb bones, places that facilitate butchering the skeleton.

Recently Rob reanalyzed the 2,500 or so animal-bone fragments from FLK that have been the focus of the hunting-versus-scavenging debate. These bones are mostly skull fragments and limb shafts. According to Rob's research, those containing marrow rather than lots of flesh are the most abundant; score one for the scavenging hypothesis.

Though original estimates for the number of bones displaying carnivore tooth marks ranged from 12 to 25 percent, Rob found that more than half the bones had

been chewed by carnivores. At the same time he also found many stone-tool cut marks and "percussion," or bashing, marks, signs of hammerstone use. Both these types of marks indicate that hominids had also been breaking open bones. The picture that emerges is one of hominids bringing parts of carcasses that had already been defleshed by carnivores, probably big cats, to the FLK site, where they broke apart the bones to get the marrow. Other carnivores came by later to polish off the remains.

"This hunting-versus-scavenging debate is a red herring," Lew Binford confessed during one of our conversations at the Institute of Human Origins. "I think the real issue is, Why do animals transport bones? I'm fairly convinced that until much later in time, when we find unequivocal, unambiguous associations of stone tools, hearths, and bones, we are not looking at diet. There's no reason to argue that what's in the site is telling you about the diet." Lew believes that the ancient archeological sites reveal aspects of hominid diet but do not inform us about all they ate or about the total range of tactics they used to obtain food.

Under the modest magnification of a hand lens or, as in these photos, the powerful magnification of a scanning electron microscope, the marks that stone tools leave on bones can be distinguished from the marks left by carnivore teeth. The tool cut marks, on the right, tend to make a V-shaped groove, while tooth marks tend to make a broader, U-shaped groove. These signatures help reveal who or what accumulated broken bones at archeological sites.
NICHOLAS TOTH AND
KATHY SHICK

Lew's statistical analysis of the Olduvai data showed a puzzling pattern. Some bones were carried from one place to another; so were some types of tools. Most of the food is consumed where it's found, but why should any be transported somewhere else by hominids? Tools made from volcanic basalt appear to have been carried greater distances than tools made of quartz, and basalt tools tend to occur around animal bones from whole body parts, suggesting that the hominids found an entire carcass. Smaller quartz tools seem to be associated with fractured lower limb bones that are isolated from the rest of the carcass and presumably were transported from somewhere else. Why did the hominids transport some kinds of bones but not others? It may have to do with how they processed bones to access food.

The hominids knew enough to find and choose raw material for stone tools from great distances. Forays for food may have included regular stops at a rock source to collect some raw material or make some tools on the spot. Lew believes that the hominids carried the quartz used for stone tools at Olduvai, because it's found over an unnaturally wide area. Apparently, though, the hominids lacked a sense of longevity about their tools. Often the tools show little or no sign of having been used before they were discarded, as though the hominids had run into a prehistoric form of planned obsolescence.

Basalt tools may have been carried by hominids on their foraging trips and discarded after the hominids found and scavenged a carcass—in other words, basalt tools came to the bones. In contrast, quartz tools may be confined to central processing places, where certain bones are brought to the tools.

As for the FLK site, the bone scatter there included

lots of lower limb bone fragments, the bones that carnivores often never get around to eating. Lew thinks that hominids brought these bones to the lakeshore to process them for the chunks of marrow inside. Most of the tools at FLK are made of locally quarried quartz. The hominids may have soaked the skin and periosteum, a membranous sheath that covers bones, in the lake before they could penetrate the bones with stone flakes. The African sun dries hides quickly and leaves them impenetrable.

The lakeshore location of FLK also makes it an unlikely site for a hominid camp. The edges of African lakes and water holes are potentially dangerous places, especially at night, when a hominid would have hunkered down in the grass like any other animal or sought shelter in a tree. The safest place at night may have been off the ground. During the day, however, the lakeshore teemed with all sorts of animal life, what Lew has called "the midday drinking club," when gazelles, wildebeest, zebra, and other herbivores come to drink at their leisure, while the carnivores are at their most lethargic, asleep in the shade of acacia trees. The absence of predators at such a time would have opened an opportunity for hominids to obtain food or prepare food that they had already scavenged.

Lew believes that scavenging was just one tactic hominids used to survive. It may not have been the main calorie-seeking strategy for hominids, but it might have been a strategy of great evolutionary significance. Scavenging and stone technology may have evolved in concert with the noticeably larger brain of early *Homo,* and the high-energy packets of marrow locked in bone would have helped fuel the energy demands of the brain. Most vertebrates devote between 5 and 8 percent of their total body metabolism to running the brain; large monkeys

Zebra and wildebeest herds often occur together in the savanna, especially around water holes. Large herbivores approach water holes in the afternoon heat when predators such as lions seek shade. Hominids may have brought scavenged meat to the water's edge at this time of day for butchering.
LENORA JOHANSON

such as baboons need 10 to 13 percent. Humans use more than 20 percent, and the brains of human infants demand half of a body's metabolism.

Hominids, Lew speculates, may consequently have scavenged marrow as a high-fat supplement for weaning children or lactating females. That might account for the dual pattern of tool and bone transport, in which only the marrow bones have been moved from where they were obtained. Lew sees bone marrow as the perfect weaning-time food—high quality in a small package. So scavenging may have been a key part of a bigger strategy of parental investment and care of the young. "How all these things fit together is the interesting question," he concluded our discussion, "not just, Did early man scavenge?"

Part of the problem in fitting all of the pieces of hominid behavior together is that Olduvai constitutes a complex range of habitats over a vast span of time. The site called FLK-NN, for instance, is very different from the FLK "living floor" where Mary Leakey found the Zinj skull. It is called the "tortoise floor" because a number of broken tortoise shells were found there with the bones of only a single large animal. This site lacks the dense concentration of tools found on the Zinj floor. Instead, there are a few scattered smatterings of stone. Lew Binford thinks the FLK-NN site captures a series of separate episodes over a long period of time.

What it really looks like, in fact, is a string of oppor-

Not far from the FLK Zinjanthropus floor and its dense concentration of tools is another site that reveals the range of ancient landscapes at Olduvai. This site, called the "tortoise floor" because of several smashed tortoise shells, preserves only a single large animal carcass and a smattering of stone tools. Little can be learned about hominid behavior by focusing on just one small area in a place as large as Olduvai.

D. C. JOHANSON

tunistic events: A hominid happens upon a tortoise and smashes open its shell to get a meal. Later a herbivore dies and its body is scavenged. More time passes. Another hominid smashes open another tortoise shell. The presence of tortoises suggests that this was a dry region, although it is not far from the FLK site and the lakeshore. The quartz tools and bone remains contain information about hominid behavior, but clearly the types of activities recorded here are different from those at FLK. Maybe tortoises were dry-season food resources for hominids.

With hypotheses like these, which attempt to factor in a site's full natural context, Lew Binford, Rob Blumenschine, and other archeologists, like Rick Potts of the Smithsonian Institution—who is currently bulldozing three-mile trenches at the Olorgesailie site in Kenya instead of the traditional square-meter test pits—are actively bringing the principles of landscape archeology to bear on the African Paleolithic. Lew's final take on who was responsible for what at Olduvai, by the way, is that *all* the archeological sites there remain equivocal. We simply don't know enough about them yet. We need more evidence, and we need to keep refining our ways of thinking about it. Like an Agatha Christie novel, the excavations at Olduvai Gorge are littered with clues to a real whodunit. It's our own brains and tools that require expanding before the *Homo habilis* installment of the human mystery moves closer to a solution.

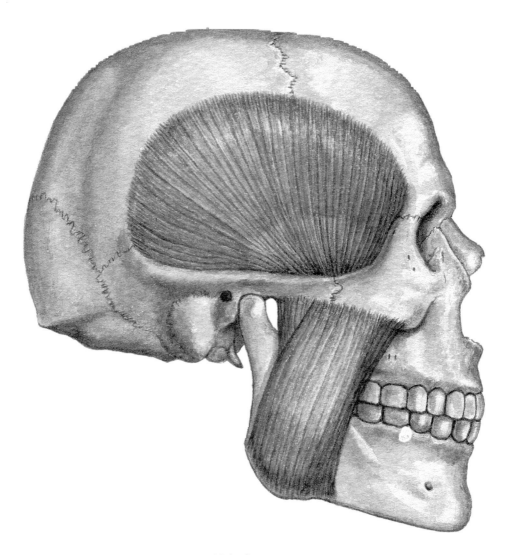

Modern human

CHAPTER FOUR

The Nutcracker People:

Australopithecus robustus

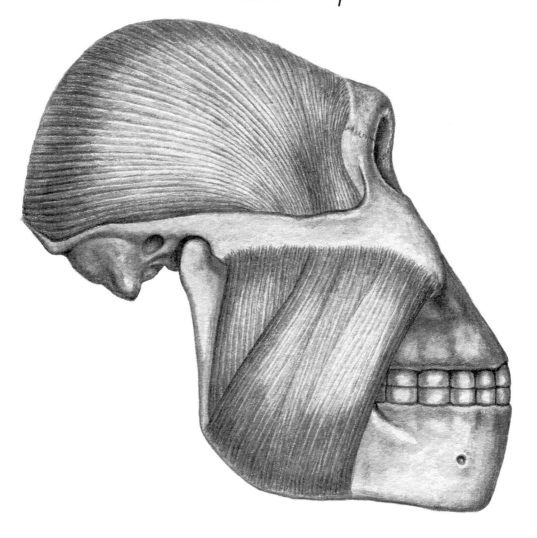

Robust australopithecine

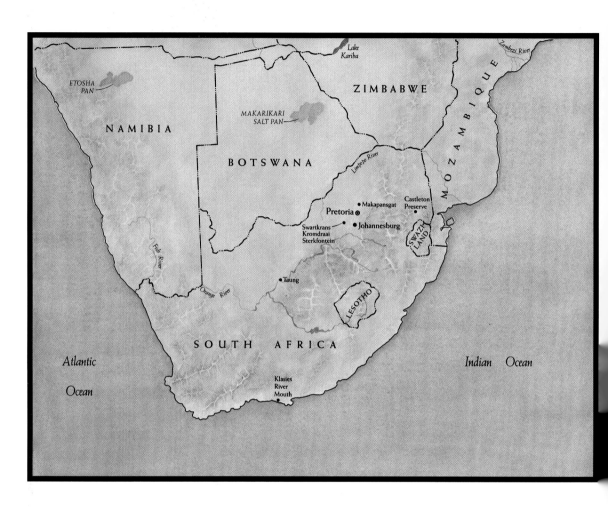

Map of South Africa with
prehistoric sites. CAROLYN FISH

PICTURE AN ANCIENT LIMESTONE CAVE IN AN exposed outcropping somewhere on the highveld of South Africa. Over this cave hangs a lone stinkwood tree. Inside, a small group of humanlike creatures about four feet tall huddle together. They have tiny crested heads, cheekbones like flying buttresses, and wide, thickly enameled, nickel-sized teeth. They are *Australopithecus robustus*, an extinct hominid species that is an important subplot of our story.

These creatures were the most fascinating characters in the whole human mystery, and they aren't even our direct ancestors. If Lucy and the *afarensis* First Family at Hadar were our species' great-grandparents, if the *Homo habilis* crowd at Olduvai were our grandparents, and *Homo erectus* our parents, then *Australopithecus robustus* are by way of being our great-great-uncles and -aunts.

Their outlandish appearance tells us that the robusts were unique among hominids before or since. They ate different foods, possibly lived in different habitats, carved out their own highly specialized evolutionary niche. They coexisted with two species of *Homo* and were our lineage's closest relatives until they died out. Yet *robustus* remained a separate evolutionary experiment; for reasons still unknown, its story ended while that of our immediate forebears went on.

In spite of the robusts' spectacular looks, their unique anatomy has only recently been studied in depth. This strange omission came about because *Homo*-centric investigators traditionally regarded this long-since-defunct group, in the words of my colleague Steven Ward, as the "chaff of hominid evolution." Why and how did these mysterious hominids evolve as they did—and why don't we currently share the planet with some third cousins who might have stepped out of a 1950s science fiction movie?

Let's go back to Lucy and her genus, *Australopithecus*. Anthropologists have come to divide the australopithecine genus into two broad groups: gracile and robust. So far Africa has given us two gracile species, *afarensis* and *africanus*, and at least three species of their robust descendants. In a sense, though, the terms *gracile* and *robust* are misleading, calling to mind as they do ballet dancers versus wrestlers; the fact is that the two groups of hominids probably did not differ much in overall body size. We don't know for sure, of course, because the fossil evidence for these species consists mainly of skulls and teeth. At the same time we need to remember that the most dramatic physical changes after hominids became bipedal took place only from the neck up; thus faces, skulls, and teeth really are the crucial evidence that allows us to distinguish one species from another.

With its flat face framed by exaggerated cheekbones and a muscle-bearing bony crest riding the tiny braincase, a robust can be identified even from the smallest fragments of skull bone. Its teeth are even more distinctive: huge broad flattened molars and premolars, or bicuspids, with an enamel coating twice as thick as that on the teeth of other australopithecines or humans. The durable skulls and teeth comprise most of the few hundred robust fossils that have been found at eight African sites—two in South Africa and six in East Africa. Apparently, robust australopithecines ranged for at least 2,200 miles across Africa.

The robusts were living at the same time—and sometimes in the same places—as their cousins the tool-using *Homo habilis* 2 million years ago and as recently as 900,000 years ago, alongside *habilis*'s descendant and our immediate ancestor, *Homo erectus*. Though these two lines of hominids clearly overlap in time and habitat, whether they lived alongside each other or to what extent they interacted are questions we can't answer now, if ever.

To find the richest fossil deposits of the evolutionary dead end we call *robustus* we must leave the East African sites we've grown familiar with in previous chapters and look down to South Africa, beyond the southernmost tip of the Great Rift Valley. South Africa presents paleoanthropologists not only with a new cast of fossil characters but with new habitats and a completely different set of conditions under which the remains of hominids and other animals have been preserved. Instead of the open terrain of rugged volcanic sediments at Hadar or Olduvai Gorge, where fossils erode easily from the ground in the rain, the early South African hominid sites are deep limestone caves, where fossils are mixed into a cement-hard melange of sand, gravel, and calcium carbonate known as breccia. Historically, these caves attracted miners blasting for lime, and many discoveries were made as fossil hunters poked laboriously through piles of rubble left in the miners' wake.

Thanks to the unflagging zeal of a young anatomy professor named Raymond Dart, the story of African paleoanthropology actually began in South Africa long before Hadar and Olduvai were excavated, during the first decades of this century. In 1924, Josephine Salmons, the only woman student in Dart's class at the University of Witwatersrand in Johannesburg, alerted her professor to some fossils found by miners at the Buxton Limeworks,

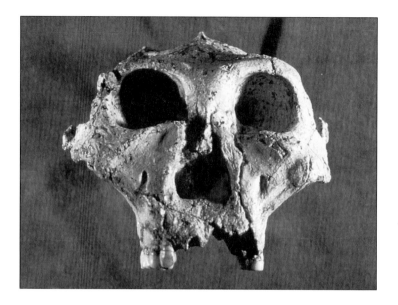

A front view of Australopithecus robustus *reveals the very flat, even dished face that distinguishes this hominid. One anthropologist has described the face as "so flat that you can almost play snooker on it."*
D. C. JOHANSON

a quarry near Taung. Dart, in his second year at the medical school, was keen to develop a comparative teaching collection of bones and had encouraged his students to hunt for fossils during their vacations, with the incentive of a small reward for the most interesting finds. His student had seen what she thought was a baboon skull on the mantel of the quarry owner's home, and Dart arranged to have some bone-laden blocks of rubble from Taung sent to him. He quickly found in this unpromising assortment the skull of a young humanlike creature.

It took Dart two months of careful work with a hammer and his wife's knitting needles to remove the rock slab that encased his precious fossil. What he exposed was breathtaking; he had before him the face of a child with delicate features and a gap-toothed grimace, along with a crystal-coat limestone cast of the brain. Dart knew this creature had died at a young age because the permanent first molar had just begun to erupt.

Realizing that he had stumbled upon something utterly new and different, Dart described the Taung child as a bridge between living apes and humans and gave it the name *Australopithecus africanus.* Dated later at possibly 2 million years, the Taung child at that time was the oldest human ancestor ever located.

Raymond Dart's announcement of this missing link appeared in the February 7, 1925, edition of the journal *Nature.* Immediately, it ignited a fierce controversy. European scientists were looking to Asia for evidence of human antiquity and did not want to believe that a young anatomist in provincial South Africa had come upon anything to do with our evolution. The Taung fossil was variously dismissed as an immature chimpanzee or a dwarf gorilla.

Raymond Dart immediately recognized the significance of the Taung skull that was sent to him from a South African mine in 1924. He spent years defending his view that the Taung fossil belonged to a hominid and eventually prevailed.

IAN EVERARD

It took several years to convince the critics. Few of them had examined Dart's specimens firsthand, so it was not widely recognized how unusual they were. Four years after the *Nature* article, Dart separated the upper and lower jaws of the Taung skull, revealing all the teeth. The following year he took it to England to argue his case. The fossil itself and its newly exposed dental evidence effectively supported his claims.

At home, Dart had a diehard supporter named Robert Broom, a country doctor and self-taught authority on the fossil reptiles of the arid Karoo region. A grandfatherly man with baggy jowls and owlishly round glasses, Broom believed Dart was right in calling the Taung child a human ancestor, and he resolved to find more fossils to prove Dart's point. In fulfilling his goal, Broom would soon introduce the world to the more robust relatives of *africanus*.

In 1936, Robert Broom retired from medical practice

Dynamited from a cave at the Buxton Limeworks in South Africa in 1924, the tiny skull of the Taung child provided the first real evidence that human ancestors evolved in Africa. The child lived 2 million years ago and died at the age of three to five years. The announcement of the skull by anatomist Raymond Dart was met with scientific skepticism outside South Africa, but further hominid discoveries in South African caves proved Dart right. This fossil is now placed in the species Australopithecus africanus.

D. C. JOHANSON

To silence critics of the Taung skull, Robert Broom set out to find other hominid fossils in South Africa. In 1938, he discovered the first example of a completely different kind of hominid: a creature with a flat face, huge teeth, and flaring cheekbones that Broom called Paranthropus robustus. IAN EVERARD

and joined the staff of the Transvaal Museum in Pretoria. Free now to indulge his passion for fossils full-time, Broom began exploring a nearby limestone cave called Sterkfontein. Aware that fossils had been found there, he asked the mine foreman, G. W. Barlow, who knew of Raymond Dart's skull, to alert him if anything similar appeared at Sterkfontein. Eleven days later, Barlow handed him a brain cast. Subsequent searching turned up much of the skull, which resembled that of the Taung child. Though it is now regarded as belonging to the same species as the Taung child, Broom—who would become notorious for seeing a brand-new species in every fossil he came upon—promptly dubbed his find *Plesianthropus transvaalensis*.

When Broom visited Sterkfontein on June 8, 1938, Barlow showed him part of a fossil hominid upper jaw with a molar sticking out of its socket. Concealing his excitement until he had haggled with Barlow over a price for the fossil, Broom later learned that the fossil had actually been found by a schoolboy on a farm called Kromdraai, two miles from Sterkfontein. Broom went immediately to the farm, and the boy's sister took him to the spot where the fossil had been found. On the spot he retrieved two more pieces of skull and some teeth. Next Broom tracked down the boy, Gert Terblanche, in school and coaxed him to part with four more fossil teeth from his pocket, each of which fit into the upper jaw. After school, the boy showed Broom where he had hidden the skull's lower jaw, and the next day Broom discovered even more of the skull at the site.

Broom realized that the Kromdraai fossil differed markedly from those found at Taung and Sterkfontein. For one thing, the face was concave, like a shallow bowl:

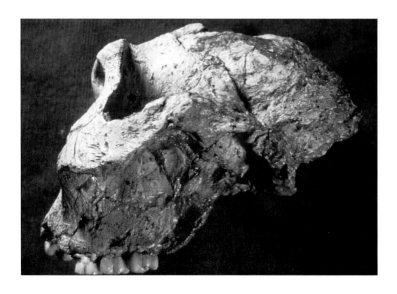

Several kinds of hominids have been found embedded in the limestone caves of South Africa's Transvaal. One of the most unusual is Australopithecus robustus, *whose huge back teeth and strong chewing muscles helped this hominid crush hard-to-chew foods such as seeds, nuts, and plants. This specimen came from the Swartkrans cave, where more fossils of this species have been found than at any other site.*

D. C. JOHANSON

Another robust australopithecine fossil from Swartkrans shows the prominent sagittal crest that runs along the top of the skull. The crest anchored powerful chewing muscles that generated tremendous biting force. D. C. JOHANSON

When he laid a pencil across it, the pencil touched only the protruding cheekbones on either side. Broom wasted no time christening this specimen *Paranthropus robustus*. For once, his name-giving proclivities were right on target. This fossil certainly was robust, and *Paranthropus* means "parallel to man." Broom, in fact, had sensed intuitively where this species belonged on the family tree. This first discovery of a robust australopithecine was to open a new chapter in the study of human origins. Though most paleoanthropologists today include *Paranthropus* within the genus *Australopithecus*, some maintain that the robust hominids are different enough to warrant Broom's distinction.

Why did the robusts look the way they did—and why so different from other hominids? The simplest answer can be found in that familiar saying "You are what you eat." The robust australopithecine face and skull is nothing more nor less than an industrial-strength food-processing machine. Those prominent cheekbones and skull-top crest are overdeveloped for one reason only: to accommodate huge chewing muscles.

I like to call the robusts the Cuisinarts of human evolution, but I think Phillip Tobias—Raymond Dart's former student, now retired from the faculty of the University of Witwatersrand—hit it right on target when he dubbed the Leakeys' *Zinjanthropus* skull Nutcracker Man. The jaws and face of a robust australopithecine operate like a nutcracker. The jaw joint is the fulcrum, and the rows of cheek teeth in each jaw are the levers, or the nutcracker handles. Compared to those of other hominids, the robusts' cheek teeth have shifted closer to the jaw joint, and that gives them more leverage for chewing. At the same time the cheekbones have shifted forward, allowing the bulky chewing muscles to generate much greater force. If you imagine these muscles as hands on a nutcracker, it's much easier to break a nutshell the farther away from the nut you place your hands on the lever.

The lower jaw of the robust australopithecines offers further evidence of their heavy-duty diet. The horseshoe-shaped—almost horseshoe-*sized*—bone widens from top to bottom, a design that resists fracture. This built-in toughness may explain why paleoanthropologists find so many *robustus* lower jaws preserved. The overall design may also have helped the jaw withstand twisting as it moved in a circle to break apart food.

The rest of the robust face seems similarly designed to withstand various stresses on the bones. The wide cheekbones help support the face, just as the flying buttresses jutting from the sides of Gothic cathedrals brace their walls and take pressure off the soaring vaults. The robust's face, however, needed even more support. On either side of the nasal cavity sit two pillars of solid bone that are the

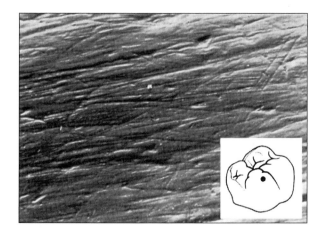

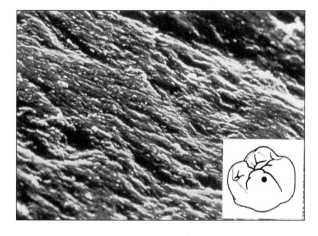

Under a scanning electron microscope, the magnified tooth surface of hominids reveals hints of what they ate. The molar from the gracile Australopithecus africanus, top, *contrasts with that from a robust australopithecine below.* FRED GRINE

strongest part of the face and act like the columns on the facade of a Greek temple. The East African robust species *Australopithecus boisei*, the name eventually given to the Zinj skull discovered by the Leakeys at Olduvai in 1959, has a further bolstering feature, a massive mid-forehead region that functions like the keystone of an arch to support the face.

Now, we modern humans have the same chewing muscles as the robusts, just not so massive (see the illustration at the beginning of this chapter). Human jaws can generate around 400 pounds of bite force, which is no mean feat. Experts judge the bite force from robust australopithecine jaws, however, to have exceeded 1,700 pounds!

What was it the robusts were eating that demanded such a specialized and rugged anatomy? The answer is fiber—*very* high fiber. We know this by examining wear marks on the teeth of the robust australopithecines. Under the magnification of a scanning electron microscope, the enamel of robust teeth reveals a series of pits that one investigator has picturesquely likened to concrete beaten with a sledgehammer. In contrast, the magnified teeth of the gracile South African australopithecine, *africanus*, resemble those of living primates that eat fruits or leaves.

Apparently, the robusts tackled almost exclusively hard foods—nuts and seeds—with tough, fibrous vegetation as a possible side course. Given their impressive equipment, for all we know they might have been eating the trees!

After his first big find, Robert Broom began work at a cave site called Swartkrans in the 1940s and here he soon uncovered more robust skulls. Typically, Broom pronounced these a separate species from the one he described at Kromdraai. He did, however, correctly recognize that the younger part of the Swartkrans cave contained a different sort of hominid, now generally regarded as *Homo erectus*, a big-brained, highly mobile hominid whose adventures we'll trace in the next chapter.

Swartkrans has produced more robust australopithecine fossils—the remains of 140 individuals so far—than any other site we have. The remains from a dozen individuals of *Homo* have also been uncovered there. From the more than 250,000 pieces of animal bone the cave has yielded, we know that at least fifty-nine large mammal species, from aardvarks all the way to zebras, inhabited the area when hominids did. The open highveld country around Swartkrans, dotted with the occasional stinkwood tree, looks much the same now as it did when hominids lived there. A river runs by the cave today; hippo and otter fossils from Swartkrans suggest that it has for some 2 million years.

Besides the tough, tedious work of finding fossils in South Africa, the other problem with the cave sites is that they lack volcanic ash and so cannot be dated by the sorts of techniques we use on rocks from Hadar and other Rift Valley sites. The dates on South African hominids, tentative at best, are estimated by comparing fossil animals found in the caves with similar bones from more reliably dated areas elsewhere. What's more, each cave has a unique geologic history.

Difficult to read as they are, however, the rock layers of the Swartkrans cave capture in several vivid snapshots the hominid and animal populations over a million years of time. Geologic evidence seems to indicate three main periods, one starting around 1.8 million years ago, another around 1.5 million years ago, and a third at 900,000 years ago. Hominids lived in or near the cave during each of these windows of time.

Decades before paleoanthropologists knew anything about who and what breaks and gathers bones, Robert Broom wrote in one of his monographs on Swartkrans: "Who killed the ape-men whose skulls we find and how is it that most are so hopelessly crushed? And how are we to explain the scarcity of bones that belonged to the ape-man skeletons?"

Unlike East African sites where hominid fossils erode easily from the ground, the caves in South Africa encase their fossils within a cement of limestone, sand, and gravel called breccia. At Makapansgat, broken bones in the breccia are stained black by the mineral manganese. Raymond Dart mistook the dark color as evidence for the use of fire by hominid hunters.

D. C. JOHANSON

To answer that question with modern techniques, we must make a detour back to the main line of australopithecines—namely, *africanus*—and another critical South African site. In 1925, a year after Raymond Dart first came into possession of the Taung skull, a schoolmaster named Wilfred Eitzman sent Dart a box of broken bones from the site of Makapansgat, another lime quarry, about two hundred miles north of Johannesburg. Two decades passed before Dart, who by that time was no longer active in paleoanthropology, finally visited the site at the urging of his student Phillip Tobias.

Impressed by its possibilities, Dart and his colleagues began work at Makapansgat in 1945. The tedious task continued for ten years. In a single year, the team sorted through six hundred tons of rubble from the mining operation. Out of this they removed ten tons of breccia and took it to Johannesburg, where, after soaking the breccia in acetic acid, they extracted a ton of bone fragments with hammers and chisels.

Apart from the tedium, the work had its dangers, too. Deadly green mambas were frequent visitors to the site, and the hundreds of feet of tunneled rock had to be shored up with braces to keep the caves from collapsing. Even though the breccia at Makapansgat is packed with broken bones, the team's efforts to locate a hominid were not rewarded until they had searched for two years. Finally, one of Dart's associates, James Kitching, a keen fossil hunter since childhood, found the back portion of a hominid skull.

Having observed that many of the Makapansgat bone

James Kitching grew up hunting dinosaur fossils in the Karoo region of South Africa and became an early associate of Raymond Dart. Kitching discovered one of the few hominid fossils found at Makapansgat, a fragmentary skull, and became convinced by Dart's idea that the broken bones at the site were hominid weapons.

D. C. JOHANSON

fragments were black—suggesting that they had been burned—Dart concluded that this new hominid had used fire and cooked its prey. Accordingly, he named Kitching's discovery *Australopithecus prometheus,* after the Greek mythological hero who defied the gods by bringing fire to mortals on Earth. This fossil and subsequent hominids from Makapansgat have since been placed in the same species as the Taung child, *africanus,* but Dart's grand name for the fossil was a harbinger of more imaginative interpretation to come.

In 1948, a juvenile hominid lower jaw was found at Makapansgat. Noting that the bone was broken on both sides and missing its front teeth, Dart concluded that the hominid had suffered a lethal blow from a fist or bludgeon. The specimen was well preserved, and the fact that it was broken and missing a few teeth could be true of any mandible I pick up off the ground at Hadar as well. This kind of damage doesn't really constitute evidence for traumatic violence. Yet Dart, doubtless influenced by the mass horrors of a recent world war, became convinced that he was uncovering evidence of humankind's violent past.

By 1955, he had also begun to argue that some seven thousand animal-bone fragments found at Makapansgat—one third of the total sample—represented the oldest known bone tools and the world's first culture. The bones included antelope anklebones, which Dart believed had been carved out on one side to form scoops; antelope horn cores that he interpreted as stabbing and carving tools; and jagged-edged jawbones he saw as cutting implements. Dart dubbed his pre-stone technology the osteodontokeratic culture, a tongue-twisting term that stood for "bone-tooth-horn," the three kinds of fossil material present at Makapansgat, which contained no stone tools whatsoever.

Dart's analysis of these bones was the first serious study of a bone collection from an African cave. Unfortunately, it was also an exercise in broad-stroke interpretation. Dart believed that the osteodontokeratic culture played a fundamental role in the development of early human thought, but the activities he attributed to the hominids do not lead us to the conclusion that they were far-thinking or contemplative. In Dart's dark vision, the australopithecines were "callous and brutal" and—judging from the preponderance of antelope skulls—headhunters to boot. The book he published in 1957 on the excavations at Makapansgat contains numerous pen-and-ink drawings of a human hand hoisting various bones in threatening positions as a vivid demonstration of how useful such bones would be for the "business of slashing, ripping or tearing."

Raymond Dart discovered thousands of broken antelope limb bones and horn cores at the ancient site of Makapansgat, a huge lime quarry where he worked for ten years starting in 1945. Perhaps inspired by memories of the recent war, Dart interpreted these broken bones as tools and weapons used by hominids to hunt each other. A more recent assessment of the bone accumulations at Makapansgat and other South African cave sites revealed that carnivores such as hyenas and leopards were responsible for the breakage.
D. C. JOHANSON

As I noted, Dart's interpretation drew heavily from his postwar environment. But just as with the Leakeys' interpretation of "living floors" at Olduvai Gorge, the impressionistic picture of "mighty hunters" that he drew of hominid behavior based on the bones from Makapansgat motivated others to take a closer and more skeptical revisionist look at the archeological record.

We saw in the last chapter how the new field of experimental archeology now allows us to analyze the telltale traces on bones at archeological sites to reveal whether or not they have been accumulated by animals; these analyses can also often show which animal is responsible. It's possible as well to infer how bones came to be deposited in the past by observing how bone collections form and change under natural processes today. That is the goal of a branch of science known as taphonomy, from the Greek word *taphos*, meaning "grave."

At Makapansgat, Donald Johanson holds the bony core of an antelope horn, one of the bones that Raymond Dart included in his osteodontokeratic ("bone-tooth-horn") culture that he attributed to the hominids that lived at this site some 3 million years ago. James Kitching explains to Johanson how lethal such a bone could be if used as a weapon.
LENORA JOHANSON

Taphonomy examines what happens to an animal's bones after it dies, what forces move, break, or otherwise influence these bones until they are uncovered.

A pioneer of taphonomic investigation is a man named C. K. Brain, recently retired from his post as director of the Transvaal Museum in Pretoria. I first met Bob Brain when I visited the museum in 1970 and was struck immediately by his graciousness to a green graduate student from the University of Chicago. He led me down a basement corridor to a thick metal door. Behind the door was a fire-engine-red brick room, the vault containing most of the hominid fossils from South Africa's caves. The fossils lay on the shelves of two tall glass-fronted cabinets on either side of the room, and each specimen was identified with a species name and a number, hand-printed on white cards like place cards at a prehistoric banquet. With no hesitation, Brain let me examine the fossil bounty of this treasure house. Every time I've met Bob since then, in South Africa and abroad, I reaffirm my first impression of him as a man of modesty and magnanimity in an ego-driven field.

In the 1950s, Raymond Dart's interpretation of the bones from Makapansgat as a highly advanced hunting and tool-using culture was accepted with little criticism, a sign that the intellectual climate was already warming up to the ideas that culminated in the "Man the Hunter" hypothesis we examined in the previous chapter. Dart had considered the potential role of carnivores in forming the broken-bone collections at Makapansgat, but he dismissed their contributions in favor of his hyperaggressive hominids. Bob Brain decided it was time to take a second look at Makapansgat and at the same time to investigate how bones accumulated at other cave sites, such as Swartkrans.

Part of Bob's evidence for reinterpreting Makapansgat came from some unlikely sources. On a chance visit to several Hottentot villages in Namibia, he was struck by the number of broken goat bones scattered among the village huts. When the villagers butchered a goat, they gave the unused bones to their dogs, who dispensed with some and left others behind. The leftovers, what Bob dubbed the "resistant residue of goat skeletons," showed a recurring pattern in bone type.

As an experiment Bob bought a goat from the village, returned it to the villagers to butcher and eat, and asked them to save him the bones they did not normally use. When the politely amazed villagers gave him their leavings, he was able to compare the damage they did to the skeleton to the damage done by the dogs. From this study and from collections made in other villages, Bob noticed that the most common goat bones were the humerus— that is, the bottom ends of the upper foreleg—and the lower jaw. These same two bones from antelopes were also the most prevalent part of the Makapansgat collection.

Bob had demonstrated that the consistent absence of certain bones could be explained by their less durable structure rather than by a hominid penchant for particular body parts. He also showed that the type of bone damage found at Makapansgat could be explained without invoking hunting by hominids. Though hominids *may* have been breaking bones at Makapansgat, he had proven more conclusively that a series of other predators and scavengers were engaged in the same activity.

As a further example of what animals can do to bones that can potentially confound paleoanthropologists, consider the porcupine. The crested porcupine, Bob learned, actually collects bones and hoards them out of sight in

underground burrows or beneath rocky ledges. Why does this rodent, whose diet consists of plants, roots, and tubers, store up piles of bones in its burrows? The reason is a rather nightmarish one, if you happen to be a porcupine. This animal must regularly gnaw on bones to keep its constantly growing incisors worn down sufficiently to continue eating. Left alone, its teeth would grow to such a length that the animal would no longer be able to feed.

Bob thinks that porcupines, who add a few dozen raw bones to their collections every year, may bring more bones into caves than any other African animal. Porcupines stash so many bones in their lairs that only a fraction ever get gnawed at all. Those that do are easy to recognize,

Donald Johanson crawls into a porcupine lair to examine some of the bones left inside. Porcupines add a few dozen new bones to their collections each year, and they may get around to gnawing only a small fraction of them.
LENORA JOHANSON

Less formidable than a hyena or a leopard, the crested porcupine is nonetheless an avid collector and chewer of bones and played a role in forming the ancient bone collections at hominid cave sites. Porcupines dig underground burrows where they store animal bones to gnaw and keep their front teeth from growing too long. The washboard-like ridges on the edge of this bone are one of the telltale traces of porcupine gnawing.

D. C. JOHANSON

once you know what to look for. The porcupines leave a washboardlike series of ridges along the edges of bones and turn limb bones into a series of circular napkin rings. These are important clues to consider in analyzing bones in archeological assemblages where porcupines have been part of the habitat at any time, ancient or modern.

Once he knew what to look for, Bob noticed that many of the Makapansgat bones had porcupine gnaw marks. Yet the greatest amount of bone damage had been inflicted by hyenas. After butchering carcasses with me at Castleton in 1992, Rob Blumenschine stopped at the Transvaal Museum to examine the Makapansgat collection firsthand with Jennifer Bishop, a former student of mine at Stanford. Scrutinizing the bones in the same way he had done with the animal bones from Olduvai's FLK, Rob and Jennifer looked for percussion marks—the divots made when a hammerstone strikes bones. Under a microscope the marks are round, shallow pits with tiny striations inside or near the edge. Often these pit striations, which are shorter, shallower, and narrower than typical tool cut marks, can be spotted with the naked eye. Carnivore teeth can also leave pits in bones, but never striations. After examining all of Dart's purported tools, Rob and Jennifer found only a handful that could not be attributed to hyena damage.

Bob Brain did hold out the possibility that some of the broken bones at Makapansgat really had been modified or used by hominids. In his office at the Transvaal Museum, Bob told me that Dart's interpretation had "an element of truth in it, but by overstating his point, he turned everyone against it." Dart had pushed his interpretation beyond the limits of the evidence, and eventually it demanded correction.

With the Makapansgat bone analysis under our belts, let's return to Swartkrans and *robustus.* Beginning in 1965, Bob Brain and his team reopened Robert Broom's excavations at Swartkrans and got an opportunity to provide an informed answer to Broom's question, Who killed the apemen? They uncovered some fascinating new evidence along the way. (Not surprisingly, Broom's own answer, following Dart's thinking, had drawn more from drama than data: The robusts, he speculated, were the powerful, club-wielding killers of the mammals whose bones lay so abundantly scattered in the cave and they in turn had been ruthlessly hunted by *Homo.*)

It's a testament to Bob's patience—and that of anyone who endures the challenge of wrenching fossils from these limestone tombs—that out of the twenty-one years of hard work that followed, fourteen were devoted simply to preparing Swartkrans for the detailed excavation; seven years alone were spent removing tons of blasting rubble that had accumulated since Broom found his fossils. Finally, the team got to the soft sediments under the breccia, and some fascinating finds began to appear.

It soon became clear that in one respect Swartkrans was no different from the other caves: Carnivores had contributed most of the bones. Most likely, many of the shattered animal bones were the remains of leopard meals hauled up into the stinkwood tree perched over the cave opening. Even some of the australopithecine fossils had

been chewed and punctured by leopards, leading Bob to suggest that the hominids were not the hunters at all—they were the prey. Bob Brain summarized his years of taphonomic work in a fascinating book published in 1981, suggestively titled *The Hunters or the Hunted?* Not all the evidence from Swartkrans can be explained as detritus from tree-stored leopard kills, though. Carnivores weren't the only contributors to the bone cache. Besides carnivore tooth marks, bones from *every time period* recorded in the cave show cut marks and percussion marks. Unlike Makapansgat, Swartkrans also yielded sporadic clusters of stone tools, mostly crude cobbles and flakes of quartz and quartzite. That raises at once an interesting question: Who made them?

In the oldest section of Swartkrans, 97 percent of the hominid fossils belong to *Australopithecus robustus;* the relatively few *Homo* fossils date from a later period. The tools, however, span all time periods in the cave. Nonetheless, most experts believe the tools belong to *Homo* and not to the robusts. For one thing, the sheer ruggedness of the robust fossils gives them an unfair advantage in long-term preservation. For another, the chaotic depositing of fossils in these caves makes exact associations very difficult to determine.

A few investigators disagree. Analyses of the robust australopithecine hand and finger bones suggested to my colleague Randall Susman—one of the trio in Chapter 2, you may recall, who swept Lucy off her feet and stuck her back in the trees—that the robusts possessed a precision grip equal to that of *Homo habilis* and were able to make the stone tools of Swartkrans. The anatomical capability to make stone tools, however, does not by itself prove the presence of tool making. (Similarly, I think that the hands of the Hadar hominids display a capability for making stone tools, but we have no evidence that they did.)

The stone tools from Swartkrans are of the butchering and carving type similar to those found at Olduvai and other sites in East Africa. If robust australopithecines ate plants, how would they have used these kinds of stone tools to process their food? If they used the stone tools for their apparent purpose—processing meat—why is their highly specialized chewing adaptation so durable over time? It seems more likely to me that the stone tools were made by *Homo*, even though the clear associations needed to prove this point are not available.

I'm not suggesting that only *Homo* among the hominids used any kind of tool at all. In fact, Swartkrans has strong evidence that the robust australopithecines used at least one implement specifically adapted for their diet. Bob Brain has marshaled a convincing case for a single type of bone tool, based on his study of about sixty bones from the site. Like Dart's Makapansgat "tools," most of these are simply limb-bone-shaft fragments from various animals and antelope horn cores. All, however, have a smooth, rounded tip at one end.

Bob found himself wondering how such a distinctive pattern might form. The answer dawned on him one day while he was excavating. "In the softer parts of the deposit I'd been using an ordinary screwdriver as a digging tool," he recalled as we drank tea by the Swartkrans site. "The end

In 1965, C. K. "Bob" Brain of the Transvaal Museum in Pretoria, shown here with Elizabeth Vrba, reopened excavations at Swartkrans. His meticulous work there has allowed a reinterpretation of the different roles that hominids and carnivores played in the bone collections that have been uncovered in several South African cave sites. D. C. JOHANSON

had gotten all worn and rounded, and that got me thinking that maybe these bones were used for digging as well."

Knowing that the landscape around Swartkrans had changed little since robust australopithecines roamed it, Bob looked for clues to what they might have dug up. He noted that certain edible bulbs and tubers were common beneath rocky scree slopes. Getting to them was the chal-

The cave of Swartkrans captures snapshots of hominid and animal life during a period from 900,000 to 1.8 million years ago. Excavations have produced fossils from 140 Australopithecus robustus *and 12* Homo erectus, *as well as bones that may have been used as digging sticks by the robusts and burned bones that could be the world's earliest evidence of human-controlled fire.* D. C. JOHANSON

lenge—unless, that is, you had some kind of tool. Bob climbed a hillside near the cave and began digging with a wildebeest limb bone that had been chewed apart by a hyena. Within half an hour, he had extracted an edible lily bulb. After several more hours of digging, the end of the bone bore a distinct resemblance to those found at Swartkrans. Enlisting his sons to help with the experiment, Bob continued to dig up tubers with different bones. Each time, the same worn, rounded pattern appeared on the tips.

Both the fossil bones and Bob's experimental tools showed crisscrossing scratches near the tip, visible to the naked eye and crystal clear under the magnification of a scanning electron microscope. Apparently, the vertical scratches formed when the bone was plunged into the soil and the horizontal scratches formed when stones in the soil scraped against the tools.

Some of the fossil bones looked so worn at the tip that they must have been used for several days. Bob began to wonder if the hominids carried these digging sticks with them. Then he noticed that the wear scratches on some specimens were obscured by a glassy polish. A similar sort of polish occurs on modern bone tools used by hunter-gatherers to burnish hides. Bob speculates that the hominids may have made hide bags to carry tools and tubers, and the glassy polish formed as the bones rubbed against the leather. A few tiny, awl-like pieces of bone— the sort of tools that could be used to puncture leather— were also uncovered at Swartkrans.

I phoned my favorite skeptic, Lew Binford, to ask what he thought about Bob's bones from Swartkrans. "Now, there's nothing in the bone marks at Makapansgat that's not known to be produced by hyenas," Lew began, "but Brain's bone splinters are different. The pattern of abrasion is not subtle, and it's consistent with digging." Near Swartkrans, there is a particular bulb that blooms right at the end of the dry season, making it easy to spot on a landscape. "Baboons dig up these bulbs all the time, but as soon as they get to a rocky area, they stop digging. Baboons dig with their fingernails. A critter with just a simple tool like Brain's bones would have a big advantage over a baboon on rocky slopes. He wouldn't have any competition from the baboon, and he could dig without tearing his fingers to pieces."

Because the digging sticks have been found throughout the Swartkrans deposits, this method of obtaining food may have had a long history. "There's no reason why robust australopithecines wouldn't have used tools," Lew continued. "They're part of the process that we all squirted out of." As I contemplated the analogy of our lineage to a tube of toothpaste, Lew, like a good scientist, qualified his statement. "Just the same, I bet the robusts aren't tool users in the same ways as other hominids because their diets are different, their settings are different. They may not even be using the same sorts of tools."

How can archeologists distinguish tools made and used by *Homo* from those made and used by *Australopithecus*? Did robust australopithecines only use digging sticks and *Homo* only stone tools? We simply cannot answer the first question with any precision. It's fair to say, though, that robusts may have been using digging sticks and *Homo* may have been using both digging sticks and stone tools.

Swartkrans contains clues to another innovation that would have been equally vital: fire. The controlled use of fire has proven tricky to demonstrate at ancient archeological sites. The evidence, such as scorched ground that could just as easily come from natural grass fire, is always enigmatic. Raymond Dart claimed that the black color of the bones at Makapansgat demonstrated early hominids' Promethean mastery of fire, but later analysis showed that these bones had been stained by the dark mineral manganese after they became locked in breccia. They had never been roasted over a campfire.

Most archeologists now accept the evidence for fire 500,000 years ago from the Zhoukoudian cave in China, which harbored numerous fossils of *Homo erectus*. From Swartkrans, however, comes compelling evidence that fire may have been around for twice as long.

After five years of excavations, Bob's team moved into the youngest part of the cave. They had found a few burned bones in the older sections, but they found further evidence here. Out of 59,488 fossil fragments removed from the youngest part of the cave, 270 bones had been burned and a larger number appeared to have been heated. The burned bones belonged to several kinds of antelope, warthog, zebra, baboon, and even *Australopithecus robustus*. Curiously, these bones came from aconfined part of the cave, a sixteen-foot-thick layer of sediment, as though fires might have been a regular event in that one small spot. Bob believes that the fires were deliberately made or tended in the cave. The hominids could have gathered fire from their surroundings and learned to control it in the cave. Even today fires break out frequently on the highveld near Swartkrans, especially in October and November, when the grass is tall and dry and thunderstorms unleash lightning. Under such conditions, carrying a flaming branch back to the cave could have been an easy matter.

When I visited Swartkrans in 1992, Bob and I built a

fire in a cave by the excavation with branches from one of the nearby stinkwood trees, and he showed me what he had learned about how bones burn. In experiments conducted with his University of Cape Town colleague Andrew Sillen, Bob had chopped an antelope limb bone into seven sections and heated the bone pieces at a range of temperatures approaching 1,500 degrees Fahrenheit for thirty minutes. When the pieces had cooled, they sliced wafer-thin cross-sections of each bone and examined them under a light microscope. At lower temperatures the bones darkened and their microscopic structure showed up more clearly than in unburned bone; when the experimental bones reached temperatures above 750 degrees Fahrenheit, they turned white and cracked.

By comparing the fossil bones to fresh ones placed in campfires under controlled temperatures, Bob concluded that many of the Swartkrans bones had been heated to temperatures between 600 and 900 degrees Fahrenheit. The majority of the burned bones, 127 of them, had been heated to even higher temperatures, which could have been reached in a campfire like the one that Bob and I made. In fact, the fossil bones had all been heated to temperatures consistent with small campfires made from stinkwood branches, the most common tree in the region around Swartkrans.

Another analysis showed that the darkened bones contained higher amounts of carbon than surrounding fossils. Unlike those at Makapansgat, then, the black color of these bones was caused by carbon residues, not manganese staining. Therefore, the burned bones at Swartkrans appear to be direct and dramatic evidence of fire, perhaps the first use of fire anywhere. Although the only hominid fossils found so far from the youngest sec-

Bob Brain and Donald Johanson built a campfire at Swartkrans to demonstrate Brain's experiments in measuring the temperatures that occur in a controlled fire. He burned pieces of antelope bone to different temperatures and noted that the damage pattern on the bones matched that found on the burned fossil bones from Swartkrans.
LENORA JOHANSON

In the youngest part of Swartkrans, Bob Brain and his team found nearly three hundred bone fragments that had been burned and heated to high temperatures. These bones came from a single patch of sediment and may be evidence that hominids made or tended fires in the cave almost a million years ago.
D. C. JOHANSON

tion of Swartkrans are nine *robustus* teeth, *Homo erectus* must have been present at that time, too, and was most likely responsible for the fires. We award fire-bearing honors to *erectus* and not to the robusts simply because fire is not present in any of the previous robust layers and only appears at the time when *Homo erectus* would have lived in the area. Along with the presence of fire, the youngest layer at Swartkrans also shows increased evidence for meat eating in the form of cut marks.

Fire is a profoundly social experience and was probably an important part of later hominid life at Swartkrans. It may not have been used for cooking meat in the Swartkrans cave, but surely it provided both warmth and protection. There is a close association between fire and the increased need for protection when caves are used as a living area. "I think that bringing bones and meat back to a cave where you sleep is very dangerous unless you have fire," Bob remarked as he poked at some white-hot bones in our experimental blaze. Did *Homo erectus* use fire to ward off leopards and sabertooth cats at Swartkrans? Of the animal remains found in the oldest section of Swartkrans, about 27 percent come from *Australopithecus robustus*, and as it is clear that carnivores accumulated most of these bones, I can't help wondering with Bob whether hominids weren't someone's favorite dinner. The last appearance of *robustus* at Swartkrans coincides roughly with the appearance of fire there. Perhaps fire helped keep *Homo erectus* from becoming a big cat's meal in quite the same numbers that the robusts did.

The youngest layers at Swartkrans capture a critical evolutionary turning point for both of the hominid lines I have tracked so far. *Homo* was about to embark on a journey beyond the African continent. Our line already had stone tools and fire to help it survive in new environments. For the robust australopithecines, meanwhile, it was the end of the line. The last recorded appearance of a robust australopithecine in East Africa was 1.2 million years ago, at Olduvai Gorge. In South Africa, the last *robustus* may have lived 900,000 years ago at Swartkrans. Whether or not that date marks their extinction is unknown. The evidence available from Swartkrans, or any other site, is simply not extensive enough to tell us what happened to the robust australopithecines. We can, however, make a few good guesses.

The East African and South African robust australopithecines probably shared similar habitats and behavior and met their ends from a similar cause. During the period that the robusts existed, spanning from at least 2.5 million years ago to around 1 million years ago, the climate changed regularly, with fluctuating cold and warm spells on a global scale. After a million years ago, temperatures dropped steadily. This sharp cooling trend may have impacted the robusts' ability to survive in several ways. First, it's likely they did not possess the fire-bearing (hence warming) capabilities of *erectus.* Second, they were dependent on a highly specialized plant diet that may have undergone modification in a cooler climate; *erectus* enjoyed a much more varied and flexible diet.

Even without climate change, herbivores have a further evolutionary disadvantage: They need to eat more to get the same amount of nutrition that carnivores do from their richer diet. The robust australopithecines, herbivores by most everybody's guess, may have found their dry habitats offering less and less to eat over the millennia, especially if their hard, tough foods were of low quality. Hominids who were nutritionally weakened in this way might have been easier prey for predators—just as in the African savanna today, when disease weakens animals, lions will stalk buffalo and other prey they would otherwise avoid. Perhaps other animals, smaller, more numerous, and more adaptable, outcompeted the robust australopithecines, who, even armed with digging sticks, could not keep up with the demand for scarce resources.

By 900,000 years ago, glaciers had spread in the Northern Hemisphere, and the next major event in human evolution had taken place. *Homo erectus*, who evolved from *Homo habilis*, may have adapted to an ecological crunch that caught the robusts unprepared. Whereas the robusts were forced to rely almost exclusively on their highly specialized teeth and chewing muscles to survive, the lineage that continued with *Homo erectus* already had a broader diet and could rely increasingly on its larger brain.

Raymond Dart's convictions about our robust relatives, if not always correct, were deeply held, yet he had the scientist's flexibility in the face of changing and better information. Bob Brain's challenge to his claim took him aback at first, but gradually he came to accept the reinterpretation and ultimately championed it enthusiastically. (Ironically, of course, Bob would soon find himself back on the other side of the fence, arguing for early bone tools from Swartkrans.) "Dart wanted to provoke discussion, a very commendable trait," Bob recalled shortly before I left South Africa. "He was more interested in the truth than in his position relative to it."

I have a similar recollection of Dart. One day in 1975 he called me out of the blue to congratulate me on discovering Lucy. I was so taken off guard that I thought at first some mischievous colleague was impersonating the legendary pioneer of early hominid hunts in Africa. In that and later conversations, Dart never disagreed with my growing confidence that the Hadar hominids represented a new species, even when it threatened to bump his beloved Taung child onto a side branch of the family tree.

Late in Raymond Dart's life, Bob Brain brought him some of the bone tools from Swartkrans. Nearly blind, Dart felt the rounded tips and asked Bob, "What do you think they did with these things?" Bob replied that he thought they were used for digging in the ground. Dart stared back in total disbelief. "That's not a very romantic explanation!" Then the old man brandished one of the bones and pointed it playfully at Bob's chest. "I could run you through with this," he cried.

Raymond Dart died on November 22, 1988, at the age of ninety-six. His ashes were scattered at Makapansgat.

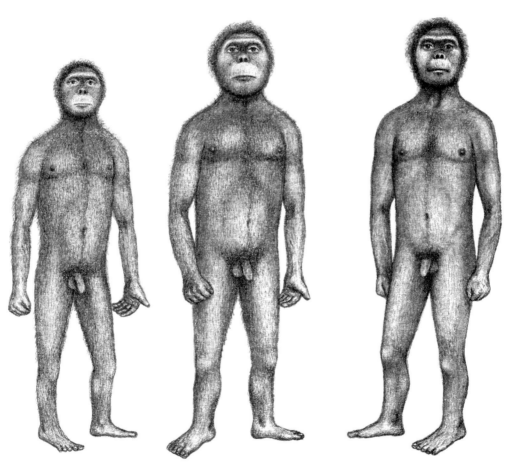

Australopithecus afarensis   *Australopithecus boisei*   *Homo habilis*

CHAPTER FIVE

Big Bodies, Big Brains:

Homo erectus

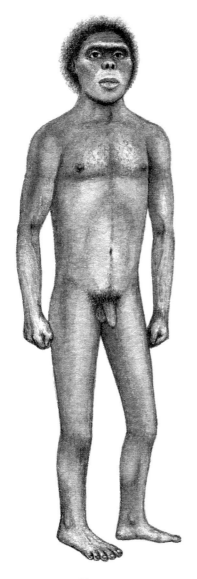

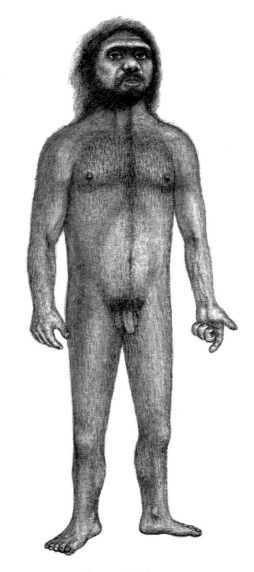

Homo erectus

Homo neanderthalensis

WHEN WE LEAVE THE AUSTRALOPITHECINES for good and move back to our own kind, genus *Homo*, something interesting happens to the evolutionary story. Narrative momentum rapidly accelerates, and suddenly a much larger cluster of turning points appears on the horizon: increasing body and brain size, epic mobility, fire mastery, more sophisticated tools. All this comes in the package loosely labeled *Homo erectus*, the evolutionary "parent" of our own species.

Though we're fairly certain *Homo erectus* lived in the Swartkrans cave around 1 million years ago, at roughly the same time as the robust australopithecines, to get to the first discovery of a fossil from this species we must jump a few continents over, another 200,000 years forward, and—on our parallel track of modern fossil finders—a century back in our own time. The find in question holds double honors: It was the first early hominid fossil to be discovered and recognized as such, and it's also— with the possible exception of a mandible recently found in former Soviet Georgia—the earliest hominid specimen known outside Africa, known as Java Man.

In the middle of the last century, years of travel and study in the island archipelagos of Southeast Asia had convinced a British biologist named Alfred Russel Wallace of the presence in nature of a principle he called "natural selection"—that is, the constant modification of organisms over time along hereditary lines of descent to maximize the number of individuals that would survive and reproduce. The concept of this built-in mechanism for biological change crystallized in Wallace's mind during a bout with malarial flu in 1858. Back in England, Charles Darwin was working on a manuscript in which he independently formulated the same ideas based on his own trips on HMS *Beagle* in the early 1830s. Once Wallace had communicated his discoveries to Darwin in a letter, arrangements were made for joint publication, in 1858, of a short paper at the Linnaean Society, in London. Darwin then hastened publication of his manuscript, which appeared as *On the Origin of Species* the following year.

Only in the last paragraphs of his monumental work did Darwin venture a vague reference to the application of evolutionary theory to the "origins of man." Wallace, in contrast, had postulated a common ancestor for primates and humans as early as 1855, in the paper "On the Habits of the Orang-Utan of Borneo," and predicted that Southeast Asia would someday reveal the "earliest appearance of the great man-like apes." That grand forecast ignited the fossil-finding passion in a young Dutch anatomist named Eugène Dubois, whose eagerness to find an ancient ancestor was matched only by the lack of knowledge he shared with most other scientists of his day about the human past. Up to that time the only recorded hominid finds were several Neandertal specimens in Europe, about whose identity investigators could not agree. Despite the uncertain prospects of this brand-new field, Dubois resigned his university teaching job, enlisted as an army surgeon, and shipped off to Sumatra, then part of the Dutch East Indies, in 1887.

Minimal military duties left him with plenty of time to hunt for fossils. More than two years of searching in Sumatra yielded nothing. An attack of malaria in 1890 led

The first discovery of Homo erectus *fossils was made by Dutch anatomist Eugène Dubois in 1891. Dubois was convinced that Asia held the evidence of our early ancestors. He went to Java as an army surgeon and made his historic finds at Trinil.*
IAN EVERARD

to his transfer to Java, where Dubois renewed his efforts. The previous year, he knew, a human fossil skull—the first such fossil find outside Europe—had been discovered in the Wajak marble quarry near Tulungagung on Java's south coast. On his first visit to the quarry, Dubois found a second human skull. Later, in hopes that they were ancient ancestors, he took both fossils to Europe for further study. (Today we know the Wajak skulls date to about 10,000 years ago and are modern *Homo sapiens.*)

Inspired to continue his quest, Dubois began exploring an area near the village of Trinil, on the Solo River, in 1891. This region of active volcanoes and rich sediments eroded by rivers and monsoon rains looked to be a promising place for fossil prospecting. Even so, Dubois had exceptionally good fortune. Using convicts supplied by the Dutch government, he dug a trench into the bank of the Solo River and was immediately rewarded with a

The tranquil Solo River in Java was the site of the "Java Man" fossils. Other sites along this river have produced many skulls and skull fragments belonging to Homo erectus *and early humans.* SHARIE SHUTE

primate's molar. The next month he found his real prize—the top of a cranium, with a low sloping forehead and heavy curved browridges. Dubois wondered at first if this piece of skull, whose facial portions were missing, belonged to an ape. When digging continued in the next dry season, a complete femur closely resembling a modern human's was unearthed about fifty feet upstream from the location of the cranial vault.

With this discovery, Dubois was convinced that he had fulfilled Alfred Russel Wallace's prediction that the remains of humanlike apes would be found in Southeast Asia and that Asia had witnessed the birth of our species. Certain that his two bones represented our common ancestor and that they came from a single individual, Dubois borrowed a generic hominid name coined by the German biologist Ernst Haeckel and called his find *Pithecanthropus* (literally, "ape-man"). As his species name he chose *erectus*. In common parlance these and subsequent fossil finds from Southeast Asia became universally known as Java Man.

Dubois returned to the Netherlands and published a description of his fossils in 1894. His announcement of a hominid ancestor, however, met the same sort of resistance and criticism among the European scientific community that Raymond Dart would encounter three decades later with his australopithecine Taung child. Some critics charged Dubois with trying to fob off part of an ape skull and a modern human femur as a single individual. Just as Dart was vindicated by later discoveries in South Africa, Dubois's ideas were to be confirmed by the discovery of similar fossils in

This monument was erected about two hundred yards from the site of Trinil, where Eugène Dubois discovered the remains known as "Java Man" in 1891 and 1893. These bones, now considered Homo erectus, *were the first hominid fossils to be found outside Europe.* SHARIE SHUTE

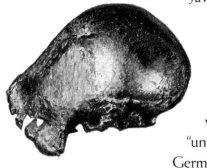

This skullcap, along with a thighbone, comprise the original "Java Man" fossils found by Dubois. He called them Pithecanthropus erectus, *but they are now considered part of* Homo erectus.

IAN EVERARD

Java as well as by the famous Peking Man fossils retrieved in the 1920s from the Zhoukoudian (literally, "Dragon Bone Hill") site, near Beijing, China. Dubois had made a discovery that would eventually force humankind to accept its evolutionary past. The highly critical response he received, however, wounded him deeply and ultimately rendered him "unaccountable as a jealous lover," in the words of the German paleontologist G.H.R. von Koenigswald, who called the Trinil specimen "the most famous, most discussed, most maligned fossil" ever found. Dubois buried his treasured fossils beneath the floorboards of his home in Haarlem, refusing to show them to anyone.

In 1936, von Koenigswald, who had spent the previous few years working in Java for a geological survey, visited the aging, ailing Dubois in the Netherlands. Cautiously, he asked for permission to see the Trinil finds. By this time Dubois had deposited the fossils for safekeeping at a museum in Leyden. Once he had ascertained that his visitor had not tried to gain access to the fossils behind his back, Dubois gave his consent to the German's request. Standing alone in the museum safe, von Koenigswald carefully examined the heavy chocolate-brown femur and skullcap. He left Leyden convinced that Dubois was right. The bones may not have come from one individual (recent evidence, in fact, suggests that they were found in geological deposits of different ages), but both belonged to a single ancestral species. Like Dubois before him, he vowed to return to Java and find more hominid fossils.

Beginning in 1937, von Koenigswald also had the good fortune to take part in several Javanese hominid discoveries. His chosen site, Sangiran, later turned up the first nearly complete skull of *Homo erectus*, a specimen known as Sangiran 17. Some forty individuals are now represented in the collection of *Homo erectus* fossils from Java—a whopping third of the worldwide total. Dubois's fossils may date back as far as a million years, and there is good evidence that this species lived and prospered in Java for the next 900,000 years.

Just who was this hominid, then, that swept out of Africa as the last australopithecines were dying off in their native continent? *Homo erectus* holds center stage in theories of human origins because it evolved from *Homo habilis* and led directly to us. In spite of the astonishingly similar skeletal remains and tools from far-flung corners of three continents, the real surprise is how little, relatively speaking, we can say about this species. One of my colleagues has referred to *erectus* as the "muddle in the middle." As with *Homo habilis*, some paleoanthropologists question which fossils should be called *erectus* and whether the fossils from Asia really belong in the same species as earlier ones from Africa. Others believe that *erectus* is not a separate species from our own *sapiens*.

The most recent evidence, largely derived from a single almost complete skeleton found in Kenya in 1984, suggests that in many ways *Homo erectus* was almost human, at least anatomically and perhaps physiologically. Even the oldest African skulls assigned to this species show features that are distinctly and essentially human. Despite the controversy, then, out of the basic cluster of evolutionary milestones clearly associated in the fossil record with this species, we can safely spin a fairly rich set of assumptions, as follows.

Bigger body and brain.   We know from the few postcranial bones we have, including the fragmentary partial skeleton found by an Institute of Human Origins team at Olduvai Gorge in 1986, that our species grandparent *Homo habilis* was built much like an australopithecine in overall body size and limb proportions. *Homo erectus*, in contrast, was the first really big hominid. Tall, thin, and barrel-chested, it was about 14 percent bigger and 20 percent heavier than *habilis* and was well adapted to long-distance ranging on the African savannas. In stature no early hominid before us came close to the aptly named *erectus*, who was tall even compared to us. The six African specimens complete enough to allow estimates of their weight and stature fall within the top 17 percent of modern human males. Comparison of fossil evidence from Africa with younger fossils from Zhoukoudian in China, the famous Peking Man site, indicates that once *Homo erectus* got big, it stayed big, varying minimally in body size over its million-year species lifespan.

Its brain size, too—roughly 900 cc for an adult *erectus*,

One third of the world's known Homo erectus *fossils come from the cave site of Zhoukoudian in China. German paleoanthropologist Franz Weidenreich reconstructed many of the "Peking Man" fossils, including this skull. Sadly, all of the original fossils were lost during World War II.*
COURTESY DEPARTMENT LIBRARY SERVICES, AMERICAN MUSEUM OF NATURAL HISTORY

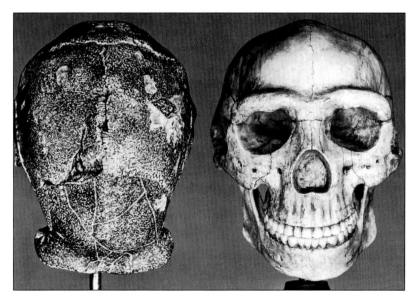

as compared with 350–400 cc for Lucy and 650 cc for *Homo habilis*—was substantially larger and remained constant.

Mobility. We know that *erectus* was able to adapt and occupy new environments, reach new horizons, and expand its geographic range far beyond that of any previous hominid, leaving Africa and spreading out across the Old World. Tools and fossil *erectus* remains have been found in Europe, India, and China as well as Southeast Asia. In Africa itself *erectus* sites—either fossils or their distinctive tool industry—include Kenya, Ethiopia, and Tanzania, where one hand ax from Olduvai Gorge has been dated at 1.3 million years.

Harry Shapiro of the American Museum of Natural History made this facial reconstruction of a Homo erectus *resident of Zhoukoudian. The cave dwellers mastered the use of fire 500,000 years ago and lived at Zhoukoudian for 200,000 years.* COURTESY DEPARTMENT LIBRARY SERVICES, AMERICAN MUSEUM OF NATURAL HISTORY

If archeologist Antje Justus's discovery of an *erectus* mandible in former Soviet Georgia is any indication, this exodus may have occurred far earlier than the traditional estimate of 1 million years ago. Early dating estimates of the Georgian mandible—found in 1991 alongside stone tools, two sabertooth cat skulls, and an elephant rib—place its age at either 1.6 million years or 900,000 years. Either date would still make this mandible the oldest known hominid fossil from Europe; the earlier date would make it the oldest hominid from anywhere outside Africa.

Fire mastery. As we saw in Chapter 4, Swartkrans shows good evidence that *erectus* made use of, if it didn't actually

The discovery of this Homo erectus *mandible from the Republic of Georgia was announced at a 1991 meeting held to celebrate the first* erectus *fossil discoveries in Java a century earlier. If the estimated age of 1.6 million years is correct, the Georgian specimen is the oldest hominid fossil known outside Africa.* ANTJE JUSTUS

make, fire at the 1 million-year mark. More recently, around 500,000 years ago, fires may have burned at the Zhoukoudian Peking Man site in China. The deposits at that cave revealed four dark layers of sediment from three to eighteen feet thick, the earliest nearly a half million years old. These layers are probably piles of ash, the remains of ancient hearths. The cave also contains lumps of cracked clay, as if these had been burned in a fire. As with Swartkrans, there is no evidence here that *Homo erectus* actually knew how to create fire. Borrowing natural fire, however, is itself no mean technological achievement and may have enabled this hominid to live at Zhoukoudian for more than 200,000 years.

Fire had the immediate effect of broadening the ecological niche of *erectus*. It increased the number of usable hours in a day, added to the range of foods eaten, improved the odds of avoiding predators, and—perhaps most important—intensified social interactions. Fire also bonds people, a necessity for small socially interacting groups.

Tools.   Heavy-duty hand axes, picks, and cleavers dominate what is called the Acheulian stone-tool industry, after an *erectus* site at St. Acheul, in France. These stone tools, sophisticated in comparison with the spheroids and simple cobbles that *Homo habilis* used, are clearly associated with butchery and suggest a major increase in meat eating. Dubbed by archeologist Alison Brooks the "Swiss army knives of the Paleolithic," the symmetrical hand axes show microwear polish consistent with use in carving both wood and meat. With some weighing as much as twenty pounds, it's hard to imagine these axes pressed into double duty as spearheads. In fact, no implements clearly identified with hunting—such as arrowheads, darts, and the like—have yet been found in *erectus* sites. These stone tools, finally, are remarkably consistent across *erectus* sites and over the lengthy span of its species life; in a million-year period, they show curiously little modification or improvement.

•   •   •

Most of these things about *erectus* were already known when, ninety years after Eugène Dubois published the discovery of his Java Man from Trinil, an amazing discovery was made on the opposite side of the Indian Ocean. In August 1984, at a place called Nariokotome, on the west shore of Lake Turkana, Kamoya Kimeu, the leader of Kenya's famous fossil-hunting team known as the Hominid Gang, was exploring a small branch of a sand river about three miles from the lake. Kamoya has

This elegantly shaped, symmetrical hand ax typifies the Acheulian tool industry, which occurs in the archeological record between 200,000 and 1.4 million years ago. Acheulian tools are often associated with the remains of Homo erectus. *Hand axes may have been Stone Age Swiss army knives, used for many tasks such as cutting plants, butchering meat, and chopping wood. Some archeologists even suggest they were thrown like a discus to bring down game.*   IAN EVERARD

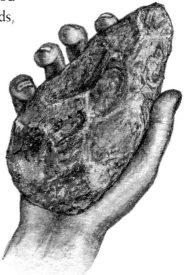

an exceptionally keen pair of eyes, sharpened during decades of fossil hunting, first with Louis and Mary Leakey at Olduvai Gorge and later with their son Richard at Koobi Fora. He has probably found more hominid fossils than any single person. As he scanned a slope covered with lava boulders this hot August day, Kamoya spotted a dark brown, matchbook-sized piece of bone, part of the frontal bone from a hominid skull.

Richard Leakey and Alan Walker, a paleoanthropologist from Johns Hopkins University, were not overjoyed to learn from Kamoya that this interesting find came out of a surface covered with lava rubble. "Kamoya keeps finding fossils where they shouldn't be," Alan recalled at a lecture in San Francisco that I attended. "Richard and I knew we were in for lots of hot, sweaty days looking for any other bits of bone." They began screening at the site and soon had recovered many more pieces of the skull. At the end of August they found the shattered face in the roots of an acacia. This pesky "wait-a-bit bush" had become notorious during the excavation for snagging the diggers' clothes, as if to attract their attention. Not until they were almost ready to give up did the workers finally search carefully around the base of the bush. Its roots had grown directly through the face.

Because the skull bones had slid downslope from some other spot, the next step was digging into the hillside. Excavations continued for five years, uncovering an almost complete skeleton. Defying the laws of probability—since ribs, with their rich marrow, a magnet for scavengers, usually don't last long enough to get preserved as fossils—even intact rib bones were found protruding from the ground. Two bones were found in each of the third and fourth seasons and nothing at all in the final

Meave Leakey and Alan Walker examine the cranium of the Homo erectus *boy during the 1984 field season at Nariokotome, Kenya. Some of the fossil-hunting Hominid Gang look on intently.*
VIRGINIA MORELL

1988 season. By the time it was wrapped up, this excavation for the remains of a single hominid had carved out an L-shaped floor about 1,400 square feet in area into the hillside and had moved more dirt than at the monumental FLK excavation at Olduvai Gorge.

The skeleton belonged to an adolescent *Homo erectus* known variously as KNM-WT 15000, the Nariokotome boy and, in the pages of *Discover* magazine, as the "most compelling pelvis since Elvis." There are no clues to the cause of death, though the boy was probably not attacked and killed by a predator. The skeleton appears healthy except for some hints of decay on the lower jaw, where the gum may have been infected. The presence of newly erupted second molars is one indication, assuming *erectus* had a rate of dental development similar to that of modern humans, that the boy died at an age of roughly twelve years. His body lay prone, facedown, in the reeds on the shore of a seasonal lake in the Omo River floodplain. As it decomposed, the teeth fell out—to be recovered in the same spot 1.6 million years later. A light current swept some of the other bones downstream. Some were apparently trampled by a large mammal, possibly a hippopotamus, and pressed into the mud.

Although skull fossils from *Homo erectus* had been previously found at the Koobi Fora site on the east side of Lake Turkana, almost no *erectus* limb bones were known until this dig, and some of those previous finds were diseased and coated with extra bone that resembled lumps of melted wax. As well as being one of the oldest and most complete examples of *Homo erectus*, the WT 15000 specimen provided a rare opportunity for in-depth analysis of an individual and permitted the first joint measurements of brain and body size in a single early hominid—a vital comparison, as we will see. Many of the bones were complete. Alan Walker, a meticulous anatomist, pieced together the WT 15000 skull from a pile of fragments, filling in missing parts of the face and cranium with bright green plasticene.

With its skull, pelvis, and much of its limb bones intact, the reconstructed skeleton allows us to examine such complicated and confounding issues as the intricate balance among factors of brain size, birth requirements, and bipedalism that was being actively worked out in our evolutionary history. Because we have a comprehensive knowledge of how this balance works in modern humans, the WT 15000 skeleton lets us see immediately how similar or different *Homo erectus* was.

Christopher Ruff, a colleague of Alan Walker's at Johns Hopkins, used the WT 15000 pelvis to produce a model for *erectus* that linked body size and shape with environmental factors. Over long periods of time, environmental factors like temperature, humidity, and rainfall exert an important adaptive influence on human body size. Humans living in cold climates tend to have broad, squat bodies. This build reduces the amount of exposed body surface area, thus limiting heat loss and the chance of frostbite. In a cold-climate adaptation, the limbs get shorter and the body does its best to take the shape of a sphere. Mammals generally tend to have shorter extremities—limbs, ears, tail—in these conditions, a phenomenon known as Allen's Rule.

Humans living in open areas with dry tropical climates, such as the Dinka of Sudan and the Maasai of Kenya and Tanzania, tend to be tall, thin, and narrow, with long arms and legs, and *Homo erectus* was no exception. To keep a constant ratio of surface area to body weight, *erectus*'s body got longer as it grew bigger. The proportions of WT 15000's limb bones, combined with evidence that Nariokotome had an equatorial climate at the time the boy lived, suggest that this hominid had a body shape like that of many African groups inhabiting hot, dry equatorial regions today. (Pygmies are adapted to a humid forest environment; their ratio of surface area to body weight is still identical with that of their larger savanna-roaming neighbors.) The Nariokotome boy is certainly the tallest early hominid ever found; if he had reached adulthood, he might have stood six feet one inch and weighed 150 pounds. Even a puny member of this species, for that matter, probably reached five feet in height and weighed in at over a hundred pounds.

Alan Walker believes that *Homo erectus* had the body shape it did because this was the best way to stay cool. Its long extremities probably allowed for easier cooling and provided more surface for sweat glands to operate. Most mammals keep cool by panting and sweating; both processes produce evaporative cooling, the loss of heat when sweat turns to steam. Humans have more sweat glands per body surface area than any other mammal except chimpanzees; our bodies are covered with them, especially at the ends of our limbs. Only the edge of our lips, the ears, and part of the genitals are exempted.

It's safe to assume that our tall, climate-adapted *erectus* ancestor also had sweat glands. That would have important implications for its choice of habitat and food. Sweating is a water-dependent and salt-dependent activity; both substances must be constantly replaced by the sweating animal. With its wider territory, *erectus* would still have needed a reliable source of water, maybe more so than less active hominid species. And one sure source of salt is the blood and flesh of animals. The added need to replenish salt in the body may have been one more factor pushing *erectus* toward greater carnivory than its predecessors.

In the Nariokotome boy's skeleton investigators uncovered previously unknown features of *Homo erectus* that set it apart from our species. WT 15000 turned out to have an exceptionally long-necked femur (a primitive feature also found in the australopithecines) and a narrow pelvis. That shortened the distance between the hip joints and increased the distance from each hip joint to the muscle that supports the pelvis during walking. Both features improved the Nariokotome boy's bipedal abilities.

One and a half million years ago, this Homo erectus *boy died in a shallow lagoon surrounded by reeds on the western edge of Lake Turkana in Kenya. In 1984, a team led by Richard Leakey and Alan Walker discovered his remains and excavated the most complete skeleton of this hominid ever found.* IAN EVERARD

"*Homo erectus* was more efficient at walking and running than we are, more efficient than any athlete," Alan insisted when I visited his laboratory in Baltimore in 1992 and examined casts of the boy's bones firsthand. "When you add up his big body size, his long narrow build, and his sweating to keep heat stress down, the story you end up with is a very tall, thin individual running around in the heat of the day chasing things. And he wasn't chasing nuts."

Why is it that we humans, accustomed to thinking that bigger is better, are no longer as tall or as fast as *erectus* was? Blame it all on cultivation. The stature of modern humans shrank after agriculture became common, around 10,000 years ago. What's more, the sedentary nature of life in agricultural societies has also been linked with poor nutrition and higher risk of disease. That *Homo erectus* was "strapping," to borrow the adjective used by Richard Leakey to describe the Nariokotome boy, also suggests that it led a healthy scavenger-gatherer lifestyle.

It looks as if this hominid as it first evolved in Africa was adapted for long-distance foraging, a capacity that later allowed it to expand its range around the world. Only later, as we evolved into our modern form, did the birth canal (hence the pelvis bones) enlarge and the length of the femur's neck shorten in our species—both adaptations at some cost to our proficiency on two feet. Among hominids and humans, however, walking and thinking have a built-in evolutionary conflict. The trade-off for the magnificent mobility *erectus* enjoyed was that its narrow pelvis set a real limit on just how big its brain could ever get.

When Owen Lovejoy studied Lucy's pelvis, he determined that *Australopithecus afarensis* could only give birth to a baby with a certain size of brain. Assuming that brain size in a newborn *afarensis* was comparable to that of a newborn chimpanzee, Lucy could have given birth to a baby with a brain this size without the difficulties that human mothers face. Lucy's anatomy, however, set serious constraints on her birth-giving capacity. Her pelvis, adapted for bipedalism, was broad through the hips, but her birth canal was narrow from front to back. Most likely, Lucy could only have given birth if the baby exited the birth canal with the skull turned sideways.

Human babies enter the birth canal from the womb in the same way. But just before actual birth—and this is a crucial difference—the skull rotates 90 degrees in order to exit the rounder birth canal that humans have evolved. And that's only one complication of modern human birth. In *Homo sapiens,* evolution reached a new compromise that favored even bigger brains, at a further cost to birthing and efficient walking. The result was one of the most difficult birth processes experienced by any mammal.

The WT 15000 pelvis was so narrow that Alan Walker and his colleagues concluded that the *only* way that *erectus* could reach the brain size it had as an adult was if it shared a fascinating quirk of modern human brain growth that is integrally related to the birth process. Humans are unique among mammals in the extent to which the brain keeps growing well after birth. The scientific term is secondary altriciality, but it's easier to think of this phenomenon as either accelerated birth or arrested development.

Monkeys and apes are born with brains half as heavy as they will ever be. A chimpanzee brain, for example, weighs perhaps 7 ounces in a newborn and twice that much in an adult. Human brains, however, are about a third of their final size in newborns; they more than double in size in the first year after birth. On average, a new-born human's brain weighs 14 ounces but reaches 35 ounces by one year. (The necessity for this adaptive stroke of genius is clear when you consider that no amount of evolutionary remodeling could ever allow the head of that one-year-old through the modern human birth canal!) The brain continues to grow for several more years until it reaches a weight of around 45 ounces, and its adult size, at age six or seven. This, incidentally, is why children's heads seem large compared to the rest of their bodies; it simply means that their brain has reached its full physical growth long before the rest of the organism.

The result of the accelerated birth effect is that, in essence, every human baby is a "preemie," born ahead of the delivery date. Gestation actually lasts for twenty-one months, and human infants are external embryos who go through a year of "prenatal" development outside the womb. During this critical year, while our brains are still in active growth, our senses are deeply engaged in storing up and interpreting sights, sounds, and all sorts of data from the environment.

What this intense development also means is that a human infant is born relatively helpless. Unlike an ante-lope on an African savanna, a newborn human cannot stand up and fend for itself within hours after birth. The consequences of our premature births include longer childhood and adolescence, more time for learning and for adopting social behavior. As paleontologist Stephen Jay Gould wrote of the Nariokotome boy, "our sexual maturation comes almost absurdly late in a Darwinian world supposedly regulated by a constant struggle to secure reproductive success and pass more genes along to future generations. . . . Slow development must provide

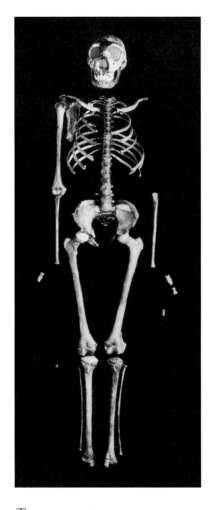

The WT 15000 skeleton, excavated by Richard Leakey and Alan Walker's team in Kenya, has shed new light on the anatomy and biology of Homo erectus. *For example, studies of the skeleton have led to provocative ideas about whether this hominid could speak and what sort of development and growth pattern it had.*

DAVID BRILL

some powerful advantage to evolve, in the face of its obvious drawbacks." In fact, much of what makes us human in the end—language, culture, social organization—may stem from this unnaturally long period of helplessness in the early part of our lives.

Just one year before WT 15000 was discovered, Robert Martin of the University of Zurich was pondering the question of when the peculiar brain-growth pattern of modern humans could have appeared in our evolution. Since the hominid pelvis set an upper limit on brain size at birth, Martin predicted that the accelerated birth phenomenon would kick in once the adult hominid brain reached a threshold size of 850 cc. This evolutionary turning point, he speculated, must have been reached just before the appearance of *Homo erectus* in the fossil record. Now it's been estimated that the Nariokotome boy's brain, if he had reached adulthood, would have been about 900 cc, a much bigger size than the customary rate of brain growth in an ape would have produced. Similarly, projecting backward, his brain at birth would have been too big to fit through his mother's narrow birth canal if the *erectus* species had followed the apelike pattern of brain growth shown among the australopithecines. Judging from the size of the opening in the pelvis for the birth canal (identical between males and females in hominids), a newborn *Homo erectus* most likely had a brain that weighed around 7 ounces. If brain growth followed a human pattern, the weight would increase by a substantial 18 ounces in the first year and by another 7 ounces before adulthood.

Using this trajectory, the total brain size of the *erectus* adult would then be between 850 or 900 cc, a figure that matches not only the estimate for the Nariokotome boy but also Martin's threshold.

Still, the adult *Homo erectus* brain was much smaller than a modern human's. The mean cranial capacity for Javanese *Homo erectus,* 900 cc, is about the size of a modern four-year-old child's brain; an average adult modern human brain measures more than 1,400 cc. "*Homo erectus* didn't have a *lot* of brain," Alan Walker allowed, "but on the other hand he wasn't a complete pinhead, either." What's even more fascinating is that the earliest members of our species, and even the much-maligned Neandertals, had brain capacities averaging *over* 1,500 cc. Some of our most recent ancestors had bigger brains than we do.

Another factor that clearly distinguishes *Homo erectus* from modern humans was revealed in some intriguing work conducted by anthropologist Ann MacLarnon, of the Roehampton Institute in London. After writing her doctoral dissertation on the evolution of the spinal cord in living primates, Ann got interested in older species, including hominids. Since only the vertebrae fossilize, for negative evidence of the spinal cord itself she had to examine the vertebral canal, that circular space in a vertebra the cord passes through.

The human backbone is divided into three regions: cervical, thoracic, and lumbar. Because vertebrae in each of these regions have slightly different shapes and structural features, it's relatively easy to say where in the spine a fossil vertebra would have been located. We humans have seven vertebrae in the cervical region, starting from the base of the skull and continuing to the shoulders. A series of twelve thoracic vertebrae in the torso forms the middle of our spine's **S**-shaped curve. Below the thoracic vertebrae are five thick lumbar vertebrae that support the lower back. At the bottom of the spine, finally, sit the sacrum and coccyx, or tailbone, both of which are made up of several fused vertebrae.

When Ann read the first published scientific article about WT 15000, one statement caught her eye. "They mentioned that the vertebral canal in the thoracic region looked small," Ann told me one evening in a London café. "I was really surprised to hear this. I'd been looking for differences between humans and primates in the vertebral canal and hadn't found many." From her own past research Ann knew that little variation exists among the spinal cords of most modern primates, a finding that suggests that unlike the brain, the spinal cord has not changed much in either primates or hominids over the course of evolution. In fact, the size of the spinal cord has stayed surprisingly constant in all mammals; a mouse's is just about the same, relative to total body size, as a dolphin's.

Ann's first impulse, then, was to doubt the accuracy of the description of the Nariokotome boy's spinal cord as smaller than a human's. Since his spine was complete except for all but one of the cervical vertebrae, she decided she wanted to study it and contacted Alan Walker. After Ann described the figures she needed, Alan and his colleague Mark Teaford measured the original fossil at the National Museums of Kenya in Nairobi. (Wisely, Ann preferred having the measurements performed on the actual fossil rather than on a cast.) All she wanted them to measure were two dimensions: the height and width of the canal within each vertebra. The only tool Alan and Mark needed was that old standby of anthropologists, a pair of calipers, which provided an intriguing story.

Although the Nariokotome boy's spine appears extremely humanlike to the naked eye, Ann's analysis turned up some surprising results. In the thoracic region, the vertebral canal for his spinal cord is only half as wide as it is in modern humans. In this feature *Homo erectus* shows much more similarity to all other primates, and presumably to earlier hominids, than it does to *Homo sapiens*. "I had actually overlooked the fact that the human canal is large in the thoracic region, compared with other primates," Ann admitted with refreshing frankness. "I missed this difference just because I thought the thoracic region was boring."

Now Ann had to ask why modern humans have a larger vertebral canal in the upper body than other primates do. She thought about what functions the thoracic region of the spinal cord could serve. She knew it didn't control arm, finger, or leg movements, but then she drew a blank. "I went back to my spinal-cord data and found I had missed another major human difference," Ann recalled. "In the thoracic region the total *size* of the human spinal cord is exactly what you'd predict from other primates. If you split it into gray matter and white matter, they all have the same amount of white matter, but humans have more gray matter than primates do."

A spinal cord contains two types of tissue: nerve cell fibers, or white matter, and nerve cell bodies, or gray matter. (The latter are not to be confused, by the way, with the "little gray cells" upstairs in the brain that Hercule Poirot always credited for his crime-solving skills.) The spinal cord serves as a messenger for nerve signals traveling between the brain and the rest of the body. If you think of the cord as a telegraph service, the fibers are the telegraph lines and the cell bodies are relay stations.

Because the thoracic region of the *erectus* skeleton had the smaller canal width of nonhuman primates and because the spinal cord of primates has a predictable ratio of white matter to gray matter, Ann hypothesized that the *erectus* spinal cord did not contain gray matter in the same amounts as modern humans' spinal cords do.

But what do we humans do with our extra spinal gray matter? In contrast to the white matter, which carries nerve signals to distant outposts, gray-matter cell bodies are associated with nerve functions close to them in the body. This suggested to Ann some extra innervation in the thoracic region itself—that is, added muscle control in the vicinity of the ribs. At first she wondered whether this extra nerve activity could have something to do with breathing, so she considered the diaphragm, the thin sheet of muscle that separates the chest from the abdomen. It turns out, though, that the diaphragm receives its nerves from the cervical region in the neck. When Ann went back to her anatomy book to see where the thoracic nerves lead, she found that the main destinations were a series of muscles between the ribs, called the intercostals, as well as some abdominal muscles. From this fact she proposes two possible reasons that modern humans might have more muscle control around their ribs than *Homo erectus.*

Reason 1:   The extra nerve activity might have to do with holding the trunk upright. This reason seemed less likely, since *Homo erectus* is humanlike, even extra-human, in its adaptations for walking. The major changes toward bipedalism occurred much earlier, some 3 million years before this boy lived and died at Nariokotome. The fact that *Homo erectus* spread so far outside Africa indicates that the species was suited for long-distance travel. Moreover, other anatomical features of the WT 15000 spine, including a widening of the vertebral canal in the lumbar region, match those associated with fully upright bipedalism in modern humans.

Reason 2: The nerves serve in the fine control of breathing, a skill necessary for speaking. Many intercostal and abdominal muscles control the volume of air in the lungs. Extra gray matter serving those muscles could function in regulating breathing, including that associated with speech. Apparently, though, *Homo erectus* lacked the nerves controlling the amount of air passing from the lungs up the respiratory tract to the mouth. Ann reached the tentative conclusion that *erectus* could not talk. "I *never* expected to find that," she confessed. "But when you find something you're not expecting, you tend to have more faith in it."

For the first time now in our mystery, the question of language has reared its head. When did our ancestors learn to communicate with each other with a meaningful set of sounds instead of with grunts and gestures? Ideas about the first appearance of language fall into two camps, favoring early and late development, respectively. The early camp argues that some form of spoken language has existed for 2 million years. The evidence includes bumps found on brain casts of early hominid fossils, which have been interpreted as Broca's area and Wernicke's area, two regions on the left side of the human brain believed to be linked with speech. Interpreting these features on fossil endocasts is a difficult game at best, however. Moreover, current physiological data suggest that Broca's area functions in controlling motor skills but may have no connection to spoken language.

The early camp also likes to argue that language was necessary for early hominids to transmit tool-making skills and other features of their rudimentary culture. As we have seen with Kanzi the pygmy chimpanzee in Chapter 3, however, sometimes a simple demonstration is worth a thousand words. Even among speaking creatures such as ourselves, watching and imitating can be easier than following spoken instruction. Language, then, is not essential for transmitting some aspects of culture. And remember the strangely unchanging stone tools of *Homo erectus*. If these hominids were talking to each other about what they were making, might we not reasonably expect more innovations to show up over the span of a million years?

The late camp, on the other hand, contends that language only arose recently—maybe only within the last 40,000 or 50,000 years. Alan Walker once counted himself part of the early camp, but lately he has shifted allegiance toward what he calls the "new heresy." He wrote in the summary chapter of a book about the WT 15000 skeleton that paleoanthropologists who argue for an early origin for human language and speech "are standing on ground that is steadily crumbling away."

In a curious historical footnote, G.H.R. von Koenigswald, the man who helped vindicate Eugène Dubois and his Javan fossils earlier this century, also suspected, though on considerably less scientific grounds, that *Homo erectus* lacked language. Describing a portrait of this hominid that hung in the Haeckel Museum in Jena, he wrote, "It is a very remarkable picture: under a tree a woman with long, lank hair sits cross-legged suckling a child. Beside her stands her husband, fat-bellied and low-browed, his back thickly covered with hair. He looks at the spectator good-naturedly and unintelligently, with the suspicious expression of an inveterate toper. It must have been a very happy marriage: his wife could not contradict him, for neither of them could speak."

If language really was a late occurrence in human evolution, then it represents only one by-product of a big brain and could not by itself have been the driving force behind expanding brain size. The dramatic spurt in brain growth that would later distinguish *Homo sapiens* from *Homo erectus* (just as *erectus*'s own expanding brain distinguished it from the australopithecines) was most likely tied to an expanding capacity for processing and keeping track of information—a further expansion and extension of those "mental maps" that even the earliest hominids possessed.

It seems likely, finally, that *erectus* became more of a carnivore than its predecessors, probably still through scavenging rather than active hunting. In the words of archeologist Nick Toth, whom we met in Chapter 3, their Acheulian tool industry, which appears well suited for processing meat, "screams butchery." This interpretation is also supported by dental evidence. Whereas the heavy pitting on robust australopithecine molars was probably caused by an abrasive fiber diet, analysis of *Homo erectus* teeth shows a wear pattern consistent with a more carnivorous diet.

We know from the WT 15000 skeleton that *Homo erectus* was a superefficient walker and probably possessed tremendous endurance. And if you're a traveling fool like *Homo erectus*, it's convenient to be a carnivore. A carnivore can eat meat from any animal and doesn't have to worry about what sort of vegetation is available. Therefore, that successful running animal *erectus*, says Alan Walker, should have been able to leave Africa very soon after it evolved—traveling in tight, supportive groups like hunting packs of other animal species.

The size of the Nariokotome boy's skeleton indicates that Homo erectus *had a tall, lean body adapted for open savanna environments. Alan Walker speculates that* erectus *may have been a formidable hunter that chased game such as wildebeest.*
LENORA JOHANSON

Exclusive carnivory, though, is actually a rare phenomenon in animals. In an average African game park, for example, only 1 or 2 percent of the animals eat meat. The reason for this lies in the nature of the food pyramid. The occupants of each layer in the food pyramid obtain only about 10 to 20 percent of the total energy of the occupants of the next lower level. By the time we get to the carnivores, who are perched precariously at the very top, the amount of packaged energy available is much smaller than that available to the herbivores they consume. Their numbers must of necessity be lower, to reflect their more limited feeding opportunities.

Despite the fact that no evidence for hunting implements has been found in any *erectus* site throughout its vast territory, some investigators continue to describe *Homo erectus* as a noble hunter. In an article called "The Costs of Becoming a Predator," Pat Shipman and Alan Walker argue that *Homo erectus* adopted a substantially more carnivorous diet than that of previous hominids and did so by aggressive hunting. Here's what Shipman and Walker predict the fossil and archeological records should contain as evidence of increased carnivory: Hominids should show signs of being faster-moving and more social, of developing better ways to process animal carcasses, and of maintaining low population densities—this last signaled either by a decrease in body size (thereby reducing the total amount of food required by each individual) or an increase in geographic range (allowing access to new food resources when the local supply gets low from population pressure and competition among carnivores).

As we know, *erectus* was the first big hominid and hence did not decrease its body size as Shipman and Walker predicted would happen in a carnivorous population competing for food resources. Significantly, however, the species did reduce its population density by dramatically increasing its range—throughout the entire Old World. I believe, however, in the absence of clear evidence for hunting, that what we see between *Homo habilis* and *Homo erectus* is a diet evolving from marginal to sophisticated scavenging. *Erectus* would have been faster getting to the carcass than its forebears, more formidable in chasing other carnivores away, more expert in processing the meat thanks to its better tools, and cleverer in finding new food resources in its wide-ranging travels.

The clear evidence that *erectus* evolved into more of a meat-craving carnivore, however, brings us back to brain size. The human brain is five times larger than the expected brain size for a typical mammal of the same body weight as a human, and the brain of *Homo erectus* was three times larger than that expected for a typical mammal of a similar body size. Although the adult human brain weighs just 3 pounds, running it drains 20 percent of our body's total energy. During that amazing growth spurt in our first year, the brain drains a full half of our body's energy.

The task of supplying that energy belongs, initially, to mothers. Human milk is rich in amino acids, proteins, and fats, and some of these ingredients help fuel brain growth. But mothers need calories to keep their infants nourished, so a diet that contained more high-protein, high-fat food, such as meat and marrow, would keep both mothers and babies well nourished through the abnormally long human dependency period. As Lew Binford reminded us in Chapter 3, "marrow is the perfect weaning-time food" for the enormous brain-fueling demands of hominid infants.

In spite of its long, nimble leap in our direction, behaviorally *erectus* still lacked some critical signatures of humanness—language, funerary rites, art. And there is the troubling matter of a tool industry that didn't change for a million years. Perhaps this seems like nit-picking in the face of a major evolutionary milestone. But a million years is a *very* long time to go with no sign of technological innovation or cultural evolution. Needless to say, it is a pattern that contrasts starkly with the archeological record for modern humans, especially within the past 40,000 years.

Why did *erectus* stay so static in its development for so long, and what critical pressure caused this lengthy equilibrium finally to shift? We are hovering now at the very threshold between hominid and human. The boundary line between genus *Australopithecus* and genus *Homo* is clearly drawn. It's not so clear where the wide-ranging but technologically conservative hominid we call *erectus* ends and our modern *sapiens* begins. How, when, and where that threshold was crossed is still a matter of intense debate in paleoanthropology today. Follow me, now, into the fray.

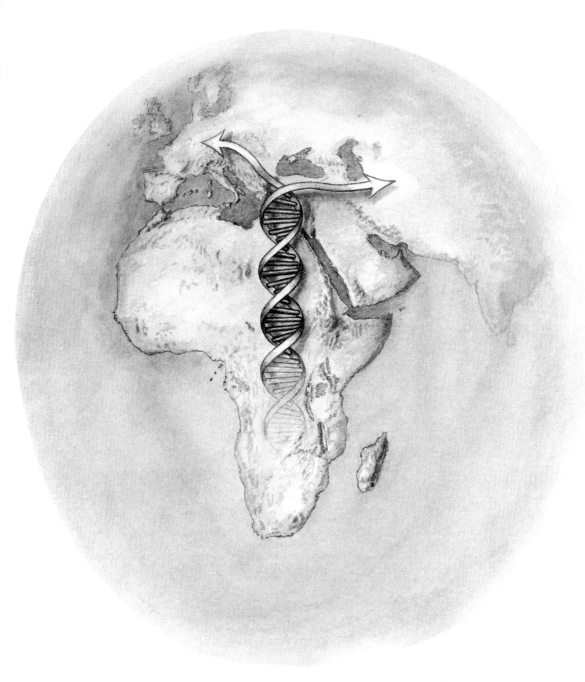

Our immediate ancestors evolved in Africa, but where did modern humans first appear?
IAN EVERARD

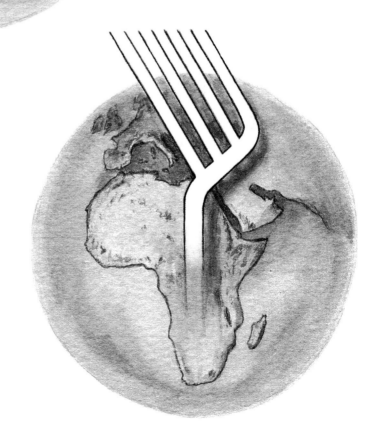

CHAPTER SIX

Looking for Eden:
"Archaic" *Homo sapiens*

*T*he Multiregional Model *(above)* argues that Homo sapiens evolved independently around the world for at least a million years after Homo erectus *left Africa. There was genetic exchange between the various populations, shown by the arrows, but modern racial differences are the product of long-term regional evolution. In contrast, the Out of Africa Model (right) argues that modern humans evolved recently and in only one location, Africa. The first modern humans left Africa within the last 200,000 years and replaced other populations of archaic humans and Neandertals in Europe and Asia. Modern racial differences all evolved within the last 50,000 years.* IAN EVERARD

IN THE SLOW UNWINDING OF THE EVOLU-
tionary sequence, we've now reached what seems to us
humans, incorrigible species-centric creatures that we are,
to be the biggest, most important event of all: the beginnings of our very own species. No one doubts that we
must look to Africa for the origin of every hominid
species as far up the line as *Homo erectus*. Now we have to
consider if we should keep looking to Africa for the origins of modern humans, *Homo sapiens*, as well. Somewhere,
at some point in the window of time between 100,000
and 500,000 years ago, our kind first appeared.

Many fossil remains from Africa, Asia, and Europe dating from this time in our prehistory—known variously as
the Middle Stone Age in Africa and the Middle Paleolithic in Europe—have been collectively lumped in a
category known as "archaic" *Homo sapiens*. It's an ill-fitting
catchall label that doesn't mean a lot. These fossils share
some features with *Homo erectus*, but they have larger brains
and show other differences, mainly in the size or proportion of various areas of the skull. Some paleoanthropologists place these fossils in one or more distinctly new
species; others think they're simply examples of the wide
range of variation that characterizes *Homo sapiens* in general.

Before us in the witness box are the two major competing theories for the origin and emergence of modern
humans, each with radically different implications for the
pace and process of evolution. At issue are the timing and
manner in which *Homo sapiens* emerged and the role

played by populations around the world in this evolutionary event. The argument boils down to two possibilities:
Did we come on the scene like a tidal wave rising from a
single region that swamped all our living predecessors?
Or was our species born in geographically separate but
analogous events that slowly overlapped each other like
spreading concentric ripples in a still pond?

The overlapping-ripple theory of human origins is
called the Multiregional Model. According to this theory,
the evolution of modern human anatomy happened at various times in various parts of the world over the last million
years. Each regional population evolved separately but not
independently, with genes flowing freely between them,
creating a mosaic pattern in which various modern human
features arise at different times and in different places.

The Multiregional Model has also been compared to a
candelabra, with our parent species *Homo erectus* squatting
at the base of the main stem. After *erectus* leaves Africa
around a million years ago and disperses throughout the
Old World, the candelabra sprouts many branches as various populations of the new species begin to emerge.
Because these local populations occupy different environments, this theory goes, they begin to develop unique
subfeatures as specific adaptations to those environments—differences that constitute the racial variations
recognized in modern populations today. All humans are
thus linked by a worldwide web of ancient lineages that
put our species' age at a venerable 1 million years.

On the other side of the debate we have the Out of
Africa (also known as the Noah's Ark) Model, which
posits Africa as the single geographical source for our
species. According to this theory, *Homo sapiens* evolved on
this continent much more recently than the Multiregional

Model allows for—within the past 200,000 years or so—and in a rapid global expansion replaced all earlier archaic populations throughout the Old World. Modern human evolution derives directly from this late tidal wave, in which neither *Homo erectus* nor "archaic" *Homo sapiens* outside Africa nor the Neandertals in Europe or the Middle East played any significant genetic role.

In this back-and-forth exchange the Multiregional Model came first. Initially championed by Franz Weidenreich, a German paleoanthropologist famous for his studies of the Peking Man fossils from Zhoukoudian, it has been with us in various forms for half a century. The Out of Africa Model, in contrast, is a young upstart; only in the past ten or fifteen years have a growing number of paleoanthropologists advanced the argument for a strictly African late origin for *Homo sapiens*. Africa was traditionally regarded as a backwater of modern human evolution because the first "archaic" *Homo sapiens* fossils discovered there—such as the Kabwe, or Broken Hill, skull found in the wall of a Zambian zinc mine in 1921—have massive faces and browridges. Mistakenly thought to be very recent, these fossils were considered too primitive to have spawned modern humans. Recent discoveries of younger, more modern-looking fossils, however, as well as the promise of new dating techniques and genetic evidence, have helped the African origin argument gather strength.

In the meantime another continent altogether, even though it was settled later than most of the Old World, has emerged as a critical if unlikely location for bolstering the Multiregional Model. Eugène Dubois may indeed have been prescient in referring to his Wajak fossils as "Proto-Australian," for the fossil evidence of Australia may pose a tough test for the Out of Africa advocates. In

August 1992 I went to Australia to examine some of this evidence firsthand.

The Willandra Lakes region of New South Wales is a chain of dry lake basins along Willandra Creek, a tributary of the Lachlan River. In ancient times a wet wilderness harboring fish, waterfowl, and other wildlife, the lakes have stood empty for the last 15,000 years. Today they are a lunar landscape of shifting sand dunes and wind-sculpted sandstone. Along the eastern lakeshore stretches a giant crescent-shaped dune known as the Walls of China—a name that proves peculiarly apt when we come to consider the possible human history of this region.

Home to the present-day Bagundji people, Willandra Lakes preserves the longest known continuous record of Aboriginal occupation in Australia: an amazing 40,000 years. The Aborigines were here when the lakes were really lakes, and they stayed on after the lakes dried up. The best record of these early colonists comes from Lake Mungo, which once covered an area of seventy-seven square miles and stood fifty feet deep. Some 30,000 years ago, people made camps here, fished for golden perch with reed nets, ate shellfish and emu eggs. They hunted animals and roasted the meat on the same bed of hot stones in shallow underground ovens that some Aborigines use today. They buried their dead in the sand with ceremony, including cremation or ritual dusting of the body with red ocher.

The man responsible for studying most of the ancient human skeletons in Australia is an anatomist and paleoanthropologist in the Department of Prehistory at Australian National University in Canberra, Alan Thorne. Decep-

This skull was blasted out of a Zambian zinc mine at Broken Hill (or Kabwe) in 1921. Perhaps 300,000 years in age, the Broken Hill skull may represent a transitional form between Homo erectus *and the first fully modern humans.* IAN EVERARD

Once the site of lush wetlands, Lake Mungo in the Willandra Lakes region of Australia is now a lunar landscape of sculpted sandstone and shifting sand dunes. The remains of more than one hundred humans have been found buried at Lake Mungo, including the skeleton of a woman who lived 25,000 years ago. This is the world's oldest evidence for cremation. D. C. JOHANSON

tively donnish with his wide-rimmed glasses and graying hair, Alan lights up like a movie marquee when conversation turns to the significance of Australia's human fossils for human evolution and the Multiregional Model he champions. I visited Lake Mungo with Alan to talk about the fossils and their implications for human origins.

The remains of more than a hundred individuals have been uncovered at Lake Mungo. The first was the skeleton of a young female, found in 1968 when geologist Jim Bowler noticed a bunched set of burned bones sticking out of a sand dune. The next year the bones were excavated in a block of calcrete, or hardened calcium. After removing the calcrete with acid, Alan Thorne had the painstaking task of piecing together the hundreds of paper-thin skull fragments in the Mungo I skull. "When I was first shown them, I thought that some of the pieces were emu eggshell," he recalled as he led me along the former lakeshore at Mungo. The bones had been deliberately smashed into pieces after burning. Alan did an exquisite and delicate reconstruction that clearly revealed the skull was *Homo sapiens.* The human female we call Mungo I died about 25,000 years ago and represents the world's oldest known cremation.

A further prize came to light in 1974, when heavy winds exposed the left side of a cranium not far from the Mungo I site. Excavation revealed an entire skeleton buried ceremoniously: its legs flexed at the knees, its arms folded across the body with the hands resting gently on the pelvis. The bones were stained pink from ocher sprinkled over the burial. The age of this male, known as Mungo III, falls between 28,000 and 32,000 years, roughly the same age as early burials in Europe that also made use of ocher. Mungo III is more robust than Mungo I but still not as

Map of China, Indonesia, and Australia with prehistoric sites.
CAROLYN FISH

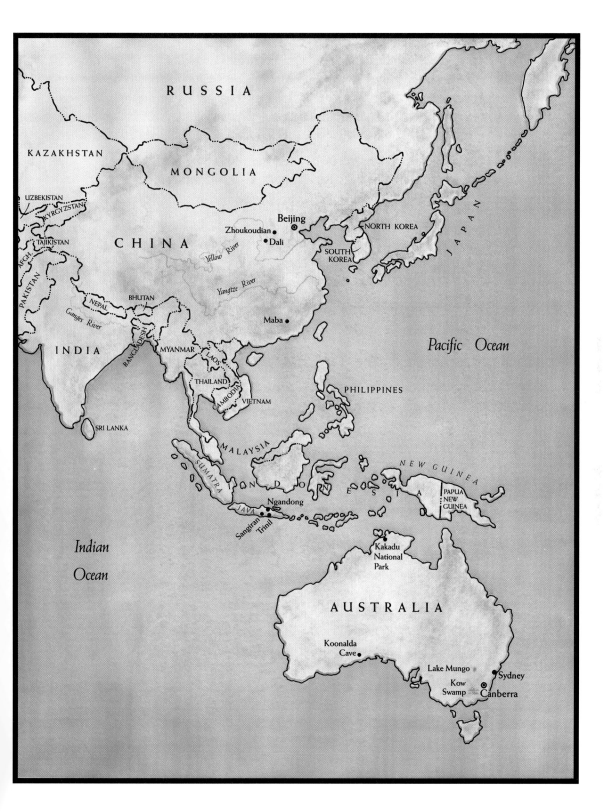

brawny as an average male Aborigine. When Alan showed me a cast of the cranium in his office before we visited the site, I was struck by how much thicker it was compared to Mungo I's. Was this simply because of gender, or could there have been more than one population at Mungo?

Alan has been thinking about this complex issue of multiple migrating populations for some time. In 1967, as he was examining some human bones in a Melbourne museum, he came across a robust, archaic-looking partial skeleton. His curiosity aroused, Alan traced the skeleton back to the spot where it had been dug up a few decades earlier, at a place called Kow Swamp, a large freshwater lake near the Murray River, south of Lake Mungo.

The next year he went to Kow Swamp himself and excavated more of the same skeleton, which was named Kow Swamp 1. Subsequent digging uncovered the remains of more than forty individuals, some buried together, with the bodies laid on both the right and left sides, the legs either flexed or extended. Some of the bodies had been adorned with bone, shell, and ivory beads, and one bore a headband made from kangaroo teeth.

Alan was struck by the thick, robust skulls, the large faces and teeth, and the dense browridges along the base of the flat foreheads that sloped back onto the crania. Using these features as his guide, he concluded that these robust fossils

Alan Thorne of Australian National University is a proponent of the Multiregional Model for modern human origins, which states that our species evolved from populations that spread around the world nearly a million years ago, after Homo erectus *left Africa. Thorne is shown here at Lake Mungo with fossils that he says represent two sequences of evolution from* erectus *in Java and in China to modern humans in Australia.*

D. C. JOHANSON

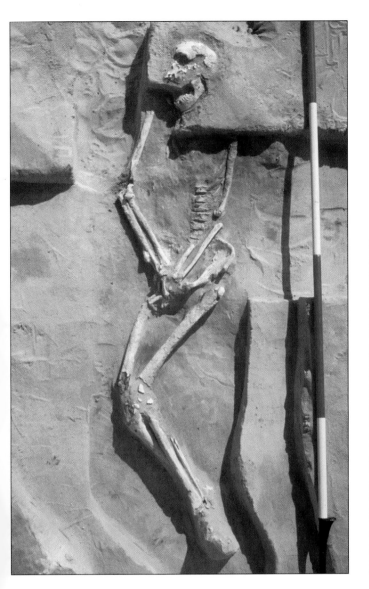

Although obscured by sand, the lower jaw, face, and skull of Mungo III appear gracile and clearly belong to a modern human. ALAN THORNE

The male skeleton known as Mungo III dates to at least 30,000 years ago. The skeleton was buried and covered with red ocher. Many human skeletons excavated from the sands of Mungo may trace back to earlier populations in China that migrated to Australia. ALAN THORNE

from Kow Swamp were the direct descendants of *Homo erectus* in Java. The surprise came when his finds were dated. Although they were considerably more "primitive"-looking, the Kow Swamp specimens were 9,000 to 15,000 years old, only half the age of the Mungo fossils. That meant that the fossils that looked more modern, the Mungo people, came *before* the robust, even *erectus*-like people at Kow Swamp. Alan Thorne had a puzzle on his hands, but he thought he had enough pieces to make out the picture. The markedly different features of their face,

jaws, and frontal bones convinced him that Kow Swamp and
Mungo represented distinct populations with separate origins,
reflecting two migrations of
modern humans into Australia.

In Alan's perspective, modern
humans in general are an
extremely diverse species in the
size and shape of our body forms.
In biological terms we are *polytypic*. "Somewhere, at the root of
our species, there's already inher-
ent a capacity for polytypism:
black, white, tall, short, fat, thin,
big nose, small nose, the whole
variation in humans," Alan told
me in his office. "Very few other
species are like that. It's part of
what makes us such an enormously successful group operat-
ing worldwide."

The real miracle, I remarked
to Alan, is that in spite of this
enormous diversity, we still manage to stay one species,
capable of interbreeding, freely exchanging genes
between populations. Alan agreed, but we parted company when he insisted that this sort of gene exchange across
space and time has been going on in our species for a million years, ever since *Homo erectus* began its cross-continen-
tal migrations from Africa into Europe and Eurasia.

I protested that I didn't think we could lump all
hominids of the past million years into the same species,

After discovering some human bones from the area of Kow Swamp in a museum, Alan Thorne visited the site and began finding more skeletons. Here is the burial of Kow Swamp 14 as it was excavated. ALAN THORNE

as the multiregionalists have proposed. Alan responded that many paleoanthropologists have become preoccupied with identifying each and every fossil rather than looking for broader biological patterns. "They put names on fossils and then say, 'If that's *Homo erectus* then it can't be *Homo sapiens* because I've already called it *erectus*,'" he scoffed.

How, I wanted to know, did his theory account for the fact that the Kow Swamp and Mungo fossils look so different? Alan told me then about the evolutionary sequences he recognizes in the human fossil record from Asia, which form the foundation of the latest thinking in the Multiregional Model. First he set out a series of casts of the Java skulls. Alan believes that these fossils represent the best case for regional evolution from what we currently call *Homo erectus* to modern humans. A third of the world's known *Homo erectus* fossils come from Java, and they span a time period from about a million to 100,000 years ago. The sequence then jumps to Australia, with the earliest robust specimens from Mungo, and continues through the younger fossils from Kow Swamp. "So there's a very clear 'Out of Java' sequence," Alan concluded, "that links the *Homo erectus* people from Java all the way through to late Pleistocene Australia."

The clincher for Alan is a set of anatomical features in the teeth, jaws, and skulls that he thinks can be traced throughout the sequence and even to living populations in Australia. These features not only distinguish the Javan fossils from other *Homo erectus* fossils found elsewhere but also distinguish modern Aborigines from other living populations. For Alan, the only explanation is morphological continuity.

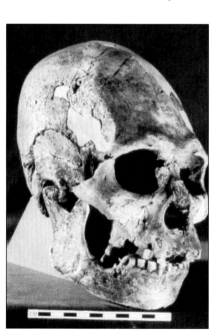

Only half the age of the Lake Mungo burials, modern human fossils found at Kow Swamp in Australia have more robust features that some anthropologists say link them with much earlier humans and with Homo erectus *from Java. Others believe that the Kow Swamp fossils are simply modern humans who evolved their distinctive anatomy in the rugged Australian environment.* ALAN THORNE

These recurring features include thick cranial bones, a big browridge that forms a thick, straight bar of bone beneath the flat, sloping forehead, and a bony shelf on the back of the skull where neck muscles attach. In addition, the protruding faces of the Java fossils have huge cheekbones and the largest teeth of any human population from that time.

Let's look at the Javan sequence in more detail. The first link comes from the site of Sangiran, where a skull known as Sangiran 17 was discovered in 1969. Many fossils had turned up previously in Java, but this was the first time that paleoanthropologists had a chance to see what an ancient hominid face from outside Africa looks like. The face protrudes forward—it is, as they say, prognathic—and has a pronounced browridge. The cranial vault is long and low, as in *Homo erectus*, and is broad at the base, angling inward toward the top of the skull. Sangiran 17 dates to about 700,000 years ago.

The Javan sequence continues with the Trinil skullcap found by Eugène Dubois in 1891. Though it is less complete than the Sangiran skull, the Trinil fossil does possess a prominent browridge and overall thick bone on the crani-

Alan Thorne compares early modern human skulls from China and Australia. He argues that certain anatomical features can be traced between these fossils and other Chinese fossils back to a million years ago.

D. C. JOHANSON

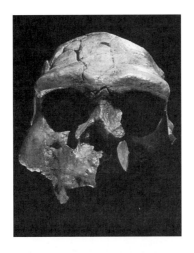
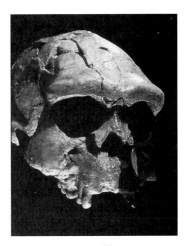

This fossil from Java, known as Sangiran 17, has a long, low braincase, a protruding face, and a prominent browridge across the forehead—features reminiscent of Homo erectus. *Believed to be 700,000 years old, this fossil forms the first link in a proposed evolutionary sequence that led to the modern humans who lived at Kow Swamp in Australia 15,000 years ago.*
NANCI KAHN

um. Alan's argument grew stronger, however, when he got to the next part of the sequence, the fossils from Ngandong, also called the Solo fossils after their river site six miles north of Trinil.

You may recall from Chapter 5 that Ngandong was the place where the German anthropologist G.H.R. von Koenigswald, following in Dubois's footsteps, looked for fossils during the 1930s. Eleven partial skulls, some skull fragments, and two lower limb bone fragments came to light, though sadly none of the skulls preserved any trace of a face. Although they share some features with *Homo erectus*, such as the large browridge, flat forehead, and thick cranial bones, the Solo fossils had larger brains than those found in *erectus*. Evolution toward modernity seemed to be occurring.

After the Solo fossils, there is no fossil evidence from Java for the evolution of modern humans until 10,000 years ago, with Dubois's Wajak skulls, the first human fossils found in Java. That's an unfortunately wide gap in the record because evidence from the missing time period could prove crucial in tilting the balance toward either the Multiregional or the Out of Africa model. The robust face and body form apparently disappeared in Indonesia after 100,000 years ago but persisted in Australia and New Guinea, where Alan thinks the early Indonesians immigrated and evolved into the robust populations sampled at sites such as Kow Swamp. Early human populations in Indonesia, then, did get replaced—that forbidden word for multiregionalists—during later migrations in the Pleistocene. Alan contends, however, that the new people came from nearby, to the north, rather than from the other side of the world, in Africa. He had explained the Javan sequence, and now he argued that the Wajak fossils and the gracile fossils from Lake Mungo provided evi-

*A*nother Javan fossil, one of eleven partial skulls from the Solo River site of Ngandong, could form an intermediate link in the evolution of modern humans in Indonesia and Australia. These 100,000-year-old fossils retain many of the primitive features of older Homo erectus *skulls but have a larger brain capacity.* NANCI KAHN

dence for a second early migration to Australia, this one from China.

Alan made a pretty convincing case for a continual sequence in Java at least until 100,000 years ago and even to the present, for a total of three quarters of a million years. The similarities between the 700,000-year-old skull of Sangiran 17 and all the Solo crania were clearly visible. Both had the barlike browridge, an inward tilt from the base of the skull to the top, a flexed occipital bone at the back, and a low ridge running down the top of the skull, called a sagittal keel. And I could see similarities in the faces between Sangiran 17 at one end and the 10,000-year-old fossils from Kow Swamp on the other, although the latter clearly had a human-sized brain. Most obvious is the shared sloping, flat forehead and big, protruding face. (As I was later to learn, though, these fossils also do show some distinctive differences.)

That was Indonesia. What about China, which yielded another third of the known *erectus* remains? The China sequence might begin as long as a million years ago if we include a flattened cranium of uncertain age from Lantian that probably belongs to *Homo erectus*. After the famous Peking Man fossils from Zhoukoudian, dated at roughly 500,000 years ago, the sequence continues with two skulls known as Maba and Dali, that clearly show the change from *erectus* to "archaic" *Homo sapiens*. No one knows how old these two skulls are, but they probably date from between 100,000 and 200,000 years ago. On the recent end of the sequence are two obviously modern skulls from the Upper Cave section of Zhoukoudian that date to possibly 25,000 years ago.

"The dating's problematic," Alan admitted of the Chinese fossils, "but the anatomy is very, very clear. Then you jump across to Australia, and here are the Mungo remains." Although the sequence in China suffers from less evidence and is more complex, Alan maintains that the argument for regional evolution is a good one. If he's right, then the ancestry of modern Australian Aborigines stems from separate migrations out of Java and China that merged in Australia.

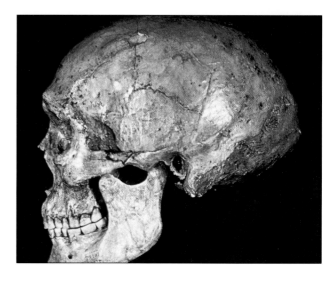

Next Alan showed me a particularly interesting fossil that added a little spice to the multiregional stew. Known as the Willandra Lakes Hominid—WLH 50 for short—the fossil had been found a decade earlier in the vicinity of the modern-looking Mungo burials. Oddly enough, however, this one looked very robust and had extremely thick cranial bones. The age of WLH 50 is unknown, but Alan suspects that it may be between 30,000 and 50,000 years old and that it may be a link between the last robust Javans from Ngandong and the late robust individuals from Kow Swamp.

The Zhoukoudian cave in China that yielded several Homo erectus *skulls also contained the skulls of modern humans that are about 20,000 years old. This specimen from the Upper Cave may link* Homo erectus *in China to modern humans in China and Australia, or it may be part of a much later human migration from Africa or Europe.* INSTITUTE OF HUMAN ORIGINS

How did they get to Australia? Alan speculated that during periods of low sea level, a craft could easily island-hop from Asia into the Philippines, to New Guinea, and beyond. It would have taken fewer water crossings to reach the north coast of Australia directly from China than to meander through the Indonesian archipelago.

In the spirit of the new archeology, Alan had performed various experiments to re-create how the first open-water crossing to Australia could have occurred.

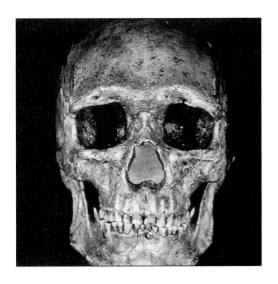

Even if their discovery of this huge continent was an accident, the first Australians had to be proficient boat builders and navigators. Techniques and knowledge already applied to shorter sea crossings enabled them to make these longer journeys, too. From earlier trips to China, Alan had observed different types of sailing craft, including bamboo rafts of the sort that have been plying Chinese waters for thousands of years. He even joined fishermen on sailing trips aboard their bamboo rafts.

To demonstrate his theory, Alan had tested the ocean-sailing capabilities of these rafts. Bamboo is a buoyant material that can tolerate ocean swells as well as rivers and bays. In Cebodas, an Indonesian village noted for growing bamboo, he had a raft built to his specifications. The result was a narrow assemblage about fifty feet long and six feet wide at the stern, with a mast and oars of bamboo and a sail stitched from woven mats purchased in the local market.

For its maiden voyage, Alan and three of the villagers from Cebodas took the raft to Pulau Seribu, a cluster of coral atolls in the Java Sea. The raft proved highly seaworthy and glided from island to island on favorable winds. This trip convinced Alan that such a vessel was perfectly capable of making even longer ocean journeys, especially when reduced sea levels shortened the distance between landfalls. There were long periods of time, for instance, when the sea level dropped so low that the Torres Strait, which now isolates New Guinea from Australia, disappeared altogether.

After he returned from his ocean experiment, Alan set

up a simulation on a computer, programming known ocean currents and wind patterns. Even with sails and steering exempted, the simulated rafts generally ended up on the Australian coast after a week, especially in runs using estimates of past sea levels. Alan believes the two routes of sea migrations, used again and again over time, explain the differences in morphology found in Australian fossils. "The stories we're trying to tell, at least biological-ly, are based on the flimsiest of evidence, but this is a nice, clear one," Alan insisted. "There are certainly two morphologies. Note, however, that none of these fossils has any features that I would describe as African. They're *not* out of Africa."

Africa is the only Old World continent crossed by the equator, and it possesses wide geographic diversity. Hominids have been there a much longer time than they've been anyplace else. All that adds up to greater gene exchange and an accordingly more complex range of fossils. On the edges of human distribution—places like China and Java in the Multiregional Model, where gene flow occurs in spurts—populations become more isolated and evolve independent features. That's why the propo-nents of this model argue that modern-day racial differ-ences can be traced back in a single region for up to a million years. As far as Alan was concerned, the only Out of Africa event in human evolution took place at least a million years ago. Ever since, we've been a single species, making the modern humans across several continents.

Alan's arguments sounded convincing to me. The Australian evidence could pose problems for the idea that *Homo sapiens* emerged first in Africa and only in Africa before spreading around the globe. But now it was time to hear the other side's story.

• • •

To find out more firsthand about the Out of Africa Model, I traveled to one of the key sites used to argue for an African origin to our species. Appropriately, this site lies at the southern tip of the continent, on the Humansdorp coast of South Africa, about four hundred miles east of Cape Town, a place of spectacular scenic beauty.

At the mouth of the Klasies River, perched on a steep cliff above a rocky beach, sits a series of five caves carved out by pounding surf. From inside, the cave entrance looks like a toothless human lower jaw, a bit of geologic irony considering what emerged from the more than seventy feet of sediments inside these caves. Klasies River Mouth, as this site is known, has produced what some paleoanthropologists regard as the earliest evidence of our kind—the first modern humans.

In 1967 and 1968, anatomist Ronald Singer and archeologist John Wymer conducted a fourteen-month excavation of the cave called KRM 1. Out of hundreds of tons of sediment they turned up thousands of stone tools made from quartzite cobbles that had washed up on the beach. They found lots of animal bones, including bones from thirty-eight species of large land mammals alone. And they found a few human fossils.

The tools included many leaf-shaped, pointed flakes and rough-edged scrapers, the sorts of implements that archeologists characterize as technology from the Middle Stone Age, the period from about 180,000 to 40,000 years ago. Yet the human fossils appeared to have the anatomical features of modern human beings and not those of Neandertals, who were known to be the Middle Stone Age toolmakers living in Europe and western Asia at roughly this same time.

The human fossils from Klasies are fragmentary, what paleoanthropologists privately call "scrappy." Nonetheless, the evidence we have—five partial lower jaws, an upper jaw, a dozen skull fragments, some loose teeth, and four postcranial bones—is highly provocative. Even though it is not intact and has badly worn teeth, the most complete lower jaw is nearly indistinguishable from a modern human's: It is lightly built, has small teeth and, most important of all, it has a chin. Though Neandertals occasionally show a semblance of one, a bony chin occurs only in anatomically modern humans. One of the skull fragments, a portion of forehead, shows no sign of the bony ridge over the eye sockets that characterizes the skulls of Neandertals and the earlier African "archaic" *Homo sapiens*. The upper

Proponents of the Out of Africa Model for modern human origins turn to the site of Klasies River Mouth in South Africa for support. A series of caves situated along the spectacular Cape coast, Klasies River Mouth yielded some human skull fragments and a lower jaw that may be 100,000 years old. PETER JONES

In addition to the human fossils, archeologists excavating in the caves found animal bones and shell middens—the remains of past meals—as well as thousands of stone tools made from cobbles that washed up on the nearby beach.
D. C. JOHANSON

end of a Klasies ulna is lightly built, like those of modern humans, and lacks the bumps and ridges found on the limb bones of the muscular Neandertals. The people who lived in the Klasies caves, in other words, looked very much like we do today.

The second striking fact about the fossils is their astonishing age. Four separate dating techniques applied to seashells, ostrich eggshells, stalactites, and other objects from the caves converge on a time within the Last Interglaciation, roughly from about 75,000 to 115,000 years ago, for the span of human occupation at Klasies River Mouth. This makes the Klasies River Mouth fossils possibly the oldest known modern *Homo sapiens* remains from anywhere in the world.

The environmental conditions that prevailed when humans first entered the Klasies caves were similar to the Mediterranean climate found on the Cape coast today. Sheltered by the surrounding cliffs, the location was easily defended. The caves served as campsites where humans accumulated most of the animal bones and ate well from a diverse diet. The menu included a wide selection of meats, ranging from antelope such as eland, kudu, and hartebeest to the extinct zebralike quagga, elephant, hare, hyrax, otter, fur seal, elephant seal, porcupine, and even penguin.

Massive middens at the site contain the remains of hundreds of thousands of shellfish, which may have been cracked and shared around a fire. These constitute the earliest evidence anywhere for the regular harvesting of coastal foods by humans, leading some to describe Klasies River Mouth as "the oldest seafood restaurant in the world." There is no evidence, however, that the occupants ate bony fish, which surely were also common and available. The caves contain very low numbers of fish and bird bones compared to those of mammals, though these animals were certainly present and their bones occur in great numbers at nearby archeological sites of younger ages.

The humans may have avoided hunting some of the more dangerous game in the area, such as bushpig, in favor of large grazing animals like the eland, Africa's largest antelope. They probably hunted only large and small animals that they could approach closely, perhaps with spears. The reason for that is simple: Bows and arrows didn't exist yet. Only at sites from the Later Stone Age, thousands of years younger than Klasies River Mouth, does clear evidence for fishing—including bone harpoons and hooks—and hunting with bow and arrow appear.

From inside, the mouth of the main Klasies River Mouth cave resembles a toothless human lower jaw. D. C. JOHANSON

Stanford University paleoanthropologist Richard Klein, who studied the animal bones from Klasies, noted several interesting features of the collection. The humans at Klasies harvested seals of all ages, for example, espe-

Women from a local village gather mussels from the shore near Klasies River Mouth. The former human occupants of the cave also harvested the rich resources found offshore, including shellfish and seals, and hunted antelope and other game.

D. C. JOHANSON

cially full adults. Nearby Late Stone Age sites, however, show a much higher proportion of young seal remains, probably nine months old and fresh from being weaned from mother's milk. Because seals in this area are born and weaned on offshore islands, they can get washed ashore in late summer after weaning. The rotund weaners would be especially vulnerable and easy to pick up and cart off to a cave. Apparently, the Middle Stone Age occupants of Klasies River Mouth did not know about the seasonal supply of weaned baby seals and took whatever they could get. Their successors at the other cave sites possessed a more sophisticated knowledge of seasonal changes in the food supply and planned for opportunities that provided the biggest bounty of food.

Much analysis remains to be done on the Klasies site. In the meantime most investigators believe hunting of some sort was now in the food-gathering repertoire of our immediate ancestors. The bone remains still suggest, though, that the Klasies people followed a "catch-as-catch-can" strategy for finding food. They were inefficient hunters, unable to exploit seasonal resources as fully as they could have, and had not yet developed basic techniques for harvesting the sea.

Klasies River Mouth is a cornerstone of the Out of Africa Model because it suggests an origin for *Homo sapiens* in Africa early enough to allow for expansion to the considerably later sites throughout the rest of the Old World. With Klasies under my belt, I headed to London in search of further evidence for this notion.

My destination was a picturesque gray-and-beige-stone Victorian building in South Kensington that has housed the Natural History Museum since 1881. This museum is one of the oldest and largest institutions dedicated to the study of nature and life, present and past. Behind the public galleries lie vast collections of preserved plants, animals, fossils—some 67 million specimens in all.

I arrived in an English drizzle and was directed to the paleontology department. There I met Chris Stringer, head of the museum's Human Origins Group and a leading proponent of the idea that humans emerged recently around the world and came first from Africa. Chris is a cordial host. After tea we sat in his office talking fossils against the muted background sound of classical music.

Now the Out of Africa Model states that modern *Homo sapiens* evolved in Africa, and only in Africa, within the last 200,000 years. The age of the Klasies fossils seems to lend weight to this theory. Multiregionalists such as Alan Thorne grudgingly accept their antiquity but are quick to point out that not all of the sparse remains at Klasies look like those of modern humans: Some of the bones, for example, are more robust than others, and though one of the four mandibles has a perfect chin, two others lack chins. I asked Chris for his response to this charge.

"Some bones are robust, but I think it's a transitional

group and that's acceptable," he pointed out. "Klasies is a population that's bordering on the modern. The mandible and frontal bone are in the modern range, but other bits are more archaic. They're old. You don't expect them to be just like modern people. Evolution didn't stop 100,000 years ago."

I wanted to know two things from Chris Stringer—first, why he thought the Multiregional Model of human origins was wrong, and second, why he thought Africa was the most likely single source for the first modern humans.

Chris had a lot to say on both points. "More important than arguing for Africa as the place of origin, I would argue for a *single* place of origin," he began. "If you're arguing for multiple origins, you've got to explain why, when modern humans appear, they show a number of similarities to each other more than they show resemblances to the specific primitive groups in each region."

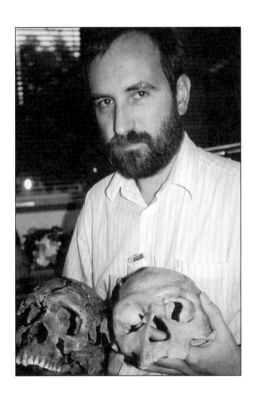

Chris Stringer heads the Human Origins Group of the Natural History Museum in London and argues that modern humans evolved first in Africa before spreading around the globe within the past 200,000 years. He holds casts of two fossils, Qafzeh 6 from Israel, left, and Jebel Irhoud 1 from Morocco, that he says support the Out of Africa Model.
BLAKE EDGAR

Such a pattern, Chris maintained, suggests that a single ancestral population possessing primitive forms of modern anatomical features dispersed widely and rapidly. The shared features among modern humans worldwide thus point not only to a common origin but a recent one to boot. "If you look at the earliest modern humans we've got from around the world, they are not like their modern regional counterparts. That, to me, says one thing, which is that modern racial variation developed recently." If human populations had evolved in place for a million years, modern people should be indistinguishable from forebears that are only 20,000 or 30,000 years old. Instead, Chris argued, most of the differences between early modern humans and present populations that we recognize as regional or "racial" characteristics evolved in the last 30,000 years.

As an example Chris turned to one of the multiregionalists' favorite regions, China. All "archaic" *Homo sapiens* have flat faces, but this feature has been used to argue for an unbroken Chinese lineage that dates back a million years. In Chris's view, however, it's equally plausible for modern Asian populations to show this primitive feature even if their immediate ancestors came from another continent. Chris took thirty-eight measurements from the Upper Cave skulls from Zhoukoudian, which, at an age of roughly 25,000 years, are the oldest Chinese modern humans that have been reliably dated. He compared these measurements to those from samples of modern-day Japanese skulls and from 30,000-year-old Cro-Magnon *Homo sapiens* skulls from France. Of the thirty-eight measurements, only ten between the Upper Cave and modern Japanese skulls showed the closest correspondence; the majority of the measurements placed the Upper Cave skulls closer to their Cro-Magnon counterparts.

Chris concluded that the Upper Cave skulls lacked the features claimed by the Multiregional Model proponents to have persisted in China for a million years. For fossils that are supposed to be part of a continuous evolutionary sequence, he told me, the Upper Cave skulls don't look Chinese.

For Chris, the most intriguing Chinese specimen is a skull from Dali, in north China, that turned up in river sediments in 1978. Dates obtained from associated animal bones suggest an age for the skull of between 180,000 and 230,000 years. The Dali skull has a lot of primitive features, including an exceptionally large browridge, thick cranial bone, and a long, low cranium somewhat similar to that of *Homo erectus*. Its brain size lies between that of *erectus* and modern humans. And it has the big, flat face that appears as a primitive feature in all early modern humans.

Based on these studies, Dali becomes a good candidate for an ancestor of modern humans, the second-best candidate after the late African fossils. Dali has the right sort of primitive face, but the overall shape of the skull is not quite modern. Chris couldn't deny the possibility that Dali might have played an independent ancestral role to later humans, and there may even be cause to consider a dual origin for humans from Africa and East Asia. But for his money, Chris picked Africa as the place with the best sequence of fossils and anatomical features that seem headed in the direction of modern humans.

"We're not dealing with certainties," he cautioned. "It may well be that such things existed in China, but we don't have them. And it may well be that they existed in Java, but we don't have them. You can make up any kind of stories about things that aren't there, but until you find them you have to work with what you've got."

That brought the discussion back to Africa. I asked Chris to explain why the African fossil record drew him to search for our immediate ancestors. He jumped from his chair and led me next door to a narrow laboratory overlooking the front lawn of the museum.

Chris pulled down a series of square, skull-sized cardboard boxes from the cabinets and set them out on the counters around me. For the first African specimen, he chose a cranium known as Jebel Irhoud 1, which was found in a cave in Morocco in the 1960s. Although the site has been difficult to date, this specimen most likely falls between 100,000 and 200,000 years in age. Chris placed the cranium next to a Neandertal from the French site of La Chapelle-aux-Saints and Qafzeh 6, the skull from one of more than a dozen modern humans from an Israeli cave.

"Which of these two, Jebel Irhoud or a Neandertal, makes a more plausible ancestor for this one, Qafzeh?" Chris asked, then answered his own question. "From my data and cranial measurements, one has to say that it's Jebel Irhoud. This is a short, broad face. It's got a relatively low nose. It's got a relatively hollow cheek region. In terms of morphology, this is a far shorter route to arrive at Qafzeh than the Neandertals offer."

I looked at the two skulls. The Qafzeh specimen clearly possessed a modern human anatomy, to my eye almost indistinguishable from bones that could be found in any college anatomy lab today. Jebel Irhoud still had robust features such as a heavy browridge, but the shape of its face and the cranium made a closer match with Qafzeh than with the Neandertal. I told Chris I could see the modern features in Jebel Irhoud, but it still looked a little primitive.

He responded that the skull would retain some primitive features, just like the Klasies River Mouth fossils do, if it belonged to a transitional population. He picked up another cast—missing the face but preserving the top, sides, and back of the cranium—that looked even more like a mosaic of modern and archaic human features. "This is Irhoud 2, found very close to Irhoud 1," Chris explained. "It was broken when it was found, and the French workers thought the back piece of the skull belonged to a modern and the front belonged to an archaic until they found the intervening pieces here."

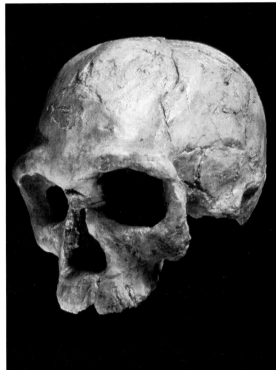

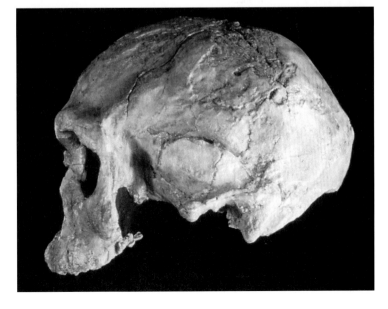

This Moroccan fossil, known as Jebel Irhoud 1, is one of several skulls used to support the view that modern humans evolved first and only in Africa. It is believed to be between 100,000 and 200,000 years old and shares several anatomical features found in the somewhat younger modern human fossils from Qafzeh in Israel.
NANCI KAHN

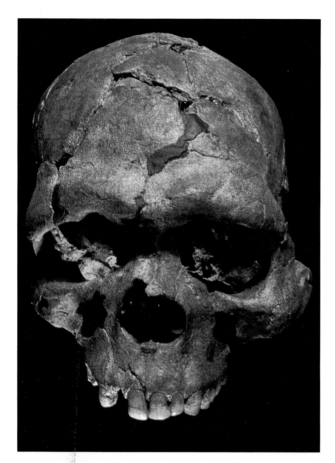

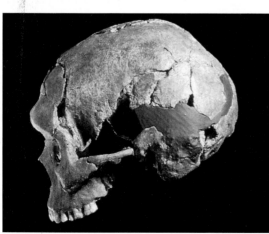

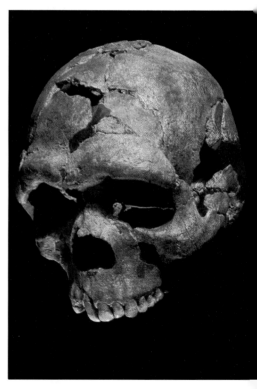

Modern human skeletons from two Israeli cave sites, Skhul and Qafzeh, have been proposed as the best link between archaic humans in Africa and modern humans found outside Africa. This specimen, Qafzeh 6, may be 90,000 years old, according to new dating techniques that may resolve the question of where modern humans first evolved.
NANCI KAHN

Africa is not just the best source, Chris argued, it's the *only* source for fossils exceeding 100,000 years in age that show this blend of primitive and incipient modern human features. As further proof he showed me the Omo 1 skull from Omo-Kibish in southern Ethiopia. It was a chocolate-brown cast with some conspicuous white gaps indicating where bone was missing and had to be reconstructed by Chris and his colleague Michael Day. Much of the back of the skull and some of the sides, the parietal bones, are intact. The mandible has a distinct chin, the cheekbones meet the face at a right angle as in modern humans, and the browridge tapers at the sides as it does in the Jebel Irhoud and Qafzeh skulls.

"Modern humans have a long and curved parietal region. Now, where do we find that?" Chris asked. "Well, it seems to be here in Omo 1, based on what we've got preserved, and we can find it to an extent on the Irhoud fossils. So I think these African ones are developing a longer, more arched parietal region, which is a significant modern feature. In particular they have this short, broad face, which is the hallmark of the earliest modern humans."

Chris believes that Omo 1 may be the oldest modern skull and skeleton because its postcranial bones are more modern in morphology than any specimens from Klasies. The uranium series dating technique, which was applied to shells from the same sediment layer where the skull was found, produced an age of 130,000 years. Chris stressed that this date should be verified by other dating techniques, but he pointed out that the sediment layer containing the skull was nearly two hundred feet beneath a layer radiocarbon-dated to almost 40,000 years ago.

Hefting the La Chapelle Neandertal, Chris showed me that Omo 1 looked far more modern, with its high forehead and long, curved sides. The Neandertal, in contrast, had a characteristically long, low forehead and cranium. Chris stressed this Neandertal was only 50,000 years old, which meant that there was much less time to evolve a modern European out of its anatomy. If Omo 1 does turn out to be one of the oldest modern human fossils, it seems fitting that East Africa's Great Rift Valley may end up holding the clues to solving the most recent mystery in our evolution as well as the earliest ones.

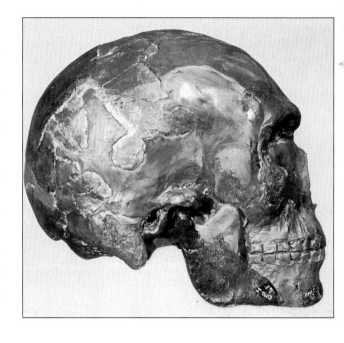

Although heavily reconstructed, the Omo 1 skull from Ethiopia clearly resembles a modern human with its flat face and expanded braincase. Its age is uncertain, but the skull may be 130,000 years old, making it the oldest known modern human fossil in Africa. M. H. DAY AND C. STRINGER

But what about "Out of Java"? Now it was Asia's turn again on the lab table. At my request, Chris laid out the Sangiran 17 skull cast—the early end of the multiregionalists' Java sequence. Next to Sangiran he placed Kow Swamp 15 from Australia—at about 10,000 years old, the young end of the sequence.

Arms folded, he stepped back. "Now, you tell me whether you think these are remarkably similar in the face," he challenged. "I just don't see it in any way whatsoever." The Kow Swamp specimen does have a flat forehead similar to that of *Homo erectus*, but otherwise the skull looks essentially modern.

To emphasize his point, Chris picked up another specimen, a complete cranium known as Kow Swamp 5. He rotated the fossil to give me a rear view of the cranium, which is high and domed like that of a typical modern human. Then he showed me Sangiran from the back, with its low, broad shape like a round loaf of bread. His last piece of evidence was a skullcap from Solo called Ngandong 5, the intermediate part of the Java sequence. I compared it with the Kow Swamp specimen. The foreheads appear similar, but the back and sides of each skull look distinct.

One significant difference between the Solo and Kow Swamp fossils shows up in the browridge, a feature that multiregionalists argue shows continuity between these scattered Australasian fossils. All the Solo specimens have a straight bar of bone beneath the forehead that reaches its greatest thickness on the sides. The Kow Swamp specimens, and other Australian material, have a browridge that reaches its greatest thickness in the middle. In the broadest terms, both possess a big browridge, and that is a primitive feature. But the details of the browridge shape suggest different origins. Although he is quick to point out that the

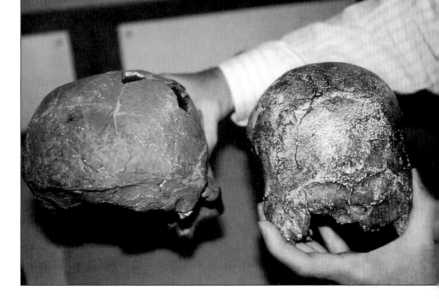

Chris Stringer displays the differences in skull shape between the Javanese fossil Sangiran 17, left, and the modern Kow Swamp 5 fossil from Australia. Rather than being part of a continuous evolutionary sequence, Stringer argues that the Javan fossil is Homo erectus *while the other is a modern human that evolved from African ancestors.*
BLAKE EDGAR

history of Australia's human occupation contains many mysteries, Chris believes that the bulk of the evidence suggests that the Australian features stem from the appearance of a radically new modern anatomy from Africa.

As for that interesting specimen from Willandra Lakes that Alan Thorne had shown me—WLH 50, the robust partial skull of unknown antiquity from near the place of the delicate-boned burials—Chris had examined this specimen himself in Australia. He agreed that it looks more primitive than any other Australian hominid fossil and is even more robust than the Kow Swamp skulls. WLH 50 has a long cranium that broadens from top to bottom, and it has a big ridge of bone on the back of the skull like the Solo fossils. On the other hand, the parietal bones that make up the sides and top of its cranium are long and curved, and they housed a modern human-sized brain. The skull is high, too, and the browridge, though big, has a modern human form.

One feature of WLH 50 that Alan attributed to its primitive Javan ancestry was its very thick cranial bone. The difference in cranial thickness between the female Mungo I and the WLH 50 specimen has been likened to that between an eggshell and an orange peel. At 19 millimeters, WLH 50 has a very thick skull—to Chris, suspiciously thick.

In *Homo erectus*, the thicker cranium was the result of thicker outer bone layers. But in WLH 50, it's the middle layer that has expanded and that creates such a thick bone. An expanded middle layer is not normal for modern humans or for *erectus*, a fact that suggests WLH 50 may be a pathological case. Thickening of that part of the cranium can be a symptom of anemia, hormonal disturbance, or old age.

Chris admitted that WLH 50 is a very primitive specimen to have in Australia more than 30,000 years ago. If modern humans had reached Australia from Africa by then, many of those primitive features should have already disappeared. No European fossils from this time look as primitive as WLH 50; the modern humans that appeared suddenly in Europe looked unlike both the Neandertals and the previous archaic humans. Chris thinks that a limited amount of gene flow might explain the odd morphological mix in WLH 50: a modern African population might have picked up genes from a more archaic-looking group while passing through Java.

"But doesn't the Out of Africa Model hold that the African emigrants totally replaced all human populations in other parts of the world?" I asked.

"I wouldn't deny that there could be *some* gene flow, some interbreeding, in these regions, and that's something that I think has been misunderstood." Chris now presented me with a compromise scenario between the competing models of modern human origins. Modern humans may indeed be a mix of different features that arose separately in Africa and Asia. Even though Africa was our point of embarkation, Asia was the hub from which humans spread to all other reaches of the globe. For much of the past million years, though, times were tough, and climates were too harsh to permit people to do as much coming and going as the Multiregional Model requires.

In this sense, the Out of Africa Model has more room for compromise than the Multiregional Model, which needs to hold true in every region. Although Chris was willing to accept a certain amount of gene flow between modern and archaic humans, the Out of Africa Model still requires a large degree of rapid and widespread replace-

ment of previous populations by the African *Homo sapiens.*
The process is often portrayed as violent invasion, but it's
possible to imagine other replacement scenarios. *Homo
sapiens* were probably more efficient at extracting energy
from nature, at exploiting resources; they were more
numerous, may have weaned their young sooner, and
probably lived longer than Neandertals or other archaic
peoples. These simple abilities may have been all the
edge they needed.

Still, the idea of replacement is a bitter pill for some
paleoanthropologists to swallow. It moves Alan Thorne
to a kind of black irony: "In the last five hundred years,
using poison, fire, bayonets, machine guns, Europeans
haven't managed to wipe out whole populations they've
set out to exterminate. So how does a bunch of hunter-
gatherers go around the world wiping out another bunch
of successful hunter-gatherers that has been around for a
million years?"

The debate over modern human origins has focused
lately on the question of replacement because of implications in the genetic evidence of the Eve hypothesis, a
stunning theory that sprouted, blossomed, and withered
like a summer wildflower within the last several years.
You may remember the provocative *Newsweek* cover of
January 11, 1988, a domestic portrait of Adam and Eve as
topless Africans. The occasion for this media blitz was
the announcement a few months before in the journal
Nature that a Berkeley laboratory a few blocks from the
Institute of Human Origins had traced a human ancestor
from genetic molecules and a computer program.

Berkeley biochemist Allan Wilson and his students
said that, using a computer analysis of mitochondrial
DNA (mtDNA), they had traced all modern human lin-

The late biochemist Allan Wilson helped pioneer the study of human origins using genetic molecules. In 1987, his laboratory announced that they had traced all modern humans back to a founding population in Africa around 200,000 years ago, an idea that quickly became known as the Eve hypothesis. IAN EVERARD

eages back 10,000 generations to a female founder (or founding population of women) living in Africa 200,000 years ago. A study that threatened to make decades of fossil hunting instantly irrelevant was electrifying, and not completely welcome, news for the field of paleoanthropology. The media embraced the idea of an African Eve with far greater alacrity. Was there really a Garden of Eden, a single place of human origin, after all?

Adept at building connections among disparate ideas, Wilson had already established himself as an innovative thinker who had confronted paleoanthropologists before and challenged their assumptions. In the late 1960s, he and his Berkeley colleague Vincent Sarich championed the science of molecular evolution by using various blood proteins to identify a molecular clock that could reveal when different animal lineages split off from each other. That research led to the then explosive idea that African apes and humans shared a common ancestor as recently as 5 or 6 million years ago. At the time, most paleoanthropologists would have placed the ape-human split at 15 million years ago or earlier.

No stranger to controversy, Wilson invited much more of it when he and a team of students, including Rebecca Cann, Mark Stoneking, and Linda Vigilant, explored the use of mtDNA as a molecular clock for the most recent split in human evolution, that of *Homo sapiens* from its ancestor. Mitochondrial DNA, which evolves ten times faster than nuclear DNA and is inherited only through the mother, belongs to the energy-producing structures inside cells. Its faster evolutionary pace allows mtDNA to be used to examine recent events in our own evolution. The premise behind the Eve hypothesis was that by examining the mtDNA of modern humans from different ethnic backgrounds, the scientists could determine how closely related each group was to each other and which group represented the oldest population.

The initial study sampled mtDNA from the placentas of 147 women, including African Americans, Asians, Caucasians, New Guineans, and Australian Aborigines. The mtDNA from Africans was far more diverse than what was found in any other group, and the shortest tree that Wilson's team found had one deep fork dividing only Africans on one branch from a mix of Africans and non-Africans on the other branch. An African origin for all human mtDNA seemed the most plausible explanation.

Not surprisingly, the Eve hypothesis had a mixed reception among paleoanthropologists. The multiregionalists insisted that the genetic evidence could be overruled by the fossils and that the supposed molecular clock must have had a broken spring. They would have been happy with a *Homo erectus* Eve in Africa a million years ago, but they could not stomach a *Homo sapiens* Eve in Africa only 200,000 years ago, especially if it meant rejecting any evolutionary role for *Homo erectus* in Asia or for the Neandertals in Europe. The Out of Africa adherents, however, embraced the Eve hypothesis like a long-lost relative and argued that genetic evidence now supported what they had surmised from the fossils.

In July 1991, Allan Wilson died of leukemia, at age fifty-six. Eve's father and most ardent advocate was no longer able to defend his provocative progeny, but a new paper that appeared in the journal *Science* two months after his death claimed to provide further proof, based on analysis of new data and wider population sampling. Just a few months after that article appeared, however, the Eve hypothesis was already unraveling. Mitochondrial Eve, like her metaphorical namesake, was about to be expelled from the genetic garden. This time the critics were not paleoanthropologists brandishing fossils but other geneticists, who had tried to construct their own trees for human origins. Geneticist Alan Templeton of Washington University in St. Louis led the attack. The trouble was not poor or inaccurate data, he argued, but misuse of the statistical computer program used to draw the tree that caused a misleading reading of the results.

Alan Templeton's first attempt at analyzing the mtDNA data with the computer program used by Wilson and his colleagues produced one hundred trees in a single run that were each two steps shorter than the revised Eve tree published in 1991. All of Templeton's trees had non-African roots.

Besides the geographic jumble in the trees, Templeton's analysis concluded that mtDNA could not be relied on as a very accurate clock. The ambiguity surrounding the actual date when modern humans emerged amounts to a full order of magnitude. Ironically, it could have happened anywhere from 100,000 to a million years ago. In other words, the date could fall into what the Out of Africa Model predicts, into what the Multiregional Model predicts, or anywhere in between. That ambiguity arises from the random variable that is evolution itself. Even if every human mtDNA had been sequenced, the rate of mtDNA evolution were known with certainty, and the molecular clock never wound down, that ambiguity would remain.

Finally, Templeton asserted, rather than arguing for an African origin, the mtDNA data tended to do just the opposite. The genetic pattern supports the idea that gene flow occurred among modern humans throughout the Old World and was an important force in our species' evolution. Populations expanded but not rapidly, and the mtDNA revealed no signs that one population completely replaced others. Instead, Templeton argued, low-level interbreeding was enough to spread modern human features around the world. That sounds like a shot in the arm for the multiregionalists, but at the end of his critique, Templeton wrote that "there is no need to postulate multiple independent origins of anatomically modern humans. All humans represent a single long-term evolutionary lineage and always have throughout the entire time period marked by mtDNA."

The evidence against the Eve hypothesis became so strong that even Mark Stoneking, one of the authors of both the initial 1987 Eve paper and the 1991 follow-up meant to quiet Eve's critics, consented to have his name included on a *Science* article in February 1992 that basically said the mtDNA data are too confusing to interpret. That Eve existed is not in dispute, but exactly where and when she lived remains unclear. Maybe humans are just too polytypic, as Alan Thorne told me, a fact that shows up in the wide variety of mtDNA, creating a sea of genetic noise we have yet to navigate without running aground.

Some genetic data still seem to support an African origin for modern humans. Nuclear DNA, for example, still shows greater variety—perhaps twice as much—among humans in Africa than anywhere else, and the likely reason is that human DNA has been evolving longer in

Africa and has had more time to diversify. Likewise, mtDNA shows greatest diversity among humans in Africa. Several geneticists who study mtDNA believe that Eve may yet have the last word on the subject. For now, however, the Eve bandwagon is a stalled vehicle. Those who jumped on it are back with their fossils again. The multiregionalists and Out of Africa-ists are arguing as heatedly as ever. Techniques improve, new evidence emerges. We're still looking for—and not quite finding—Eden.

CHAPTER SEVEN

Neandertal Enigma:

Homo neanderthalensis

The French village of Les Eyzies, located on the Vézère River in Perigord, has been called "the capital of prehistory" because dozens of archeological and prehistoric art sites dot the surrounding countryside. Nearby limestone caves such as Lascaux and Font-de-Gaume contain stunning examples of ancient paintings. BLAKE EDGAR

It WAS A COOL OCTOBER EVENING IN 1992, and I had just eaten one of the most memorable meals in my life. In the refined atmosphere of the Restaurant du Centenaire, a Michelin two-star bastion of gastronomy gracing the sleepy village of Les Eyzies in the heart of France's Dordogne region, the sumptuous five-course dinner had featured a notable entree: filet of young deer with tomato-fig tart.

It seemed highly appropriate to be eating deer meat in the Dordogne. Humans have been doing that here for many, many thousands of years. Les Eyzies itself, rightly dubbed the "capital of prehistory," lies within a twenty-mile circle of several dozen caves and rock shelters that have yielded some of the first important physical and cultural remains of early Europeans. Not far from the restaurant is the Abri Cro-Magnon, a tiny rock shelter cut out of the limestone citadel that looms over Les Eyzies, where, in 1868, a railway worker uncovered bones while digging. Subsequent excavation revealed the remains of five 30,000-year-old human skeletons—three males, a female, and an infant—alongside the bones of reindeer and mammoths. Ever since, the name Cro-Magnon has been synonymous with modern humans, people just like ourselves, who scraped the skins from the reindeer they hunted and shaped their antlers into bone tools, weapons, and personal ornaments.

I found my thoughts being pulled even more strongly toward an older but equally famous Dordogne resident as

I strolled through Les Eyzies after dinner. Above the shop roofs loomed a medieval stone fortress built into the limestone cliff that since 1918 has been home to the National Prehistory Museum, a treasure-house of art and artifacts culled from the region's rich archeological sites. Next to the museum, spotlights illuminated a large limestone statue, a humanlike figure bent slightly at the waist, huge, muscular arms dangling at his sides as he gazes thoughtfully across the Vézère River: *Homo neanderthalensis.*

Neandertal! This enigmatic group, the source of all our popular "caveman" stereotypes of prehistoric humans, has seized the modern imagination like no other early ancestor. There are, of course, good historical and cultural reasons behind the lengthy love/hate relationship both scientists and the general public have conducted with the Neandertals. Theirs were the first human fossils found in modern times, though their significance went unnoticed for decades. Theirs were the first fossils found in Europe,

A statue of Neandertal man stares out across the Vézère River and the rooftops of Les Eyzies. Several nearby sites yielded the bones and tools of this unique hominid, and Les Eyzies is also home to the site of Cro-Magnon, a name synonymous with the first modern humans in Europe.
BLAKE EDGAR

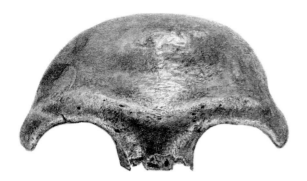

In 1856, the Feldhofer Quarry in Germany's Neander Valley yielded this fossil skullcap and several limb bones. Though these weren't the first Neandertal fossils ever found, this site lent its name to the burly hominid who lived in Ice Age Europe. IAN EVERARD

where most of the early anthropologists worked and where these investigators located—mistakenly, as it turned out—the birthplace of humankind. In the end, ironically, the much-maligned Neandertals would prove to be Europe's *only* original contribution to the human evolutionary record, and a side branch at that.

Alongside the growing pool of hard information we continue to gather about them, however, runs the much richer tradition of the invented Neandertals, born simultaneously with the first recorded discovery of this species in the mid-nineteenth century. Let's briefly trace this fictional character's notorious career before we take a close look at facts and speculations that are based on the real fossil record and recent discoveries.

Modern Neandertal folklore begins in August 1856, when parts of a skeleton—a thick skullcap with a sloping forehead, and several limb bones—were uncovered in a cave being quarried for limestone in the Neander Valley near Düsseldorf, Germany. No one knew quite what to make of these bones, and no one had seen anything like them before—or so they thought. In fact, several Neandertal fossils had already been discovered in various parts of Europe, but hindsight was needed to recognize them for what they were. By the time the Neander Valley find occurred, evolutionary theory was in the air and scientists had already begun to clamor for evidence of human evolution. The fossils caused an immediate stir.

The first guess—that the bones belonged to a stray Cossack from the Napoleonic wars who had crawled into the cave to die—gave way to multiple attempts at scientific description. From a study of the Neander Valley skullcap, the English anthropologist William King was the only initial investigator to recognize the significance of this group's distinctive anatomy. Without even seeing their facial bones—the Neandertals' most striking feature—he decided that they fell outside the range of modern humans and presciently coined the name *Homo neanderthalensis* in 1864 to reflect their species' status. King's ideas would be ignored for more than a century, however, and he himself later changed his position.

As similar bones and skulls were identified from various parts of Europe (culminating in the discovery of two skeletons from a cave in Spy, Belgium, in 1888), it was finally established that they belonged to a single type and were not simply isolated genetic freaks. Belgian anatomist Julien Fraipont declared the handful of fossils to represent a "bestial form of humanity," short and stocky, with powerfully built bones. It fell to the French anthropologist Marcellin Boule, however, to create the image of the Neandertal that endures to this day in popular imagination. From an arthritic skeleton found at La Chapelle-aux-Saints in 1908, Boule judged the Neandertals to be primitive, apelike brutes whose "energetic and clumsy body" he contrasted sharply with the exemplary *Homo sapiens* from Cro-Magnon, "who had a more elegant body, a finer head, an upright and spacious brow, and who have

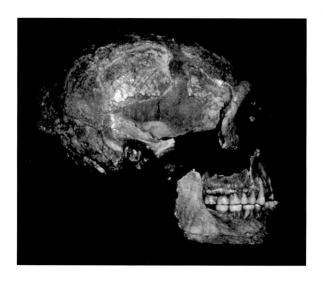

Two Neandertal skeletons, including this skull, were found at the site of Spy in Belgium in 1886. The Spy finds came thirty years after the fossil discovery in Germany's Neander Valley and convinced scientists that the Neandertals were a real example of a fossil human. INSTITUTE OF HUMAN ORIGINS

left, in the caves which they inhabited, so much evidence of their manual skill, artistic and religious preoccupations, of their abstract faculties, and who were the first to merit the glorious title of *Homo sapiens*!"

Single-handedly, Boule had established a near-indelible image of Neandertals as slouching, hunchbacked hulks that lasted for decades and deeply penetrated popular culture. His was also the first of many such obligatory comparisons linking Neandertals—always to their disadvantage—with the later "invincible" Cro-Magnons. In this vaudeville team Neandertals were invariably cast as foil or, at best, second banana to the real star, our very own species.

Around the imaginary Neandertal "brute" a rich literary history began to collect. In his story "The Grisly Folk," written in 1921, H. G. Wells described this character as "hairy or grisly, with a big face like a mask, great brow ridges and no forehead, clutching an enormous flint and running like a baboon with his head forward, and not like a man with his head up. He must have been a fearsome creature for our forefathers to come across." Implicit in Wells's depiction—and mirroring Western colonial attitudes of racial superiority as well—is the conviction that the Neandertals were not human; they were not Us but the Other.

Wells's view of Neandertals as doomed hominids hunted to extinction by encroaching modern humans was shared by a later British writer, William Golding, in his 1955 novel *The Inheritors*. Writing in the same postwar atmosphere that so influenced Raymond Dart, however, Golding reversed the terms by presenting his Neandertals as gentle, telepathic herbivores ruthlessly crushed under the heel of invading blond, bestial Cro-Magnons, a clear

reference to Nazi Germany and its racial euthanasia practices. Jean Auel, in her 1980 novel *The Clan of the Cave Bear*,
also sympathetically endows her Neandertals with telepathic powers far greater than those Golding allowed
them, but her Cro-Magnon heroine, Ayla, is "tall, blonde,
slender, and smarter" than her Neandertal peers.

As cultural perceptions shifted, scientific attitudes
toward Neandertals also began to change. The Us/Other
distinction broke down, and many experts were ready to
grant Wells's "grey-haired, wolf-like monsters" full citizen-
ship within *Homo sapiens*. Gradually the notion that Neandertals were our direct ancestors gained hold among
scientists. At a symposium in 1956 celebrating the centen-
nial of the Neander Valley fossil discovery, anthropologists
William Straus and A.J.E. Cave presented a paper in which
they attacked Boule's interpretation of the La Chapelle
skeleton that had grown to a widespread stereotype.

Although Straus and Cave noted anatomical differences in Neandertals absent from any living human population, their analysis of the La Chapelle bones showed that
Boule had ignored the obvious signs of disease and that, in
fact, Neandertals did have an upright posture. Unable to
resist some hyperbolizing of their own, Straus and Cave
said of a hypothetical Neandertal that "if he could be rein-
carnated and placed in a New York subway—provided
that he were bathed, shaved, and dressed in modern clothing—it is doubtful whether he would attract any more
attention than some of its other denizens."

As this revisionist view of Neandertals gained increasing numbers of adherents, other experts continued to stress
the unique set of features in the Neandertal skeleton, especially the face. In an issue of the magazine *Science '81*,
anatomist and illustrator Jay Matternes attempted to flesh

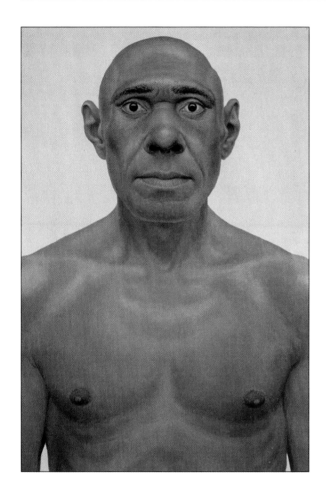

Anatomist and illustrator Jay Matternes attempted to flesh out the face of a Neandertal using fossil skulls found at the Shanidar cave in Iraq. Despite the bulbous nose and prominent browridge beneath the forehead, Matternes's Neandertal, which appeared on the cover of Science '81 *magazine, looks remarkably like a modern human.* JAY MATTERNES

out the face of a male Neandertal from fossil casts, particularly specimens from the Shanidar cave in Iraq. Matternes rendered his Neandertal male as bald, with a bulbous nose, brown eyes, and bushy eyebrows growing from his prominent browridge. Yet the impression left by this portrait is of a being that could easily pass as a modern human. One astute reader even pointed out that Matternes's reconstruction bore a startling resemblance to Pablo Picasso.

A deep split in informed thinking, in fact, still exists about who *Homo neanderthalensis* really was: one of Us—i.e., a direct ancestor—or an Other, an evolutionary dead end on the same order as the Nutcracker People. Although Boule exceeded the boundaries of scientific reserve, his hunch that Neandertals and early modern humans such as the Cro-Magnons were two distinct groups is being considered anew by many paleoanthropologists. Where he erred was in seeing Neandertals as primitive and apelike. They were nothing of the sort—in evolutionary terms, their distinctive features are more evolved and specialized than many "primitive" features of *erectus* retained in *Homo sapiens*.

Putting aside our cultural and species biases—if such a feat is ever really possible—what do we really know, or have good grounds for assuming, about this mysterious group? Large amounts of new information accumulated in the last decade have raised many new questions, but here are the basic facts we know about them.

The immediate ancestors of the Neandertals probably entered Eurasia from Africa sometime before 300,000 years ago; Neandertals and modern humans may have embarked on separate evolutionary tracks at least 200,000 years ago. The fossil record from this time remains fuzzy, and so far there are few clues to pinpoint the immediate ancestors of Neandertals. One likely source is in the Charente region of France, at sites such as Fontechevade and La Chaise, believed to be around 200,000 years old. Excavations at La Chaise in the 1960s and 1970s by André Debenath turned up eighty human fossils. The skull fragments look like those of *Homo sapiens*, but the teeth are Neandertal, as though this population had just begun to acquire the specialized cold-adapted features that set them increasingly apart from our own ancestors. The site of Atapuerca, in northern Spain, discovered by cavers at the bottom of a fifty-foot rock chimney, has yielded some seven hundred bones from at least thirty individuals. Three partial skulls were found at the site as recently as 1992. All these bones, which appear to be 300,000 years old, reveal an anatomy that looks to be intermediate between that of *Homo erectus* and Neandertals. The Atapuerca fossils may be giving a glimpse of the Neandertals' immediate predecessor.

Neandertals as we know them first appear around 130,000 years ago and disappear from the fossil record around 35,000 years ago. They probably evolved in Europe, and that remained the center of their range, thanks to barriers of geography and climate. Neandertals lived in the shadow of glaciers, bounded by the Atlantic Ocean to the west, by the Mediterranean to the south, and by ice sheets to the north. They traveled as far south as Gibraltar and moved down through the Anatolian plateau to Israel and the Near East. As far as we know, they never got to Africa.

"More than anything," Chris Stringer once told me, "what made the Neandertals was ice." The so-called "classic" Neandertal anatomy is particularly suited to the extreme cold of the Ice Age European continent on which they lived in caves, rock shelters, and open-air camps. Their most striking facial feature, a bulbous, protruding nose, may have served the dual purpose of warming and humidifying inhaled cold air on one hand and radiating excess body heat to prevent overheating from exertion on the other.

And—to judge from the massive skeletons, stout limb bones, and prominent muscle marks—the Neandertals really exerted themselves. The upper-body musculature of this group can only be called awesome. Their arm and leg bone shafts were thicker than those in modern humans and thus able to withstand extreme stress; their shinbones could take three times the stress that a modern human shin can take without breaking. Their knee and ankle joints were also larger, which may mean they put more pressure on these bones in daily life than on more injury-prone cartilage.

The Neandertals, then, lived extremely physically active—and physically stressful—lives. They lived hard and died at younger ages than Cro-Magnons did. Judging by comparative studies of baby-teeth wear marks, they probably weaned their young at a later age, which has implications for long-term population growth. It's been speculated that a shorter nursing period allowed *Homo sapiens* to increase our populations more quickly by decreasing the spacing between births.

Next to these hardy specimens, though, we modern humans are frail, vulnerable, puny creatures—hardly invincible conquerors, and a far more likely candidate, at first glance, for the role of evolutionary loser. The Neandertal brain, on average, even exceeded ours in size, though that is probably because everything about them was big. Unfortunately, we don't know what they used their big brains for, since their tool industry, known as the Mousterian, remained unchanged for the duration of their species' lifespan.

Their beautifully crafted flint tools, however, did manage to keep them alive under conditions that no other type of human seems to have managed to endure. And Neandertals showed a considerable advance over the *Homo erectus* "Swiss army knife" hand ax; they had different tools for different functions, such as meat cutting, hide scraping, and woodworking. Stone points were probably hafted to wooden poles and used as spears, and the Neandertals may have been skilled workers of animal skins to create leather clothing. Some experimental studies lead us to believe they ate a lot of meat—their diet may have been, according to one investigator, somewhere between a wolf's and a fox's—which would certainly have been a cold-climate adaptation, too. From the hearths found in some Neandertal caves, we can be confident that they had mastered fire making, a skill that would have been vital for their survival.

Some archeologists, including Lew Binford, have argued that Neandertals lacked crucial behaviors found in modern humans. Based on his study of Neandertal sites in the Dordogne region of France, Lew believes that Neandertal mating pairs spent little time together and had no semblance of a nuclear family. Males and females ate different foods, used different tools, and performed different tasks. Lew said that Neandertals, unlike modern humans, never modified their environment to suit their needs; in caves, for example, they simply tucked their bodies in among the natural contours to sleep.

Most important, according to Lew, Neandertals may have lacked what he called "planning depth," the ability to anticipate future events and future availability of food. They could not predict patterns in a dynamic and changing landscape. "There's more salmon in bear dens in the Dordogne than at any archeological sites," Lew said. "The Neandertals just weren't bringing salmon back to the caves in any numbers. It's hard to imagine fully modern man in a salmon-rich environment behaving that way."

Other archeologists disagree strongly with his interpretations, and it's fair to say that we can deduce some real evidence of social behavior from the fossil record. Signs of long-term trauma and injury found in some Neandertal skeletons indicate that individuals were cared for by others during periods of helplessness. The most striking evidence for care, however, is the presence of burials inside Neandertal caves. Although interpretations of burial rites have sometimes been exaggerated, Neandertal skeletons at several sites have been discovered in flexed posture within carefully dug pits.

Where a skeptical archeologist like Lew balks at this interpretation of what he calls "practical disposals" of stinking dead bodies, my friend Yoel Rak disagrees. "I doubt they were buried just because they smelled. They could just be dumped outside the cave. Instead there was

care and premeditation. They dug a hole and put in the body. There was some spiritual connection, because the bodies stay in the cave with the occupants."

Whether or not Neandertals possessed language, finally, remains a matter of debate. Though they may not have been fully equipped for modern language, it seems unlikely to me that Neandertals sat silently around the campfire in their caves. We'll examine some compelling new fossil evidence for the presence of language from Israel, and that brings me to the latest chapter in the Neandertal saga. Although Europe may have been the center of their range, a crucial new archeological sequel to the story of the "real" Neandertal is being written in the Middle East, especially in Israel. The emerging evi-

Paleoanthropologist Yoel Rak believes that the anatomical differences between modern humans and Neandertals preclude them from belonging to the same species. He is shown here with fossils from two caves in Israel, an early modern human from Qafzeh, left, and a Neandertal from Amud.
D. C. JOHANSON

dence from seven cave sites, all but one in Israel, has taken us much further down the road to understanding them as a species.

The new installment begins with a tale of two caves on a mountain already famous for other reasons. Not far south of the Israeli port of Haifa is the mountain known as Mount Carmel, on which are situated, a mere three hundred feet apart, the "cave of young goats," Skhul, and the "cave of ovens," Tabun, which British archeologist Dorothy Garrod began excavating in 1929. At Tabun she

Map of the Middle East with prehistoric sites. CAROLYN FISH

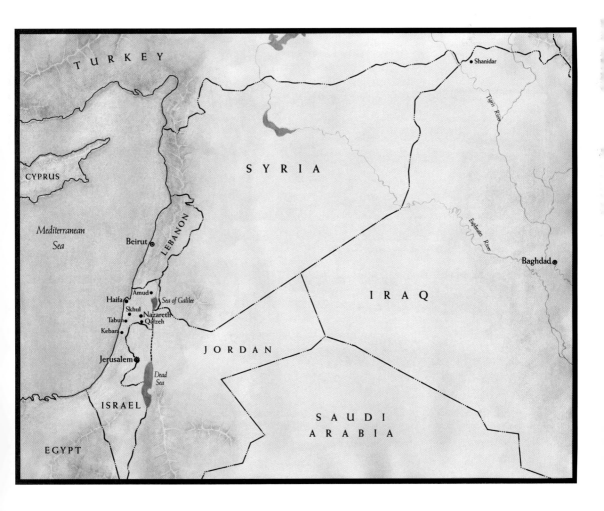

found numerous stone tools that resembled Middle Paleolithic (Middle Stone Age to us Africanists) flint flakes from the Mousterian industry in Europe that is associated with Neandertal fossils. In 1931 Garrod uncovered the first Neandertal from the Near East in a burial containing a skull and partial skeleton, as well as bones from at least one more individual.

That same year a young American anthropologist named Theodore McCown continued the work at Skhul. After two seasons McCown had found eight human burials, both adults and children. All the skeletons had their limbs folded in such a way that there could be no question these people had been given a deliberate burial. As more finds continued to be made at Skhul, McCown collaborated with the prominent English anatomist Sir Arthur Keith, then nearly retired, to study the skeletons from Skhul and Tabun, which had just been dated—mistakenly, as it turned out—at 40,000 and 80,000 years, respectively.

The two men noted the Neandertal-ness of the partial female skeleton and male mandible from Tabun, but when they came to the Skhul remains they were puzzled. These skeletons looked different—namely, far more modern. The faces were robust, but they lacked the projecting midface typical of Neandertals. Although they recognized distinct differences between the bones from Skhul and Tabun, the close proximity of the caves convinced McCown and Keith that the fossils came from a single, variable population, which they described as "in the throes of evolutionary change." The two caves, they believed, captured a snapshot of the earlier Neandertals from Tabun as they were evolving into the later modern humans from Skhul. This view became widely accepted and later includ-

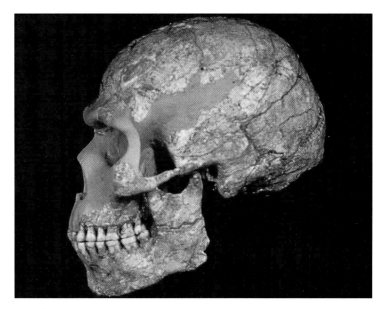

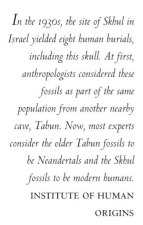

In the 1930s, the site of Skhul in Israel yielded eight human burials, including this skull. At first, anthropologists considered these fossils as part of the same population from another nearby cave, Tabun. Now, most experts consider the older Tabun fossils to be Neandertals and the Skhul fossils to be modern humans.
INSTITUTE OF HUMAN ORIGINS

ed the idea that the Skhul and Tabun fossils demonstrated crossbreeding between Neandertals and modern humans. At the time, based on erroneous dating of the caves, such a sequence seemed reasonable because they believed the Tabun fossils to be twice as old as those from Skhul.

Now comes another tale of two caves in Israel—in this case, some distance apart. One site, Kebara, overlooks the Mediterranean coast about eighteen miles south of Haifa and seven miles south of Skhul and Tabun. The other site, Qafzeh, lies just south of the Biblical town of Nazareth, about eighteen miles east of Mount Carmel. While McCown was digging up his bounty of fossils at Skhul, a French archeologist named René Neuville began excavations at Qafzeh. Neuville's excavation trenches exposed the skeletons of seven anatomically modern humans similar to those from Skhul, including a pieced-together skull that he nearly lost to his pet boxer when he left it on a rock to dry.

Work at Qafzeh continued in the 1960s under the direction of Bernard Vandermeersch of the University of Bordeaux. During thirteen years of excavation he found the remains of at least eight more people, along with stone tools and many other animal bones. Because of their modern appearance these human remains were dubbed Proto–Cro-Magnons. If Cave and Straus's Neandertal would not look out of place in the sub-

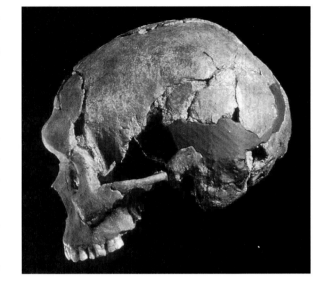

way, then these specimens would not look out of place in a college human anatomy class. Their mandibles have a distinct chin, their faces are short and broad, and the back of their cranium lacks the distinctive occipital bun found in Neandertals.

Because the Qafzeh finds resembled those from Skhul, they fell easily into the accepted sequence that the Neandertal population at Tabun had simply evolved into the more modern-looking population at Skhul and Qafzeh. But then studies of the fossil species of microvertebrates, especially rodents, suggested that the age of the Qafzeh site had been greatly underestimated. This new dating evidence argued that Qafzeh and its "modern" population might be as old as 80,000 to 100,000 years— possibly the oldest Middle Paleolithic site in the Levant.

The new dates for Qafzeh, proposed in 1980 by Van-dermeersch and archeologist Ofer Bar-Yosef at a scientific meeting in Lyon, met with universal disapproval. The ideal choice for a new excavation that might resolve the

Another cave in Israel, Qafzeh, contained the remains of many modern human burials. Recent dating of these fossils to around 90,000 years old upset traditional ideas that Neandertals evolved into modern humans in the Levant and established that the two groups co-existed in the region for tens of thousands of years.
NANCI KAHN

quandary posed by Skhul, Tabun, and Qafzeh was the site of Kebara. Archeologists had worked this site over a number of decades and it still held many untouched ancient deposits. Work began again in 1982, just as renewed interest in the origin of modern humans and the evolutionary place of Neandertals had begun to build. In a model of collaborative endeavor that lasted over a decade of field and lab work, the Kebara team turned up a fascinating record of Neandertal life.

In the summer of 1983, the team made a spectacular discovery: a robust, nearly intact male Neandertal skeleton that lay in a narrow burial pit. Covered by twenty-five feet of sediment in a layer that definitely dated to the Middle Paleolithic, the skeleton—now known as Kebara 2 and nicknamed Moshe—had a complete set of arm bones and vertebrae, ribs, the pelvis, even a tiny bone in the throat, called the hyoid, that had never before been preserved in a fossil hominid. Unfortunately, Moshe lacks most of his lower limb bones and, apart from the lower

Archeologist Ofer Bar-Yosef was one of the first to suggest that the Qafzeh site had an ancient age. After excavating at Qafzeh, Bar-Yosef helped lead excavations at another Israeli cave, Kebara.

D. C. JOHANSON

jaw and one upper tooth, his skull is also missing. It's possible that the skull was removed as part of the burial process, but that remains a mystery. The bones showed no sign of trauma or injury, and none had been chewed by carnivores, a clue that the body had lain undisturbed since its burial.

The hyoid bone that was found behind Moshe's mandible had special significance for the debate over whether Neandertals had language. The U-shaped hyoid is the only bone in the human skeleton that does not attach to another bone but rather to the cartilage that makes up the larynx in the throat; the "Adam's apple" in our throats is actually this bone-cartilage package of hyoid and larynx. Because it anchors muscles that connect to both the larynx and the tongue, the hyoid is also an important component of the anatomical equipment that permits speech.

Some scientists had argued that the flat base of Neandertal skulls meant that their larynx sat higher in the throat than it does in modern humans, thereby ruling out the capacity for speech in Neandertals. They also speculated that a Neandertal larynx and hyoid would have probably resembled a chimpanzee's. One of the Kebara team members was Yoel Rak, the paleoanthropologist who finally found a skull at Hadar in 1992. On one of Yoel's yearly trips to work at the Institute of Human Origins, we talked about the Neandertal language debate. "The notion that Neandertals couldn't speak was an absurd

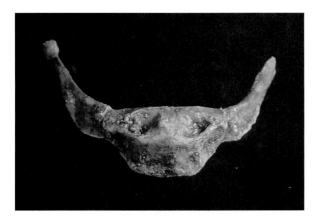

notion to start with," Yoel asserted. "Intuitively, I couldn't accept it, even before the hyoid bone was found. The fact that we found a Neandertal hyoid that looks exactly like a modern hyoid may constitute the proof that the larynx of the Neandertal was also like a human's."

Besides his hyoid, Moshe gave us the first complete Neandertal pelvis ever recovered. Because the pelvis contains a lot of spongy bone, only its densest parts tend to fossilize; it can also be easily damaged in hasty excavations. Moshe's pelvis showed distinct differences from the modern human pelvis, fueling the latest argument that Neandertals do represent a different species. Yoel said that Moshe's hip sockets face sideways more than they do in modern humans, suggesting that Neandertals had a different posture and gait. Whereas the *Homo sapiens* face remained somewhat primitive compared to the specialized features of Neandertals, Yoel thinks the opposite occurred with the pelvis: Neandertals retained a primitive pelvis shape as modern humans evolved a specialized, shock-absorbing pelvis. Either of these cases illustrates the principle of mosaic evolution, in which some parts of the body retain a primitive state and others evolve, like Lucy's apelike skull on top of her humanlike lower body.

As the Kebara excavation continued, important information about Neandertal activities began to emerge. Each find added detail to a picture of Neandertal life that had previously been painted with fairly broad brush strokes. The cave, it turned out, had been a kind of giant trash bin, accumulating thousands of years' worth of dirt and refuse as humans, hyenas, and other animals came and went. Along its north wall an especially huge pile of animal bones, mainly from large mammals, had built up over time. Blocks and cobbles of flint quarried from sources a few miles from the cave also showed up in the bone pile, along with discarded flint flakes. This suggests that the work of making tools took place inside the cave. Could this separate pile of bones and stones have been a Neandertal garbage dump?

Answering that question required careful examination of the bones. As Bob Brain had done with the bones from the Swartkrans cave in South Africa, the Kebara team scanned their bones for clues as to whether Neandertals or carnivores brought them into and broke them inside the cave. Some of the bones, particularly lower limb bones from gazelles, had gnaw marks, punctures, and etching from stomach acids, suggesting that carnivores had played a role in accumulating the bones. But the presence of so much stone-tool debris, the more numerous burned and cut-marked bones, and the fact that many of the bone concentrations occur in the same layers as the hearths all support the conclusion that the bone buildup took place while hominids lived in the cave. Apparently, the Neandertal residents intentionally swept, tossed, or dumped their trash along the north wall of the cave. Later, carnivores came in and gnawed on the bones.

The cave appeared to be more heavily occupied during

Excavations at Kebara lasted for ten years and uncovered a wealth of new information about Neandertal life. Fire pits were found where Neandertals apparently roasted meat and wild peas, and at the back of the cave was a garbage heap of animal bones and discarded tools made of flint brought from miles away. OFER BAR-YOSEF AND BERNARD VANDERMEERSCH

its Neandertal period (63,000 to 45,000 years ago) than during its later period of occupancy (42,000 to 28,000 years ago). Traces of carnivore activity increase during this later period, so the Neandertals may have been able to keep predators at bay, perhaps with fire. Kebara contains numerous hearths, proof that the Neandertals used fire and a strong indicator that they knew how to start fires on their own. Plant remains in the burned layers revealed that both grass and woody plants had fueled the fires; charcoal came from a type of oak that grew near the cave. Some of the hearths had a thick layer of ash that may have been spread out to make a warm sleeping surface. Except for the absence of stones used to retain heat, these rounded, bowl-shaped hearths were very much like those found in the younger layers and at other Upper Paleolithic sites associated with *Homo sapiens* remains—a tantalizing indication of shared cultural features between Neandertals and modern humans.

More than 25,000 Mousterian stone tools at least an

The sediments in Kebara preserve several hearths, such as these circular pits viewed from above. This is solid evidence that the Neandertals who occupied Kebara had mastered the use of controlled fire. OFER BAR-YOSEF AND BERNARD VANDERMEERSCH

A typical stone tool from Kebara is this stone point, which may have been hafted on to a pole and used as a spear tip. Many of the points excavated at Kebara have impact fractures suggesting their use as projectiles, and the tools may have also been used as knives for carving meat. IAN EVERARD

inch long have been recovered from Kebara. One of Ofer Bar-Yosef's doctoral students at Harvard, John Shea, studied more than seven thousand tools from both Qafzeh and Kebara for traces of microwear that might indicate how the tools were used. He also reproduced similar artifacts and put them to work as projectiles, butchery knives, hide scrapers, bone and wood carvers, plant mashers, and other tools to see what kind of wear resulted.

The most common task for stone tools seemed to be woodworking, followed by butchery. Plants may have been cut for bedding or to remove brush for fires, and the hominids from both caves seem to have worked hides, perhaps making use of leather. Burned seeds of wild peas and a smaller number of burned bones turned up in the hearths, along with a number of flint flakes. It's likely that peas and meat were intentionally roasted for eating, and the flint flakes got kicked into the fire by accident.

From Kebara comes incontrovertible evidence for hunting: triangular pointed tools exhibiting a high incidence of double use as both projectiles and knives. Besides their butchery marks, the pointed tips had truncated fractures, as if they had hit hard objects. Ofer said that the impact wear found on the Kebara points was identical to that seen on arrowheads from modern human Neolithic sites.

Kebara has a high, arched entrance and a strategic location at the intersection of two valleys, where the cave's occupants could have tracked the movement of animal herds on a coastal plain for a considerable distance. The pattern of gazelle and deer bones found at Kebara fit

Rows of banana plants encroach on the entrance to Kebara today, but 60,000 years ago this cave was home to Neandertals who hunted deer and other game.
OFER BAR-YOSEF AND
BERNARD VANDERMEERSCH

with a strategy of ambush hunting by Neandertals, possibly at close range with spears. By studying gazelle teeth and determining the age of individual animals, the team learned that gazelle had been hunted at Kebara in both winter and summer.

There is less evidence for the use of hafted spear points at Qafzeh, but the inhabitants there may have hunted with wooden spears that did not preserve. Evidence for wooden spears has been found at a few Neandertal sites in Europe, most notably the Mousterian site of Lehringen in Germany, where a twelve-foot preserved yew spear dated at 120,000 years was found lodged between the ribs of an elephant. Overall, however, the level of technology and behavior found at Qafzeh, where the much older *Homo sapiens* remains occurred, appears identical to that of the Neandertals at Kebara.

Ofer Bar-Yosef and Bernard Vandermeersch had already argued that people first lived at Qafzeh between 80,000 and 100,000 years ago, but no one listened—until

1988. That's when Hélène Valladas, an archeologist at the Center for Low-Level Radioactivity in Gif sur Yvette, France, stunned the skeptics with her results from a new dating technique known as thermoluminescence (TL). Spanning the time range between 50,000 and 300,000 years, thermoluminescence is an invaluable new archeological tool. It fills the gap between the outer limits of radiocarbon dating (about 40,000 years) and other techniques used for the early hominid sites such as Hadar.

Valladas and her colleagues had already employed the TL technique to determine that the earliest occupation at Kebara took place 60,000 years ago. This was also found to be Moshe's age and fit in with the accepted view that Neandertals had evolved directly into later *Homo sapiens.* The shock came when Valladas dated twenty burned flints collected at Qafzeh in layers that harbored the human skeletons. The TL dates placed humans at Qafzeh at least 92,000 years ago, and a similar age was found for the *Homo sapiens* at Skhul by another team of scientists using a related dating technique, called electron spin resonance (ESR), on tooth enamel from a gazelle found near the human remains.

The new early dates for Qafzeh had several immediate effects. They demonstrated that when early *Homo sapiens* lived at Klasies River Mouth in South Africa, others of the same species had already occupied the Levant, at least 30,000 years before the Neandertals appeared in the region. By this further proof of the presence of modern humans in and near Africa at a very early date, they gave the Out of Africa Model a boost. And they seriously undermined the by-this-time conventional evolutionary sequence of Neandertals as our direct ancestors. The additional fact that the Tabun site is probably older than

the original estimate of 80,000 years suggests that Neandertals came before *and* after more modern-looking
humans in the Near East.

Paleoanthropologists now had to face the fact that
these two closely related hominids coexisted in their separate identities for tens of thousands of years. Since their
remains had never been found together at the same site,
however, the extent of possible interaction remains completely unclear.

So now the question was: How do two similar yet distinct groups of hominids that apparently share the same
level of technology survive independently of each other
in the same place for so long? It's a problem in which the
evidence from anatomy collides with the evidence from
archeology, for without the fossils we would certainly
conclude from cultural evidence alone that the same
species of human lived in Qafzeh and Kebara.

This is the point Ofer Bar-Yosef makes to support his
view that Neandertals and modern humans should not
be considered separate species. When so little cultural
change is evident either between Qafzeh and Kebara or
between the Neandertal and modern human levels at
Kebara, Ofer asked, how can there be two separate
species?

Ofer stood his ground on this question when I caught
up with him in Israel in August 1992 at Hayonim, the
"cave of the pigeons," site of his latest excavation. "I don't
think these are different species," Ofer told me. "I see
them as two populations with a degree of isolation
between them. I don't see a reason to induce a biological
change to explain the transition from the Middle to the
Upper Paleolithic." Ofer not only accepts the possibility
that Neandertals and modern humans interacted in the

Archeologist Ofer Bar-Yosef has begun excavations here at Hayonim Cave in Israel to find traces of the first people to enter the Levant, perhaps from Africa. He believes that the fossil hominids who began living in these cave sites at least 100,000 years ago belong to a single species, because the stone tools and other evidence of culture are indistinguishable among the various sites. D. C. JOHANSON

Levant, he thinks they could have interbred as well. Moshe, the Kebara 2 skeleton, is not only fairly complete, he is also very robust—the most robust hominid of its age known from Israel. It serves as a reminder that these fossils have a high degree of anatomical variation, even more than those from Europe. That could be a sign of genetic mixing as populations moved to and from the Levant. Between 64,000 and 75,000 years ago, Europe experienced an especially cold climate, and even the hardy Neandertals may have been forced to evacuate and head east. Ofer thinks that places such as the Balkans or the Anatolian Plateau in Turkey became uninhabitable.

Neandertals could have easily moved from Turkey into Israel by following the Mediterranean shoreline.

I asked Ofer what conclusive evidence he thought it would take to resolve the question of whether Neandertals and modern humans are separate species. "We need to go back to the field and find more fossils and try to get DNA out of them," he responded. "The solution won't come from a frozen Neandertal. The solution will come from waterlogged Neandertals. Now, with global warming, many lakes are going down, and what we need to find is a waterlogged Neandertal site."

There are indeed bog people from northern Europe that have been perfectly preserved. A 10,000-year-old human brain was found in a Florida peat bog and, in 1991, a receding glacier in the Tyrolean Alps revealed the preserved body and belongings of a 5,000-year-old hunter-gatherer. Finding some Neandertal DNA, then, is not entirely inconceivable.

Other investigators strongly disagree with Ofer's position. When Yoel Rak looks at the bones from Qafzeh and Kebara, he sees two species. As far as Yoel is concerned, the task falls to archeologists like Ofer to figure out why two species share the same culture. The degree of anatomical difference between modern humans and Neandertals has definite biological implications; the fossils cannot simply be shoehorned into subspecies. Subspecies tend to be divided by behavior and minor differences in size and color—features that often don't fossilize. The differences between Neandertals and modern humans exceed those found in the skeletons of the two living chimpanzee species and in hyenas, which are not only separate species but separate genera, the biological notch above a species.

This partial cranium from Zuttiyeh in Israel may represent an early member of the "proto–Cro-Magnon" people of the Skhul and Qafzeh caves who alternated occupation of the Levant with Neandertals. At least 100,000 years old, the fossil lacks many distinctive Neandertal features but resembles some early African modern human fossils such as Jebel Irhoud.

D. C. JOHANSON

Some anthropologists argue that the Kebara and Qafzeh skeletons show even more differences than do African bushmen and Arctic eskimos, the two extremes of variation in modern human populations. The European Neandertals have a body shape that clearly seems adapted for cold climates, and even Moshe down in Israel goes way off the scale toward the most wide-hipped, sphere-shaped, and cold-adapted of modern human populations.

Like Ofer, Yoel sees the Neandertals as an isolated population. Yet they could move east, and they spread at least as far east as Teshik-Tash, in Uzbekistan. Yoel thinks that the geographic range of Neandertals expanded and contracted eastward in response to the advance and retreat of glaciers. At the coldest times, even those western European Neandertals with the most "classic" features of their species ended up in Israel for a time. "There is no doubt in my mind that the Middle East is some sort of borderline, a very broad borderline, between Neandertals and *Homo sapiens*," Yoel explained to me in the library at the Institute of Human Origins. That doesn't mean that modern humans and Neandertals necessarily interacted in Israel. "In the Mousterian period there were fluctuations in the territories of these different forms," Yoel continued, "and the caves of Israel were sampling whoever was in the vicinity. One time it was the Neandertals. Then it was

Homo sapiens. Then something in between. And this is apparently the source of the complexity that we find."

As for the fact that the two hominid groups had similar tools, Yoel said, "That's still a big question, but let's say they do. Maybe it stems from a common ancestry. After all, the Mousterian goes back 150,000 years." The Mousterian tools Ofer Bar-Yosef is turning up at the Hayonim site bear some resemblance to those from Klasies River Mouth and a few sites in North Africa. Ofer thinks this might be the "Out of Africa industry," but cautions that it's hard to tell from artifacts which way people were moving. Maybe they were going *into* Africa.

Not surprisingly, the Out of Africa advocates readily accept the two-species hypothesis. When I visited Chris Stringer at the Natural History Museum in London, he stressed the differences between Neandertals and *Homo sapiens* as part of his critique of the Multiregional Model for human origins. Chris also pointed out that modern Europeans today look different from the first *Homo sapiens* in Europe, as represented by fossils like Cro-Magnon. The multiregionalists cite this difference as evidence that Neandertals evolved into modern Europeans, but when one employs Allen's Rule, as we did in Chapter 5, the story is not that simple. "It is argued that the body shape of Europeans today is in some ways similar to the body shape of Neandertals," Chris said. "Now for me, that's because they live in comparable environments. It's not as cold now in Europe as it was, but modern Europeans show, to some extent, cold adaptations in their body proportions. So do Neandertals. But if we look at the earliest modern humans in Europe, they don't show these cold adaptations."

Neandertals have a ratio of lower to upper leg bone

lengths identical to that of the present-day people of high-latitude Lapland. Short, squat Neandertals, with the sphere-shaped body that minimizes heat loss, stand at the opposite extreme from *Homo erectus*, who had a tall, thin body adapted to the hot equatorial African sun. Neandertals also stand at the opposite extreme from early modern *Homo sapiens* like the people from Skhul, Qafzeh, and even Cro-Magnon. "If Cro-Magnons have a significant Neandertal component," Chris asked, "why do they show a maximal difference in body shape from Neandertals? There are a whole lot of body-shape features that suggest Cro-Magnons were fundamentally hot-adapted. They've got a tropical body shape, which doesn't fit with the Neandertals or with modern Europeans."

Chris lined up the Neandertal skull from the French cave at La Chapelle-aux-Saints alongside the male skull from Cro-Magnon. "I think most people agree now that Neandertals have what seems to be a very specialized facial morphology," he began. "The middle of the face is pulled out. The nose is *enormous*. It's very long, it's large, it's voluminous. The cheekbones are swept back. And we have a cranial vault that's very rounded—it's almost spherical in rear view—long and low, with a bulge in the occipital region. And we have this double-arch browridge." The ridge above the Neandertal's eye sockets was curved like the top rim of a pair of round spectacles. "Now, here's Cro-Magnon," Chris continued, "and this face is about as different as you can get."

His point was compelling. The face of Cro-Magnon is flat, broad, and short. Its cheekbones form almost a right angle, first parallel to and then perpendicular to the face, unlike the Neandertal cheekbones, which sweep back like jet wings. The eye sockets, or orbits, are low and square, compared to the high, round sockets of the La Chapelle Neandertal. I also noticed immediately that Cro-Magnon had a canine fossa, a depression in the upper jaw beside the root of the canine that gives modern humans their distinctive "sunken" cheekbones. The La Chapelle Neandertal, with a suite of specialized facial features that modern humans never evolved, lacked this feature.

Yoel Rak, the australopithecine face expert, has recently studied the Neandertal face as well. Yoel found that the face of Neandertals has a "profoundly different architecture" from that of modern humans. It's often possible to distinguish a Neandertal from a modern human just by looking at the mandible; Neandertals lack bony chins. The biggest difference, however, occurs in the middle of the face. The Neandertal nasal bones are flared out almost perpendicular to the rest of the face, like saloon doors swung open by a gunslinger in a Western, and form a lid over the large nasal cavity. Yoel thinks the Neandertal face evolved as an adaptation for handling heavy forces with the front teeth, which probably gripped objects like a vise. Most of the wear seen on Neandertal teeth occurs on the incisors, and these front teeth have bigger crowns and roots compared to the others. The fact that their front teeth are frequently found eroded down to the roots indicates that they used these teeth, and not their molars (as modern humans do), for crushing food. The long, low shape of the Neandertal cranium may have also evolved in harmony with the muscles that helped turn the front teeth into an extra pair of hands.

There was a time when I shared the sentiment that Neandertals belonged in our own species and I said as much in my first book, *Lucy: The Beginnings of Humankind.*

Over the last decade, however, my opinion has changed. Like Chris and Yoel, I'm convinced that Neandertals belong in a separate species from ours and that they were an experiment in human evolution that ended in extinction. Why, after we have stripped away the "primitive brute" bias of previous generations, are we so reluctant now to accept that another species very similar to us occupied part of the planet at the same time that we did, as recently as 35,000 years ago? When I visited Alan Thorne in Canberra to talk about the Multiregional Model, I couldn't resist baiting him a little on this score. "I'm convinced that Neandertals are a separate species and have nothing to do with our ancestry," I told him.

Alan gave me a searching look. "Are you perfectly satisfied that you aren't carrying any Neandertal DNA?"

"Yeah, I'm satisfied."

"Because that will be the acid test, you know"—he paused for full effect—"when we find some Neandertal mtDNA. They're working on it with that Neandertal vertebra from Shanidar, you know."

I know. And we'll see.

• • •

Whatever label we wish to put on this remarkable group, I still long to know what happened to the Neandertals. There are many examples in natural history of a successful animal species diminishing and disappearing quickly when faced with stiff competition from a new species, often an outsider who has taken up residence in the first species' range. It's natural for populations to be in flux as their numbers rise and fall in response to changing conditions in the environment. All things being equal, when a species has plenty of food, water, space, and shelter, it will experience a population explosion. If a species suffers from too much predation, competition, disease, and habitat disruption, its numbers will dwindle.

The mysterious overlap we see in marginal Neandertal occupations like Israel also took place in their main habitat, Europe. *Homo sapiens* had appeared in central Europe at least 35,000 years ago and in western Europe a few thousand years later. Neandertals disappear at about the same time, after an overlap of several thousand years. What might have happened during this interval?

A case in point is a French cave site called Saint-Césaire, where a Neandertal skeleton was uncovered in 1979. Applying the thermoluminescence technique to burnt flints found with the skeleton, a French team dated the skeleton to roughly 36,000 years ago, making it one of the latest known Neandertals. The stone tools associated with this skeleton were the real surprise. They belonged to a *Homo sapiens* technology, called the Chatelperronian industry, that overlapped in time with another industry, known as the Aurignacian, that was made by the first populations of modern humans in that region. Not long after this time Chatelperronian tools disappear altogether from the archeological record.

The presence of these tools in a Neandertal site was tantalizing in the extreme. Was the Chatelperronian industry, always thought to be a modern human invention, actually a contribution by late Neandertals? Or did the Neandertals simply mimic the technology of their neighbors the modern humans? If Neandertals learned these techniques from modern humans, we have to wonder what our ancestors might have gained in return. Did we beg, borrow, or steal from the Neandertals some of their secrets for surviving in glacier-covered valleys that helped us expand our own range? These are questions without answers. What lies more within the realm of speculation is this question: *Why* did they die out? The traditional answer has always been evolutionary replacement by modern *Homo sapiens.* I can think of many other examples of alien species wiping out native ones—usually, in fact, in the wake of purposeful or inadvertent introductions by humans. We humans have been playing ecological roulette since we began to spread around the world. Could it be that we played an active role in extinguishing one of our own kind, the Neandertals? That's certainly been the stereotypical model—evolutionarily successful Cro-Magnons murdering gentle or brutish (take your pick) Neandertals in our march to world conquest.

The fossil evidence from Europe does show a dramatic and sudden transition from *Homo neanderthalensis* remains to those of *Homo sapiens,* a fact that supports the view that the latter replaced the former. In the Middle East, though, the puzzling presence of *Homo sapiens* well before their *Homo neanderthalensis* cousins in the Israeli caves demonstrates that the story has extra layers of complexity. That's why it's so critical to sort out just what went on in these various caves for the past 100,000 years.

An interesting scenario for the fate of the Neandertals has been proposed by Ezra Zubrow of the State University of New York at Buffalo. A mathematics student who helped excavate at Qafzeh one season, Zubrow decided to become an archeologist instead. He combined both passions to construct a startling population model that suggests the Neandertals needed only a tiny tilt in the wrong direction to plunge them toward extinction. In a scientific paper composed in a refreshingly spritely style, Zubrow described the geographic expansion of Neandertals as "a leisurely stroll through Europe," in contrast with the more recent spread of modern humans "at a jogger's pace which rapidly became an all-out sprint."

Zubrow's model is grounded in logic and statistics, not the fossil record. To build it, he borrowed the concept of the life table from population biology. Just like a timetable tracks the schedule of trains, the life table is a grid that keeps track of the fate of members of a population from birth until death. A population's death rate can be affected by such factors as disease, accidents, and competition for food.

His first assumption was that *Homo sapiens* and Neandertals were interacting populations that overlapped in both time and space. Nonetheless, Zubrow believed that both populations lived in low densities, walking for weeks at a time without seeing any other individuals except kin or band members. On occasion, though, perhaps during foraging trips or while following game across the land, the two populations did encounter each other. He assumed that these encounters did not result in retreat and that some interaction—including competition for food, fighting, and trade—took place. He also used previous studies that indicated a lower life expectancy (around forty years) for Neandertals than for *Homo sapiens.*

The model also assumed that while the presence of *Homo sapiens* had an impact on the survival of Neandertals, the Neandertals had no reciprocal influence on the survival of modern humans. When either population increased beyond a certain size, the odds that Neandertals would become extinct quickly increased. A mere 1 or 2 percent increase in the death rate would have been enough to start the Neandertals spiraling toward extinction after just fifteen generations. Within thirty generations, or less than a thousand years, they would have been wiped out. A 7 percent rise in the death rate would have brought extinction in half as much time.

With both populations starting equal and neither receiving any edge in longevity or mortality, the Neandertals consistently lost. Given ten times as many individuals as the *Homo sapiens* population, they still went extinct. A lower rate of death among *Homo sapiens* invariably caused a higher rate of death among Neandertals. The fact that life expectancy between the two groups differed most at younger ages would have added to the long-term impact on the Neandertals' survival.

This model lets us draw an important conclusion. It's easy to assume that *Homo sapiens* did something right and Neandertals did something wrong because we are here and they're not. The fact that modern humans survived, however, was by no means an inevitable outcome. Differential reproduction and survival is what drives evolution so that one population survives, another doesn't. We may never know why, for evolution carries no guarantees for any species, including ours. We weren't better than they were; we were somehow simply better adapted, a difference amounting to no more than some slight competitive edge.

In other words, even though the Neandertals died out, they didn't actively fail. They didn't necessarily goof up or get killed off. It's just that *Homo sapiens* succeeded, probably by accident. We don't need to feel sorry for them, either. They had a respectable species life and left their mark. Let Ofer Bar-Yosef's affectionate description of the Neandertals at Kebara serve as an epitaph for a close relation and most unusual species: "Listen, these guys were eating peas; they were hunting. Everything was fine."

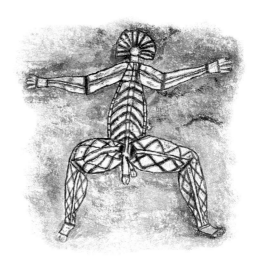

CHAPTER EIGHT

The Human Revolution:

Homo sapiens

One of the most desolate spots on Earth is the Nullarbor Plain of southern Australia, which ends abruptly in these sheer cliffs that drop three hundred feet to the ocean. Despite a lack of resources, humans have survived on the Nullarbor for thousands of years. D. C. JOHANSON

STRETCHING THE LENGTH OF THE CENTRAL coast of southern Australia is a desolate region known to the continent's European population as the Nullarbor Plain. Their nineteenth-century forebears found the most striking feature of this hot, dry, barren expanse, the world's largest alkaline plain, to be its absence of trees—hence the bleak Latin sobriquet. For settlers from the industrial West, the Nullarbor meant hardship and loneliness, a place to be cursed, crossed, conquered. For the descendants of its first colonizers, the Aborigines, however, it is Undiri, bare and clean like a bone, an ancestral home of formidable antiquity alive with myths crisscrossing two hundred miles and 40,000 years. In what may be the earliest and longest example of human adaptation to a desert, Aborigines retained their original nomadic life-style in Undiri/Nullarbor and adjacent areas until just a few years ago.

Like Zhoukoudian and other fossil-rich cave sites in China, the Nullarbor is a karst landscape, an interconnected chain of vast caves and blowholes formed as acidic groundwater percolated through limestone and slowly wore it away. Today it remains a sacred location for Aboriginal rituals. In its catacombs, say the stories passed down for thousands of generations, lurk devils and spirits known as *manu*. In the eastern part of the Nullarbor dwells the giant snake Wanambi, whose breathing reaches the surface through the deep limestone vents.

Our Western scientific knowledge about this vast plain is still sparse. Despite the Nullarbor's 132 known archeological and anthropological sites, its prehistory is poorly studied compared to that of sites like Lake Mungo and Kow Swamp. Many of its caves have no Western names, and only a few have been explored by archeologists. One of these pioneer investigators is Rhys Jones, an archeologist at Australian National University in Canberra. Rhys, an effervescent Welshman with red hair and beard and ruddy cheeks, cuts a Falstaffian figure and is known to his colleagues as the "prehistory cowboy." After spending many years studying the early settlement of Tasmania, he began working at sites on the northern and southern ends of Australia that are helping to fill in the big picture of how and when humans spread around the globe.

In August 1992 I came with Rhys and the NOVA film crew to Koonalda Station, an old sheep-shearing outpost where the rusted remains of a dilapidated petrol station bore testimony to failed past attempts to transplant a Western lifestyle to Undiri. The uncompromising nature of this landscape made me profoundly uneasy. By the time humans came to live on the Nullarbor, they had learned to adapt to the most adverse environments imaginable. These people were more resourceful than their hominid African ancestors. In stark contrast to the open African savannas, with their large water holes and fruit-bearing trees, the Nullarbor forced its human population to rely on whatever resources lay hidden in its own bleak landscape for their survival. And survive they did, for forty millennia.

The purpose of our visit to Koonalda Station was to explore a special cave. About an hour's drive from the coastal cliffs, Koonalda Cave is a monstrous sinkhole that appears to bottom out on

The location of this water hole would be a vital piece of knowledge for surviving in the harsh environment of the Nullarbor, as Aborigines have for more than 20,000 years. The Aborigines weave environmental features into an intricate mental map of the landscape. D. C. JOHANSON

Archeologist Rhys Jones is pushing back the date of the first human arrival in Australia. On the continent's southern coast he is excavating a cave where humans lived 40,000 years ago, and stone tools excavated from northern Australia may be 20,000 years older. D. C. JOHANSON

A huge sinkhole in the surface of the Nullarbor, Koonalda Cave was first explored at least 24,000 years ago by humans who mined precious nodules of flint for stone tools from the limestone walls. The cave remains a sacred site for Aborigines today.
D. C. JOHANSON

the other side of the Earth. This karst crater seems like the last place where one would expect to find evidence of early human occupation. If it seems remote and isolated today, though, the cave and its environs were much more so for a long period during its human occupation. The Nullarbor still had scrub vegetation when humans first explored Koonalda at least 24,000 years ago. But around 18,000 years ago, when the world climate cooled, glaciers grew, and seas shrank, the cave sat not 5 but 125 miles inland, smack in the middle of an arid plain now permanently treeless. Somewhere during the time between 12,000 and 16,000 years ago, when sea levels rose back dramatically, Koonalda was abandoned.

We had obtained permission from local Aborigines to enter the cave, and Maurice Miller, one of the Wirangu people who have occupied the Nullarbor successfully for thousands of generations, joined us as their representative. Maurice is a cosmopolitan Australian in beige slacks and a knit sweater, but he has kept intact his deep respect for this place, his people's past, and his inherited responsibility to care for the land. He still brings his children to the Nullarbor and shows them the secrets of finding tubers and water in a land that seems to offer nothing but open space.

Maurice fears that the customs of the Wirangu, and

Maurice Miller, a member of the Wirangu group of Aborigines, reveals a hidden water hole in the otherwise stark, dry Nullarbor Plain. In Wirangu legend, the first man and woman on Earth emerged from the sea and climbed through vast limestone caverns to reach the surface of the Nullarbor.
D. C. JOHANSON

all Aboriginal culture, are eroding like the limestone in the caves. That's why he brings his children to the Nullarbor to teach them the old ways; he believes it is his responsibility to protect what's left of his people's past and infuse it with life and meaning for the next generation. Maurice told me bluntly that he was ambivalent about the comings and goings of transient visitor groups like ours in these sacred places. I understood his position, which is shared by many countries that have moved to control and preserve the management of their earliest heritage in the wake of an intellectual imperialism that has too long prevailed.

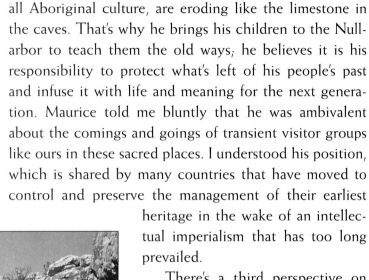

The entrance to Koonalda Cave can be approached only after scaling a precipitous cliff. A series of caverns and narrow passages wind from the entrance to an underground lake and some of the world's oldest known art.

D. C. JOHANSON

There's a third perspective on this problem, though. Paintings fade, old skills are forgotten, and oral traditions can change or be lost between generations. Ironically, what helped kill the old ways can at least preserve their artifacts. In spite of its invasive and destructive effect on traditional culture, technology can be a force for preservation and continuity. Now more than ever we're equipped to document and preserve art and culture for the future—through film, video, and other, newer technologies.

When I first arrived, Maurice graciously shared with me one of a thousand strategies that made his people successful exploiters of the Nullarbor. Leading me to a spot on the plain where angular stone slabs seemed to lie scattered in no particular order, he pointed to one small group of rocks. Immediately, I saw that these rocks had been carefully arranged by human hands to form a perfect arc around a single rock in the middle. Maurice lifted the central stone to reveal a perfectly round hole full of water, barely a foot in diameter but deeper than an arm's length.

In terms of human mental development, here was a dramatic measure indeed for the length of the journey from Hadar to Undiri. Knowing how to return to such a spot—having the social and cognitive skills to share symbolic communication in the form of the marker rocks and an inner mental map on which to commit this site firmly to memory—was as vital to the early colonizers of Australia 60,000 years ago as had been the ability to deflesh and dis-

Donald Johanson examines some of the abstract finger engravings on the wall of Koonalda Cave. The first appearance of art, a symbolic representation of the world, occurs during a creative explosion evident in the archeological record that signals the arrival of modern human behavior.
LAUREN SEELEY AGUIRRE

articulate an animal carcass for our African ancestors 2 million years earlier.

In the cool subterranean air of Koonalda Cave we descended a steep downhill path between chalk-white limestone walls until we were two hundred feet beneath Undiri's surface. Dark patches of flint nodules, the resource that first lured Maurice's ancestors here, jutted out of the limestone walls. In the old days Koonalda was a quarry where the precious flint chipped out of the rock was fashioned outside the cave into stone tools.

From a cavern big as a cathedral we entered a smaller pitch-black chamber scattered with boulders. The beam from my light glanced along the wall and I stopped in my tracks. Every inch of the soft limestone walls within reach of human hands had been finger-incised into a meandering series of swirling lines. (Similar patterns in European cave art have been called, for want of a better term, "macaroni.") The designs ended abruptly in a sharp curve just above arm's reach.

Charred pieces of the fire sticks carried into Koonalda by the artists have allowed archeologists to estimate the age of this artwork: 20,000 years for the fire sticks and 24,000 years for a deeper cultural level in the cave. These dates make the Koonalda engravings older than almost all of the fabled prehistoric art in French and Spanish caves, such as Lascaux and Altamira. And Koonalda is not unique. Other sites lie nearby, and rock art elsewhere in south Australia has been tentatively dated at 30,000 to 42,000 years.

What compelled people to make these abstract marks, whose uniformity seemed to mirror the surface of the land above us? In central Australia, such wavy lines can signify the snake, and we know that the Nullarbor is the mythic site of a giant serpent. But the same marks are also found throughout the Old World. South African archeologists David Lewis-Williams and Thomas Dowson suggest that the origins of image making lie in just these sorts of basic symbols that forge a link between two-dimensional lines and three-dimensional objects. They also posit a neuropsychological model for the analogous grids, lines, and curves found in Old World cave art, which they believe reproduce actual forms seen during the shamanistic trance state and are thus "fixed mental images of another world."

Whatever the meaning of the Koonalda engravings may be, what we realize at once is that Neandertals did not make marks like these. Neither did "archaic" *Homo sapiens* nor *Homo erectus.* The wavy lines on the walls of Koonalda Cave are an electrifying signal that something in the evolutionary record had changed dramatically. Like their counterparts in European and African caves, the Koonalda engravings indicate the presence of an artistic mind, the capacity to perceive and represent some aspect of the world in abstract terms.

This art began suddenly to show up in the archeological record all over the world only between 40,000 and 50,000 years ago—a relatively recent point in our record of the human past and a time many paleoanthropologists have begun to view as the period of the "human revolution." Ofer Bar-Yosef has seen it in the archeological record of Israel, and others cite its appearance at European sites. The revolution took place during the period of time we call the Upper Paleolithic (Late Stone Age in Africa), which may have begun at least 40,000 years ago in Africa and the Middle East and was established in western Europe at least by 30,000 years ago. Perhaps the difference in timing coincided with a westward migration of those *Homo sapiens* who occupied the former range of Neandertals.

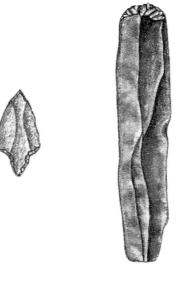

By about 100,000 years ago, as the Qafzeh and Klasies River Mouth sites indicate, *Homo sapiens* had gained its identifying physical features: the high rounded cranium, reduced teeth, prominent chin, and relatively gracile body. But our distinctive culture did not emerge until much later in our history as a species. And as paleoanthropologist Richard Klein has pointed out in his book *The Human Career,* "Plainly, it was culture and not body form that propelled the human species from a relatively rare and insignificant large mammal 35,000 years ago to a geologic force today, impinging as a natural selective agent on all other species."

For many archeologists, the scenario begins around 50,000 years ago, after a period of slow cultural development, with a dramatic change in the archeological record that they connect with an explosive spread of ideas across the Old World. We recognize this change most immediately through the work of those crucial cultural messengers, the artists. Artists historically play pivotal roles in fomenting cultural and political revolutions. It now seems that they may have always played such a role and that art was at the center of the revolution from which fully modern humans emerged.

In the Upper Paleolithic, archeologists recognize a greater variety of stone tools overall, more tools specialized for distinct tasks, and the first examples of style in toolmaking. Our immediate ancestors were more efficient at obtaining food and may well have been the first truly proficient human hunters. Other signs of advanced material culture proliferated. The Neandertals probably had burials, but they had no grave goods, communal graves, ocher markings, rocks covering the graves to protect them from scavengers, and others signs of ceremony.

Some investigators, including Richard Klein, propose that whatever lay behind this major transformation in human behavior may never reveal itself to archeologists. The cause may have been some kind of neurological leap forward, a biological re-wiring in the brain 40,000 or 50,000 years ago that enabled humans to manipulate culture and the environment in a way—and to an extent—never possible before. This would have been a breakthrough adaptation with dramatic consequences, like the ones Owen Lovejoy thinks allowed the evolution of bipedalism, and, later, big brains. Although human biology and behavior had evolved at a similar pace in the past, the "human revolution" split the two processes and caused an acceleration in the evolution of behavior, and of culture. We may not be able to measure it in brain capacity, skull shape, larynx position, or tooth size. But what happened so profoundly impacts the archeological record that we know immediately these people are identical to us.

How paradoxical that the most striking archeological signature of the full-blown emergence of our own human species (which we have so self-congratulatorily dubbed "wise man") turns out to be not new and better hand axes but symbolic art. It is precisely nonutilitarian art that bears the greatest significance in showing that modern humans had made the leap to assigning value to objects that went beyond practical day-to-day needs. Symbolic and spiritual thinking are in many respects the same process.

Then there is the matter of language. All art speaks a visceral and universal language; we may not always understand what it says, but it evokes emotion and invites us to respond. The use of abstract symbols in art is also a prerequisite skill for spoken or written language. When we want to express ourselves, to offer an opinion, often we begin by saying, "I think." The act of thought and the act of self-expression are not just linked, they are inseparable. Could the archeological record of the past 40,000 or 50,000 years be giving us clues that art, language, and cognitive thought all emerged recently as linked, interdependent phenomena? Did they spark the fuse for the first cultural revolution—the human revolution?

The late Allan Wilson, proposer of the Eve hypothesis, went so far as to speculate that language itself arose as a mere mutation in the DNA of mitochondria. He dubbed this hypothetical change the "Chomsky mutation," in honor of MIT linguist Noam Chomsky, who has championed the idea that all language has a genetic base. Language, Wilson suggested, made a biological barrier that *Homo erectus* could not overcome, and the use of language allowed modern populations to invade new areas and overtake the archaic humans. He argued that if language had been strictly a nuclear DNA mutation, then if

On the edge of the giant sinkhole at Koonalda, Donald Johanson and Rhys Jones discuss how archeologists can find evidence for the first appearance of modern humans by studying ancient art and symbolism. PETER JONES

invading Africans mated with resident archaic humans elsewhere the language gene could be inherited in any offspring. If language was a mitochondrial mutation, however, it would not be passed on from modern human men to the children of archaic human women, and they would lose a survival edge that may have prompted their extinction. Sitting around a campfire outside Koonalda, I spoke of these things with Rhys. "One of the most challenging things that Aboriginal culture presents us with is this paradox, which some of the more perceptive first Europeans saw," Rhys told me. "You see a man standing. He has almost no clothes on. He has very little technology, just the barest minimum number of things to live. He lives sometimes in the harshest places, in an open, vast area. And yet this same person has a complexity of language, including different languages to speak with different members of his family. There are secret languages. He has very complex kinship relationships with people in his family. He has trading networks across desert areas of continental scale, and he has built a cognitive map of this landscape. This cognitive map is put in terms of real things like wells, or animal tracks, or sources of excellent raw material for making stone tools. But it is also intellectual or religious, in the sense that it is posited in a story or an idea of how the world was formed. It's a worldview that is projected into the past. They had a theory of the creation of the world through ancestral heroes coming through a flat, empty country, shaping the landscape. The essence of this theory still resides within the land."

In a landscape that did not permit much material complexity, the Aborigines substituted mental complexity. To a typical hunter-gatherer survival strategy they added layers of drama, magic, and spirituality. Aboriginal culture revolves around the concept of the Dreamtime, that is, the ancestral past, when mythological beings created the land, gave it shape and life, and passed on a sacred law for its protection. Modern Aborigines are the keepers of that law, and their oral traditions are rich with stories of Dreamtime creation. To the Aborigines, people and land are inseparable, physically and spiritually. The strength of such ties is difficult for most Westerners to grasp, as we come from a culture that has largely contained, or even severed, our connection with nature. The indissoluble connection between land and spirit our ancestors devised as the deepest cornerstone of their culture is an evolutionary marker we have come very close to abandoning.

In the past, Eurocentric scholars conventionally looked to the Neandertals' successors, the Cro-Magnons, and their spectacular cave art as the epitome of the new *Homo sapiens* mind and culture. I have seen the rightly acclaimed prehistoric art in many caves of western Europe and in the Drakensburg Mountains of South Africa—the animal friezes of Lascaux that parade across the wall in polychrome splendor and the amazing hand-sculpted horses of Cap Blanc.

For me, the far more ancient designs in Koonalda Cave hold their own special fascination. The people who made these designs showed up in Australia well before Cro-Magnons arrived in Europe and kept their culture virtually intact through modern times. The Aborigines, the people and their practices, constitute the world's oldest surviving culture, one with a dignity of depth and firmly planted in the Pleistocene past. They are our direct living link with our own human past and heritage. As such they deserve our immense respect as well as our scholarly interest.

I posed to Rhys the old question: What makes a human? Was the Koonalda art a first step or a last one? Did we become human inch by inch or all at once?

"My guess is that we will very quickly be able to establish that early on, whatever early is, the whole lot was there. Bang. They were us. And before that they weren't us; they were something different. Then something decisive happened."

I asked Rhys if he agreed that these interrelated cultural artifacts represent a major revolution, like the agricultural revolution or the industrial revolution. Wasn't this a major cognitive revolution—a new perception of the world and the possibilities within it? There must have been something magical happening, something that wasn't possible until this creative explosion.

Rhys Jones and geologist Bert Roberts (standing in pit) are excavating Allen's Cave, a coastal site not far from Koonalda that preserves evidence of human occupation beginning 40,000 years ago. Roberts is an expert in a new dating technique that gives an age to rock sediments from the amount of light released when a sample is heated in a laboratory.
D. C. JOHANSON

Rhys nodded. Many archeologists attribute the onset of modern human behavior to some critical cognitive edge, and until recently few bothered to search for signs of this edge beyond western Europe. "What is exciting is that for the first time we have a global perspective on it," he added, emphasizing the role that Australia has played in our expanded archeological awareness. Rhys reminded me of the water barriers that had held back animals for millions of years and kept Australia isolated. Yet by 60,000 years ago, judging from current evidence, humans had crossed the sixty-mile-wide water barrier, and all of Australia lay before them. The problem facing archeologists, he told me, can be simply stated: How can we test that?

It's safe to say that Rhys Jones and his colleagues will get the answers they want from dating. Grounded in the hard sciences of geology and physics, the new sophisticated dating techniques such as thermoluminescence give power and precision to the interpretive stories we spin. Rhys is working with geologist Bert Roberts to determine

Vast marshes and billabongs support life beneath the rugged Arnhem Land escarpment at Kakadu National Park in northern Australia. The region is still home to the Gagudju people and harbors the earliest evidence of human presence in Australia as well as striking examples of rock paintings. D. C. JOHANSON

the date of human arrival at sites on both ends of Australia. One site just west of Koonalda Cave on the southern coast, Allen's Cave, preserves the longest continuous archeological sequence in all of arid Australia. It may be the second oldest campsite on the continent, with one date suggesting that human occupation here dates back 40,000 years. On the northern side of the continent, in Kakadu National Park, where Rhys and Bert first collaborated in 1988, samples of sediment associated with stone flakes, red and yellow ochers, a grindstone, and other artifacts gave dates between 45,000 and 61,000 years ago.

Kakadu, across the continent from Koonalda, offers not just ancient dates but a living glimpse at the cognitive and artistic achievements of the Pleistocene. Aborigines from seven different language groups once occupied the land in Kakadu and remain as traditional owners, rangers, and cultural guides. Some one thousand rock-painting sites have been documented at Kakadu.

Although the exact age of the art remains a mystery, the earliest paintings may be more than 20,000 years old, and the tradition continued unbroken, though evolving through several distinct styles, until recently. Artists coated the rocks with a paste of white and yellow pigments made from clay as well as a red watercolor pigment from iron oxide that seeped into the sandstone. The Aborigines believe that only the most recent layers of paint have been laid by people; the rest of the work they credit to spirit artists.

Stranded in the middle of a billabong, the sacred Gagudju creation rock embodies Indjuwanydjuwa, the spirit ancestor who created the animals and the people, who were entrusted with caring for the land and were taught how to live off it.

D. C. JOHANSON

Within sight of the creation rock, a shelter protects sacred paintings, including a yellow whale and a depiction of Indjuwanydjuwa. Pigments were ground and mixed in the round depressions at the base of the shelter. D. C. JOHANSON

Unlike most of European prehistoric rock art, which depicts animals, Australian rock art often represents people, their activities, and artifacts of their culture, such as digging sticks, fire sticks, and dilly bags. The paintings also offer a unique record of past associations of people and animals. Images of emu, wallaroo, bandicoot, rock python, echidna, and crocodile are common, and some images have been interpreted as representations of now-extinct animals such as the Tasmanian wolf.

Profound environmental changes also were reflected in these rock paintings. Between 7,000 and 9,000 years ago, the river valleys in Kakadu were flooded, forming the tidal flats and wetlands found today. Rising water forced many of the animals depicted in early art farther inland, and new species, as well as more symbolic mythological figures, took their place in the art. A common subject is the giant perch, or barramundi, a fish that remains a vital food source for Aborigines to this day.

Along with these changes in the landscape reflected in the content of the art came a distinctive new style of art for this rugged Arnhem Land region of north-central Australia as well. Some of the barra-mundi paintings I saw when I visited Kakadu National Park had been made with white pigment in the "X-ray" style, a technique of showing the body outline as well as details of the internal organs and skeletons. By depicting internal bones and organs, these paintings serve as a metaphor for the inner life of the subject and offer a vivid example of abstract thought. The Aborigines say that the friendly *mimi* spirits inhabiting the escarpment who created the first rock paintings taught them how to execute these "X-ray" paintings.

One of the prominent Aboriginal groups living in Kakadu are the Gagudju. Today their once-vital culture is kept alive by the three hundred or so living members. One of these elders is Bill Neidjie, a burly man with curly white hair and a bushy beard, a weathered face, and a jagged scar across the bridge of his nose. He is the philosopher of his people, concerned with enforcing and imparting the Dreamtime law. Other elders care for the various creation stories and the songs performed during burial rites. The land of Kakadu itself serves as school and library for Gagudju culture and its Dreamtime stories.

Bill took me to an overhang above a billabong, a

The ancestral spirit figure Indjuwanydjuwa is the life force of the Gagudju people. The Gagudju trace their origins to this being, who gave them life after he became stuck in a billabong and turned himself to stone so that he could always be seen.

D. C. JOHANSON

marshy area choked with red lilies. This was Warrayangal, a sacred burial site for the Bunitj clan to which Bill belongs. In his deep ceremonial voice, Bill warned me that if I fell asleep here in the rock shelter, I would sleep forever. The wall was coated with colorful paintings depicting dramatic historical events. There was a yellow whale next to a human figure brandishing a harpoon, an image that signified the coming of Balanda, white people, to Kakadu. Nearby there were more traditional images, including X-ray style depictions of barramundi, the giant perch.

Then Bill showed me a human figure painted in white, holding a dilly bag. The figure had huge round eyes and a flat nose, gangly arms, and stubby legs. This was more than just another painting, though. This image was the most important being in Gagudju philosophy, Indjuwany-

Some Aboriginal paintings represent more recent historical events. This ship depicts the colonization of Australia by Europeans. D. C. JOHANSON

djuwa. Bill told me the story of Indjuwanydjuwa, an old man who had
crossed the northern plains with his family after Warramurrungundji, the Earth
Mother, made the land. Indjuwanydjuwa
taught the Gagudju people how to hunt
and live off the land, so he is revered as
their life force. He stopped at the billabong below us to drink some water, but
his legs were too short for him to get
across it. "And he stuck in the mud and he
stay for good," Bill related. "He say, 'I
can't make it. Can't go dry land, get back
that cave.'" Unable to reach the rock shelter where Bill and I stood, the place
where Indjuwanydjuwa once camped
with his family, he reshaped the land simply by pointing his hand. He created animals around him—the long-necked
turtle, the barramundi, the goanna lizard.
He laid down the law for his people to
follow and take care of the land here at Kakadu, and
elders like Bill Neidjie bear the responsibility of following
this law, or as they call it, "looking after the country."

"He created this country. World, huh. You call it
'world' now, but Aborigines, they say 'the country,'" Bill
continued. "He made all this country what it look like
now." Bill pointed to a mammoth ovate boulder protruding from the billabong on an eroded stone pedestal.
Coated white with guano, this was the Gagudju creation
rock. It represents Indjuwanydjuwa himself, having
turned himself to stone for an eternity. "Government
making law now, but what about this one?" asked Bill,

*Separated from the handprints in
French prehistoric art by thousands
of years and thousands of miles,
ancient and modern symbols meet
in this recent Aboriginal painting
of a hand beneath a suspended ax.*
D. C. JOHANSON

A common symbol in Aboriginal rock art, handprints represent the identity of the artist and convey a uniquely human form of self-awareness and expression.

D. C. JOHANSON

acknowledging Indjuwanydjuwa's presence in the billabong. "He's sitting there, my law."

• • •

Western scholars have been studying Pleistocene art in other parts of the world for more than a century. Carved and engraved bits of bone and other portable art were discovered in France as early as 1833, but no one knew the extent of their antiquity. Although ancient art sites such as Niaux in the French Pyrenees were already known in the 1860s, they were forgotten. The famous Altamira site in Spain, discovered in 1879, went unrecognized and Niaux was only "rediscovered" in 1906. General scientific acceptance of the antiquity of the European cave art only came in 1902, after the discovery of several more sites, especially in the vicinity of Les Eyzies, home to our earlier Neandertal cousins. Eighty-five percent of the roughly two hundred western European cave-art sites that have been found so far occur in Spain and France. These countries, especially France—whose Périgord region occupies some 3,000 square miles and is one of the world's richest repositories of cave art—have dominated studies and interpretations of Paleolithic art even though Australia has many more such art sites.

If the appearance of art was indeed a global phenomenon, then the ancient traditions in Australian art may have much to tell us about the earliest European art and the difficulties in extracting meaning from it. Modern investigators are looking more and more to the living Pleistocene culture of Australia for clues to both the technique and meaning of the art of early modern *Homo sapiens* in the rest of the Old World.

One of these new investigators is Michel Lorblanchet, archeologist and painter. A student of the late André Leroi-Gourhan, the most influential French scholar of Paleolithic art, Michel has helped to revise Leroi-Gourhan's long-standing interpretation of cave paintings as hunting narratives depicting game as a magical way to secure success at the hunt. Drawing from still-living traditions among the Kakadu rock painters of Arnhem Land, he seeks to learn about the "dialogue between the artist and the cave" and sees a universal statement about the land recurring in Paleolithic art around the world.

With his mop of curly white hair, petit goatee, and beret, Michel is the very picture of the Gallic *artiste* in quest of an understanding of the mind and craft of the

Map of France and northern Spain with prehistoric sites.
CAROLYN FISH

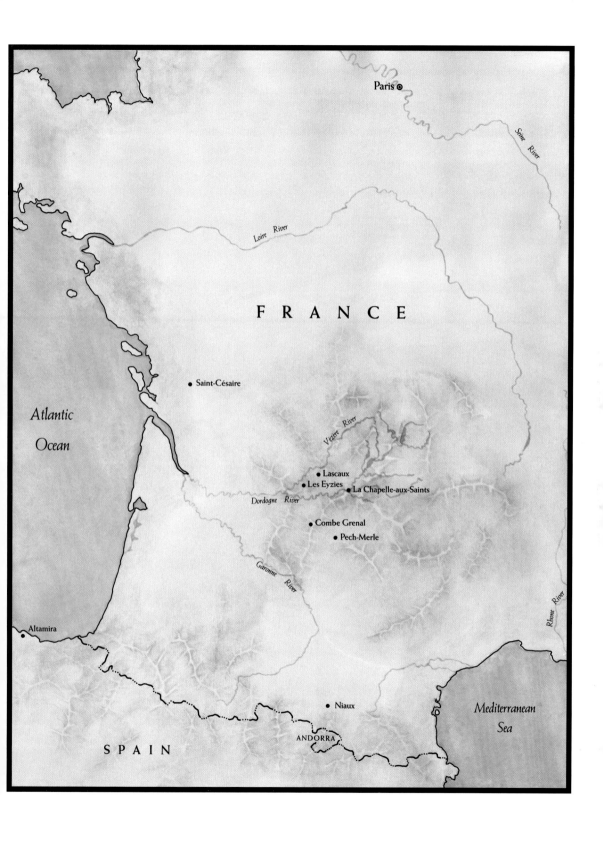

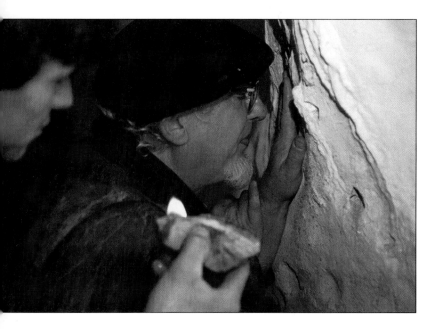

ancient Renoirs. "I think it's very important to see the real process, the real rock art," Michel maintained. To learn firsthand about this "real process"—how and why prehistoric European artists created their works—he spent four years studying the painting techniques of Aborigines in north-central Australia's Arnhem Land, where artists produce dramatic images in red ocher by spitting on fragile sandstone walls. Michel quickly realized that such a technique would have worked on the uneven limestone canvases of the Quercy or Périgord regions. "I learned how to do paintings by spitting in Australia because Aborigines used to draw paintings this way, especially on rugged walls or on more friable rocks. It's easy to do paintings without touching the wall," Michel explained. "That's the main use of the spitting technique."

The spitting technique probably began for practical reasons, but it became a cultural and even spiritual tradition in Arnhem Land, and perhaps in Europe as well. For Aboriginal artists in Australia, the act of painting is a direct passage to the Dreamtime and helps to keep its creation stories alive. Spitting has spiritual implications as well. In an article about his technique in re-creating cave art, Michel wrote: "The method of spit-painting seems to have had in itself exceptional symbolic significance to early people. Human breath, the most profound expression of a human being, literally breathes life onto a cave wall."

Michel confessed that Australian rock art won't give us the answers to all our questions, but it teaches us how to think about rock art, how to approach it as scholars. In Australia he also learned the life of the rock-art sites. These sites are always used by successive generations, and the paintings are always reinterpreted and integrated in the new mythology. "There is no single meaning," Michel told me as we sat inside a cave in Quercy, France. "Each figure has a different meaning. It depends on the figure; it depends on the generation. Even in the same generation, one image can have several meanings."

Back in Europe, Michel put Aboriginal techniques and his own painting skills to work in some fascinating rock-painting experiments. In an experiment conducted in 1979, Michel memorized the twenty-five animals in the "Frise Noire," or Black Frieze, of Pech-Merle, a cave in the Quercy region southeast of the Périgord, and reproduced the whole 6-by-22-foot panel on a blank limestone canvas in another cave. This feat of copying took a mere hour and a half and convinced Michel of two things: that the original frieze had been made by one artist and that a talented artist could have created even highly detailed figures in a very short space of time.

In a separate experiment, Michel re-created the smaller spotted-horse frieze from Pech-Merle that may be 18,000 years old. In this famous work two large horses oppose each other with overlapping flanks. A half-dozen handprints surround the horses, which are covered with 212 black dots and additional red dots. Michel spent thirty-two hours of hard work on this project; he estimates the original took a week. Animal bones, some with cut marks, had been found at the foot of the frieze, and these may have been the leftovers of an artist's lunch break.

On a blank wall in a nearby cave Michel demonstrated how handprints like those in the spotted-horse frieze from Pech-Merle were painted. One hypothesis holds that the artist blew paint through a hollow bird bone, but Michel insists that this technique leaves big blotches of color and does not allow fine control for detail. He thinks the artist used a different method, and his Australian training gave him a good idea which one.

Michel put the red ocher–water mixture in his mouth and added a third ingredient, saliva, to give his paint the right consistency and help it adhere to the wall. He

Lorblanchet believes that the spitting technique not only enables paint to adhere on the friable limestone walls of French caves but also allowed the prehistoric artist to transfer identity to the painted image and breathe life into it.
D. C. JOHANSON

chewed for several minutes, his lips and teeth turning brick-red, and then he was ready to begin. Placing his left hand flat against the wall, Michel bent his head close and began spitting rapidly. Keeping his lips pursed like a trumpeter's, he moved his head around the edge of his hand and fingers. The percussive sound from his lips was surprisingly loud, reminding me of rapid distant gunfire. It took several coats of paint to make a handprint, and each time Michel lifted his left hand from the wall, he carefully replaced it by applying each fingertip first before lowering his palm.

"The first time I did the handprints I was amazed at seeing the image of my hand," Michel confessed to me. "It's a strange feeling," he admitted. "Like being exposed to the sight of people, like being nude."

"You don't recognize the anatomy of your hand until you do that?"

"Not at all. But once you do, you never forget it or mistake it for another person's." Michel came to learn every contour of his hand from painting it, and he believes it is a recognizable mark. "Every hand has a personal

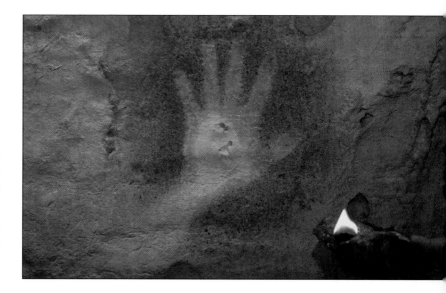

The finished handprint resembles those known from several French cave sites including Gargas and Pech-Merle. Such handprints may have represented the signature of an artist. D. C. JOHANSON

shape," he said. "It's better than a signature." In Australia, Aborigines can tell who has passed through an area before them from the painted handprints left behind, and Michel thinks the handprints in French caves had a similar purpose. What's more, his study of the handprints in Pech-Merle convinced him that they were all made by the same hand, that one person painted the spotted-horse frieze.

After completing his handprint, Michel opened a book of photographs from Lascaux and studied an image of a horse head like an artist consulting a sketch. Michel examined the cave wall and found a tiny imperfection that would become the horse's eye. He had to stand on planks to reach this part of the wall, and I imagined prehistoric artists using wooden ladders or scaffolds. The artists of Koonalda Cave did not appear to have used scaffolding, but in Lascaux the cave wall contains holes that once held scaffold beams.

Using the flat edge of his hand as a stencil, Michel began to sketch the outline of the horse by spitting his charcoal pigment mix. When the black outline was done, Michel switched to red ocher to fill in his sketch, then spattered charcoal dots along the neck to make the mane. His final touch was to accentuate the outline to create contrast with the inside of the figure. Michel's finished product was not as complete, not as "alive," as the Lascaux original, and he readily admitted that. By attempting to make a facsimile of this so-called primitive art, Michel has come to view these ancient artists as true masters.

"The *action* of painting may be more important, or as

Artist Michel Lorblanchet even mimics the lighting of his prehistoric forebears to re-create cave paintings. He places a lump of goose fat from a jar on a stone lamp and lights a rope wick. A pound of animal fat can burn for a full day and produces no soot, which could damage a painting.
D. C. JOHANSON

important, as the result, the image," Michel told me. "The breath is probably the most important part of an individual, and by spitting the paint on the rock, the painter was being transformed into the horse. He became the horse." Michel believes that there could be no more direct connection between a work and its creator.

One of the most interesting and promising developments in the study of European cave paintings has come from analysis of the individual ingredients of the pigments themselves. This work has been pioneered by archeologist Jean Clottes and physicists Michel Menu and Philippe Walter. "Both of us are trying to be archeological physicists," Michel Menu told me at his office in the research laboratory of the Louvre Museum in Paris. The use of such high-powered techniques as scanning electron microscopy, gas chromatography, and X-ray diffraction allows these physicists to confirm or refute interpretations made from little or no hard evidence. "The human imagination is fertile, but to prove these speculations is sometimes difficult."

An important example of how such new techniques will expand our knowledge of prehistoric art came from the site of Niaux. One of several art sites in the French Pyrenees, Niaux is a vast cave with a huge mouth. At the entrance, visitors carry lanterns inside for the half-hour hike to the galleries deep within the cave. About a half-mile beyond the first paintings is a gallery adorned with bison, horses, and ibex sketched in black beneath a domed, cathedral-like ceiling. This is the famous Salon Noir, which seems to have been a sort of sanctuary for the human hunters and artists. Scholars had formerly argued on stylistic grounds that all the paintings in Niaux, including the Salon Noir, had been executed at the same time.

The new pigment studies by Menu and Walter showed otherwise. "Looking with another eye, with the eye of light microscopes and scanning electron microscopes, we were able to point out two major phases in the fabrication of Niaux," Michel told me.

By analyzing fifty-nine red and black paint samples obtained from different images in the cave, the Louvre researchers concluded that the artists had specific recipes for their paints, using mineral ingredients available near Niaux. The two main recipes differed in the type of mineral extender added to make the paint go further, spread better, and preserve without cracking. The first recipe used an extender of potassium feldspar, which also showed up on objects from another site of known age and could therefore be dated to around 12,900 to 13,940 years ago. The second pigment recipe used an extender mixing potassium feldspar with black mica or biotite that made the paint darker and more spreadable. This pigment, used in the Salon Noir paintings, was datable from stone artifacts in an associated cave nearby, thus proving that the Salon Noir paintings were made at a later time than other art in Niaux.

The Salon Noir paintings also showed signs of greater planning. "We now know that these major paintings in the Salon Noir were made after an initial sketch with charcoal," Michel Menu said. "We were able to find all the steps that you'd find in a modern easel painting: the choice of a support for the art, the sketch, and the final application of paint." Paintings from elsewhere in Niaux lack

Michel Lorblanchet studies a photograph of a horse painting from Lascaux before attempting to recreate it from memory. He has reproduced some of the more complicated friezes of the Pech–Merle cave from memory and believes that skilled prehistoric artists produced these works in a few days. D. C. JOHANSON

The first step in re-creating the Lascaux horse is to make a charcoal sketch outlining the head and body. D. C. JOHANSON

Lorblanchet used his hands as a stencil to direct the pigment that he spat to form the horse's head, neck, and mane. He admits that the finished product is less "alive" than the original, confirming his opinion that prehistoric cave painters were the Renoirs of the past. D. C. JOHANSON

the preliminary sketch, a circumstance suggesting that the Salon Noir was indeed a special place, where greater care was taken in producing art.

The chance use of charcoal in the Salon Noir sketches allowed Niaux to make more news recently as one of few prehistoric sites where a date could be determined directly from a painted image. Along with a team of researchers Hélène Valladas, who previously stunned paleoanthropologists with her thermoluminescence dates from the Israeli caves Qafzeh and Kebara, recently obtained radiocarbon dates of 13,000 years for images of bison from the Salon Noir of Niaux (very close to those predicted by the pigment study) and 14,000 years from the Spanish caves of Altamira and El Castillo. The experiment showed that good dates could be obtained directly from the paintings without damaging them, since the dating technique requires that only a minuscule sample of organic material be scraped off the cave wall with a scalpel.

Cultural and spiritual meanings resonate in other types of art made by early moderns. We are inherently attracted

This bison from the Salon Noir gallery of Niaux was painted after the artist first made a charcoal sketch, indicating that great care and planning went into decorating this part of the cave. Charcoal from some of these sketches has been radiocarbon dated to around 13,000 years ago.
IAN EVERARD

to art hidden in the dark recesses of deep caves, but more than two thirds of Upper Paleolithic art sites occur in once-exposed rock shelters or in shallow caves. I think deep-cave sites like Lascaux were special, sacred places, and the art within them could be called "invitational," accessible only to certain individuals. Then there was "public art," art designed to be viewed by all who passed. Such public art might have served as a monument or territory marker. As the *Homo sapiens* population density rapidly grew in Ice Age Europe, the issue of territoriality would have loomed large.

The third category, portable objects such as painted stones, carved figurines, and engraved bones, might be called "personal art." These include the famous "Venus figurines" found throughout Europe and central Asia, which were probably fertility charms or god images. Tools show elaborate animal and abstract designs. All are different manifestations of the same simultaneous and universal phenomenon: the great leap forward we call the "human revolution."

In the grand scope of geologic time, the human revolution happened just seconds ago. Like any revolution, it was tumultuous, and some of its repercussions have not been fully felt even yet. Humans modern in both body and behavior have lasted maybe half as long as the Neandertals and merely a twentieth of the lifespan of Lucy's species. We cannot dare to assume that evolution anointed our short-lived species to take a heralded place among life on Earth. We are only one part of the evolutionary process, very possibly yet another side branch, like the Nutcracker People and the Neandertals—not its preordained culmination. Once we recognize that fact, possibly we will attain the wisdom to survive the revolution that has brought us thus far.

Storytelling, like art, is a distinctive trait of humans that is grounded in memory and symbolism. The story I've just told is based in the methodology of Western science as well. In one sentence my story line is this: Human beings the world over share a deep African past during which the present shape of our bodies evolved and a much more recent revolution that saw the beginnings of our modern minds. But much along the way—many of the whys, hows, and whens—remains beyond our grasp.

I'd like to think that paleoanthropologists, archeologists, geneticists, and linguists will keep pooling their talents to unravel the human mystery. Just as physicists strive for the elusive Grand Unified Theory that links the laws of nature from the structure of subatomic particles to that of the universe, paleoanthropologists should strive

Just outside the town of Les Eyzies, the Cap Blanc rock shelter preserves a spectacular, fifty-foot-long sculpted frieze of almost life-size horses, bison, and deer. A modern human burial was found at the base of the sculpture.

D. C. JOHANSON

for a unified theory of human origins that marshals evidence from fossils and genes, from art, artifacts, and language, all on a foundation of firm dates bolstered by physics and geology. Only then will we near the end of our exploration and—as T. S. Eliot wrote—arrive where we began and know that place for the first time.

One last story. At Kakadu National Park Bill Neidjie's son, Jonathan Yarramarna, has followed in Bill's footsteps, walking a tightrope between two cultures for the sake of the Gagudjus' and Kakadu's future. Like his father, Jonathan works as a park ranger, but he also joins Bill on visits to the sacred dreaming sites, or to the quarry at Djirringbal, where the Gagudju once came to make stone tools, like their ancestors before them.

A few years ago, Bill took Jonathan to the site of Hawk Dreaming, the sacred home of Garrkine, the

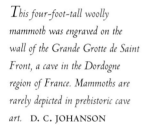

This four-foot-tall woolly mammoth was engraved on the wall of the Grande Grotte de Saint Front, a cave in the Dordogne region of France. Mammoths are rarely depicted in prehistoric cave art. D. C. JOHANSON

brown falcon that taught the Gagudju people to fish. Bill's own father had brought him to this place when he was eight years old. On the rock wall is a small white hand stencil that Bill made during this visit. Bill showed Jonathan how to make a paint of white clay and water, grinding the clay with a stone in a rock depression at the base of the wall. Then Jonathan took a mouthful of pigment, placed his hand on the wall, and created his own handprint. In doing so he forged a link with a personal and collective human past—with his father's child-sized handprint, with the handprints that are among the oldest known painted images at Kakadu, and with handprints from Pech-Merle and all over the Old World.

Bill believes it is important to pass on the Gagudju stories, not just for his own people but for all people. At the deepest level the Aborigines teach the rest of us what being human means. Their lessons about caring for the land must be learned by everyone. When Stanley Breeden and Belinda Wright traveled to Gagudju country a few years ago on assignment from the National Geographic Society, Bill summed up his people's worldview for them in a simple, eloquent statement:

All these stories
Tell of earth, animals, Gagudju people.
Our blood, animals' blood and sap of plants.
It all the same, we all the same.
The old people, they know this,
That why for thousands and thousands of years
This country not change.
This is our culture, our story,
Your story.

GLOSSARY

Acheulian The stone-tool industry commonly associated with *Homo erectus* and characterized by hefty butchering tools such as pointed hand axes and flat-edged cleavers.

Allen's Rule A biological generalization that mammals living in colder environments will have shorter limbs and stockier bodies to reduce heat loss.

"archaic" **Homo sapiens** An ambiguous term for fossils from Africa, Asia, and Europe that are intermediate in form between *Homo erectus* and modern humans and that range in age from 100,000 to 500,000 years old.

australopithecine Belonging to the genus *Australopithecus*.

Australopithecus The earliest hominid genus, which appeared in Africa at least 4 million years ago and went extinct about 900,000 years ago. There are at least five known species in this genus.

bipedalism A form of locomotion marked by habitual walking on two legs. Bipedalism is a fundamental feature used to define hominids.

cut marks Microscopic scratches on the surface of an animal bone that tend to have distinctive V-shaped grooves and that indicate meat and muscle were removed from the bone using stone flakes.

femur The thigh bone, the largest human bone.

Great Rift Valley An ancient geological feature most prominent in eastern Africa, where the action of earthquakes and volcanoes created ideal conditions for burying and preserving bones. Many early hominid fossil sites have been discovered in the Great Rift Valley.

hominid   A member of the family of primates that includes modern humans and our extinct ancestors in the genus *Homo* and the genus *Australopithecus.*

hyoid   A U-shaped bone that makes up part of the larynx in the throat and is the only human bone that does not connect with another bone.

Homo   The genus that includes our species, *sapiens,* and our non-australopithecine ancestors, including *Homo erectus* and *Homo habilis.*

humerus   The upper arm bone in the human skeleton.

ilium   The largest of the three innominate bones in the pelvis.

innominate   The bone that comprises three fused bones that make up each side of the human pelvis.

mandible   The lower jawbone.

microwear   Microscopic scratches and polish on the surface of stone tools or hominid teeth that might reveal how various tools were used or what types of food certain hominids ate.

mitochondrial DNA (mtDNA)   The genetic material inside the mitochondrion, an energy-producing unit of a cell, which has been studied to calculate the antiquity of modern humans. Some mtDNA studies suggest that modern humans arose first in Africa around 200,000 years ago.

Mousterian   The stone-tool industry associated with Neandertals and with archaic humans in Africa after 200,000 years ago, characterized by small flake scrapers and pointed flakes that may have been hafted onto sticks.

Neandertal   A member of a strong, large-bodied species of genus *Homo* that lived in Europe and the Middle East between 130,000 and 35,000 years ago.

niche   The ecological space and role filled by a particular animal, sometimes referred to as an animal's profession.

Oldowan   The earliest recognized stone-tool industry, dating to around 2.5 million years ago and characterized by cutting flakes and angular chopping tools.

paleoanthropology   The study of human origins and evolution.

paleomagnetism   A technique for determining the age of rocks by analyzing the magnetic field polarity of certain minerals in the rock.

Paranthropus   A name that some paleoanthropologists use to categorize the species of robust australopithecines as a separate group from the other species of *Australopithecus.*

pelvis   The bowl-shaped arrangement of bones that supports the upper body and anchors the muscles that enable humans to walk upright on two legs.

percussion marks   Distinctive, striated pits on the surface of an animal bone that indicate the bone was broken by human hands using a hammerstone.

postcrania   A collective term for the bones in the human skeleton below the skull.

secondary altriciality   A unique human phenomenon of rapid brain growth, during which the brain doubles its size in the first year of life, that may have been a feature of our ancestor *Homo erectus.*

taphonomy   The study of the processes that disturb and damage bones before, during, and after burial.

thermoluminescence   A technique for dating burned flint or ceramics found at archeological sites that spans the critical period in human evolution from 50,000 to 300,000 years ago. Thermoluminescence measures the amount of light emitted by electrons as heat forces them out of a crystal and converts that measurement into an age.

tibia   The larger bone in the lower leg that forms, with the femur, the knee joint.

ulna   The bone in the lower arm that forms most of the human elbow joint, sometimes called the funny bone.

BIBLIOGRAPHY

Arensburg, B., L. A. Schepartz, A. M. Tillier, B. Vandermeersch, and Y. Rak. "A Reappraisal of the Anatomical Basis for Speech in Middle Paleolithic Hominids," *American Journal of Physical Anthropology,* 1990, 83:137–146.

Arsuaga, Juan-Luis, I. Martinez, A. Gracia, J. Carretero, and E. Carbonell. "Three New Human Skulls from the Sima de los Huesos Middle Pleistocene Site in Sierra de Atapuerca, Spain," *Nature,* April 8, 1993, 362:534–537.

Asfaw, Berhane, C. Ebinger, D. Harding, T. White, and G. WoldeGabriel. "Space-based Imagery in Paleoanthropological Research: an Ethiopian Example," *National Geographic Research,* Autumn 1990, 6(4):418–434.

Asfaw, Berhane, Y. Beyene, S. Semaw, G. Suwa, T. White, and G. WoldeGabriel. "Fejej: a New Paleoanthropological Research Area in Ethiopia," *Journal of Human Evolution,* August 1991, 21(2):137–143.

Asfaw, Berhane, Y. Beyene, G. Suwa, R. C. Walter, T. D. White, G. WoldeGabriel, and T. Yemane. "The Earliest Acheulean from Konso-Gardula," *Nature,* December 24, 1992, 360:732–734.

Auel, Jean M. *The Clan of the Cave Bear.* New York: Crown, 1980.

Bahn, Paul G., and J. Vertut. *Images of the Ice Age.* New York: Facts on File, 1988.

Barinaga, Marcia. " 'African Eve' Backers Beat a Retreat," *Science,* February 7, 1992, 255:686–687.

Bar-Yosef, Ofer. "Mousterian Adaptations: A Global View," in *The Fossil Man of Monte Circeo: Fifty Years of Study on the Neandertals in Latium.* Quaternaria Nova, 1, 1990–91, 575–591.

————. "The Role of Western Asia in Modern Human Origins," *Philosophical Transactions of the Royal Society, London* B, 1992, 337:193–200.

Bar-Yosef, O., B. Vandermeersch, B. Arensburg, A. Belfer-Cohen, P. Goldberg, H. Laville, L. Meignen, Y. Rak, J. D. Speth, E. Tchernov, A.-M. Tillier, and S. Weiner. "The Excavations in Kebara Cave, Mt. Carmel," *Current Anthropology*, December 1992, 33(5):497–550.

Blumenschine, Robert J. "Characteristics of an Early Hominid Scavenging Niche," *Current Anthropology*, August–October 1987, 28:383–407.

————. "Man the Scavenger," *Archaeology*, July–August 1989, 42(4):26–32.

————. "Breakfast at Olorgesailie: The Natural History Approach to Early Stone Age Archaeology," *Journal of Human Evolution*, 1991, 21:307–327.

Blumenschine, Robert J., and J. A. Cavallo. "Scavenging and Human Evolution," *Scientific American*, October 1992, 90–96.

Bower, Bruce. "Talk of Ages," *Science News*, July 8, 1989, 136:24–26.

————. "Neandertals' Disappearing Act," *Science News*, June 8, 1991, 139:360–363.

————. "Erectus Unhinged," *Science News*, June 20, 1992, 141:408–411.

Bowler, Peter J. *Theories of Human Evolution: A Century of Debate, 1844–1944.* Baltimore: The Johns Hopkins University Press, 1986.

Brain, C. K. *The Hunters or the Hunted?: An Introduction to African Cave Taphonomy.* Chicago: The University of Chicago Press, 1981.

Brain, C. K., C. S. Churcher, J. D. Clark, F. E. Grine, P. Shipman, R. L. Susman, A. Turner and V. Watson. "New Evidence of Early Hominids, Their Culture and Environment from the Swartkrans Cave, South Africa," *South African Journal of Science*, October 1988, 84:828–835.

Brain, C. K., and A. Sillen. "Evidence from the Swartkrans Cave for the Earliest Use of Fire," *Nature*, December 1, 1988, 336:464–466.

Breeden, Stanley. "The First Australians," *National Geographic*, February 1988, 173(2):266–289.

Breeden, Stanley, and B. Wright. *Kakadu: Looking After the Country—The Gagudju Way*. Brookvale, NSW: Simon & Schuster Australia, 1989.

Broom, Robert, and J. T. Robinson. *Swartkrans Ape-Man*. Pretoria: Transvaal Museum Memoir No. 6, 1952.

Brown, Michael H. *The Search for Eve*. New York: Harper & Row, 1990.

Brown, Peter. "Recent Human Evolution in East Asia and Australia." *Philosophical Transactions of the Royal Society, London* B, 1992, 337.

Cane, Scott. "Heritage Values of the Nullarbor Plain," Draft Report to D.A.S.E.T.T., July 1992.

Cann, Rebecca L., M. Stoneking, and A. C. Wilson. "Mitochondrial DNA and Human Evolution," *Nature*, January 1, 1987, 325:31–36.

Cavallo, John A. "Cat in the Human Cradle," *Natural History*, February 1990, 53–60.

Clottes, Jean, M. Menu, and P. Walter. "New Light on the Niaux Paintings," *Rock Art Research*, 1990, 7(1):21–26.

Conkey, Margaret W. "A Century of Palaeolithic Cave Art," *Archaeology*, July–August 1981, 34(4):20–28.

Coppens, Yves, and B. Senut, eds. *Origine(s) de la Bipédie chez les Hominidés* (Cahiers de Paléoanthropologie). Paris: Editions du CNRS, 1991.

Dart, Raymond A. *The Osteodontokeratic Culture of Australopithecus prometheus*. Pretoria: Transvaal Museum Memoir No. 10, 1957.

———. *Adventures with the Missing Link*. Philadelphia: The Better Baby Press, 1982.

Dayton, Leigh. "Australia, the Oldest School of Art?," *New Scientist*, August 8, 1992, 9.

Delson, Eric, ed. *Ancestors: The Hard Evidence*. New York: Alan R. Liss, 1985.

Dorozynski, Alexander, and A. Anderson. "Collagen: A New Probe into Prehistoric Diet," *Science,* October 25, 1991, 254:520–521.

Fagan, Brian M. *The Journey from Eden: The Peopling of Our World.* London: Thames and Hudson, 1990.

Flood, Josephine. *Archaeology of the Dreamtime: The Story of Prehistoric Australia and Its People.* New Haven: Yale University Press, 1990.

Foley, Robert, and R. Dunbar. "Beyond the Bones of Contention," *New Scientist,* October 14, 1989, 37–41.

Gibbons, Ann. "A 'New Look' for Archeology," *Science,* May 17, 1991, 252:918–920.

Gillespie, D., ed. *The Rock Art Sites of Kakadu National Park.* Canberra: Australian National Parks and Wildlife Service, Special Publication No. 10, 1983.

Gould, Stephen Jay. "The Most Compelling Pelvis Since Elvis," *Discover,* December 1985, 54–58.

———. "A Novel Notion of Neanderthal," *Natural History,* June 1988, 16–21.

Graves, Paul. "New Models and Metaphors for the Neanderthal Debate," *Current Anthropology,* December 1991, 32(5):513–541.

Grine, Frederick E., ed. *Evolutionary History of the "Robust" Australopithecines.* Hawthorne, N.Y.: Aldine de Gruyter, 1988.

Grün, R., and C. B. Stringer. "Electron Spin Resonance Dating and the Evolution of Modern Humans," *Archaeometry,* 1991, 33(2):153–199.

Hill, Andrew. "Causes of Perceived Faunal Change in the Later Neogene of East Africa," *Journal of Human Evolution,* 1987, 16:583–596.

Johanson, Donald, and M. Edey. *Lucy: The Beginnings of Humankind.* New York: Simon and Schuster, 1981.

Johanson, Donald, and J. Shreeve. *Lucy's Child: The Discovery of a Human Ancestor.* New York: William Morrow and Company, 1989.

Klein, Richard G. *The Human Career: Human Biological and Cultural Origins.* Chicago: The University of Chicago Press, 1989.

————. "The Archeology of Modern Human Origins," *Evolutionary Anthropology*, 1992, 1(1):5–14.

Leakey, Mary. *Disclosing the Past*. London: Weidenfeld and Nicolson, 1984.

Lewin, Roger. "The Unmasking of Mitochondrial Eve," *Science*, October 2, 1987, 238:24–26.

————. "Stone Age Psychedelia," *New Scientist*, June 8, 1991, 30–34.

————. "Rock of Ages—Cleft by Laser," *New Scientist*, September 28, 1991, 36–40.

————. "A Hip Theory for Human Evolution," *New Scientist*, November 16, 1991, 20.

Lorblanchet, Michel. "From the Cave Art of the Reindeer Hunters to the Rock Art of the Kangaroo Hunters," *L'Anthropologie*, 1988, 92(1):271–316.

————. "Spitting Images," *Archaeology*, November–December 1991, 44(6):24–30.

Lovejoy, C. Owen. "The Origin of Man," *Science*, January 23, 1981, 211:341–350.

————. "The Natural Detective," *Natural History*, October 1984, 24–28.

————. "Evolution of Human Walking," *Scientific American*, November 1988, 118–125.

Marean, Curtis W. "Sabertooth Cats and Their Relevance for Early Hominid Diet and Evolution," *Journal of Human Evolution*, 1989, 18:559–582.

Mellars, Paul, and C. Stringer, eds. *The Human Revolution*. Princeton: Princeton University Press, 1989.

Noble, William, and I. Davidson. "The Evolutionary Emergence of Modern Human Behaviour: Language and Its Archeology," *Man*, June 1991, 26(2):223–254.

Nyamweru, Celia. *Rifts and Volcanoes: A Study of the East African Rift System*. Nairobi: Thomas Nelson and Sons, 1980.

O'Connell, James F., K. Hawkes, and N. B. Jones. "Hadza Scavenging: Implications for Plio/Pleistocene Hominid Subsistence," *Current Anthropology*, April 1988, 29:356–363.

———. "Hadza Hunting, Butchering, and Bone Transport and Their Archaeological Implications," *Journal of Anthropological Research*, Summer 1988, 44:113–161.

Ovington, Derrick. *Kakadu: A World Heritage of Unsurpassed Beauty*. Canberra: Australian Government Publishing Service, 1986.

Potts, Richard. "Home Bases and Early Hominids," *American Scientist*, July–August 1984, 72:338–347.

Rak, Yoel. "The Neanderthal: A New Look at an Old Face," *Journal of Human Evolution*, 1986, 15:151–164.

Rensberger, Boyce. "Facing the Past," *Science 81*, October 1981, 2(8):40–51.

Roberts, Richard G., R. Jones, and M. A. Smith. "Thermoluminescence Dating of a 50,000-Year-Old Human Occupation Site in Northern Australia, *Nature*, May 10, 1990, 345:153–156.

Roberts, Richard G., and R. Jones. "The Test of Time: Physical Dating Methods in Archaeology," *Australian Natural History*, Summer 1991–92, 23(11):858–865.

Rukang, Wu, and L. Shenglong. "Peking Man," *Scientific American*, June 1983, 86–94.

Shea, John J. "A New Perspective on Neandertals from the Levantine Mousterian," *Anthroquest*, Spring 1990, 14–18.

Shipman, Pat, and A. Walker. "The Costs of Becoming a Predator," *Journal of Human Evolution*, 1989, 18:373–392.

Soffer, Olga, ed. *The Pleistocene Old World: Regional Perspectives*. New York: Plenum Press, 1987.

Spencer, Frank. "The Neandertals and Their Evolutionary Significance: A Brief Historical Survey," in *The Origins of Modern Humans: A World Survey of the Fossil Evidence*. New York: Alan R. Liss, 1984.

Stanley, Steven. *Earth and Life Through Time*. New York: W. H. Freeman, 1986.

Straus, William L., Jr., and A.J.E. Cave. "Pathology and the Posture of Neanderthal Man," *Quarterly Review of Biology*, December 1957, 32(4):348–363.

Stringer, Chris. "The Asian Connection," *New Scientist*, November 17, 1990, 33–37.

————. "The Emergence of Modern Humans," *Scientific American*, December 1990, 98–104.

————. "Replacement, Continuity and the Origin of *Homo sapiens*," *Continuity or Replacement: Controversies in* Homo sapiens *evolution*. Rotterdam: A.A. Balkema, 1992.

————. "Reconstructing Recent Human Evolution," *Philosophical Transactions of the Royal Society, London* B, 1992, 337:217–224.

————. "Secrets of the Pit of the Bones," *Nature*, April 8, 1993, 362:501–502.

Tattersall, Ian. "The Many Faces of *Homo habilis*," *Evolutionary Anthropology*, 1992, 1(1):33–37.

Templeton, Alan R. "Human Origins and Analysis of Mitochondrial DNA Sequences," *Science*, February 7, 1992, 255:737.

————. "The 'Eve' Hypothesis: A Genetic Critique and Reanalysis," *American Anthropologist*, March 1993, 95(1):51–72.

Thorne, Alan, and R. Raymond. *Man on the Rim: The Peopling of the Pacific.* London: Angus & Robertson Publishers, 1989.

Thorne, Alan G., and M. H. Wolpoff. "Regional Continuity in Australasian Pleistocene Hominid Evolution," *American Journal of Physical Anthropology*, 1981, 55:337–349.

————. "The Multiregional Evolution of Humans," *Scientific American*, April 1992, 266(4):76–83.

Valladas, H., J. L. Reyss, J. L. Joron, G. Valladas, O. Bar-Yosef, and B. Vandermeersch. "Thermoluminescence Dating of Mousterian 'Proto–Cro-Magnon' Remains from Israel and the Origin of Modern Man," *Nature*, February 18, 1988, 331:614–616.

Valladas, H., H. Cachier, P. Maurice, F. Bernaldo de Quiros, J. Clottes, V. Cabrera Valdes, P. Uzquiano, and M. Arnold. "Direct

Radiocarbon Dates for Prehistoric Paintings at Altamira, El Castillo and Niaux Caves," *Nature*, May 7, 1992, 357:68–70.

Vigilant, Linda, M. Stoneking, H. Harpending, K. Hawkes, and A. C. Wilson. "African Populations and the Evolution of Human Mitochondrial DNA," *Science*, September 27, 1991, 253:1503–1507.

von Koenigswald, G. H. R. *Meeting Prehistoric Man*. New York: Harper & Brothers, 1956.

Walker, Alan, and R. E. Leakey, eds. *The Nariokotome* Homo erectus *Skeleton*. Cambridge: Harvard University Press, 1993.

Ward, S. C. "Taxonomy, Paleobiology and Adaptations of the Robust Australopithecines," *Journal of Human Evolution*, 1991, 21:469–483.

Wells, H. G. "The Grisly Folk," in *H. G. Wells: Selected Short Stories*. Harmondsworth: Penguin, 1958.

Wheelhouse, Frances. *Raymond Arthur Dart: A Pictorial Profile*. Sydney: Transpareon Press, 1983.

White, J. Peter, and J. F. O'Connell. *A Prehistory of Australia, New Guinea and Sahul*. New York: Academic Press, 1982.

Wilford, John Noble. "Critics Batter Proof of an African Eve," *The New York Times*, May 19, 1992.

Wilson, Allan C., and R. L. Cann. "The Recent African Genesis of Humans," *Scientific American*, April 1992, 266(4):68–73.

Wolpoff, Milford, and A. Thorne. "The Case Against Eve," *New Scientist*, June 22, 1991, 37–41.

Wood, Bernard. "A Remote Sense for Fossils," *Nature*, January 30, 1992, 355:397–398.

———. "Origin and Evolution of the Genus *Homo*," *Nature*, February 27, 1992, 355:783–790.

ABOUT THE AUTHORS

World-renowned for his discovery of the Lucy skeleton, DONALD JOHANSON *is president and founder of the Institute of Human Origins in Berkeley, California.* LENORA JOHANSON *is a journalist, photographer, and documentary filmmaker. She was a producer for the NOVA series entitled* In Search of Human Origins, *and has produced films for the* BBC, WNET, Nature, *and* National Geographic Explorer. *Among her awards are the prestigious Cine Gold Eagle, the National Cindy Award, and the Missoula Film Festival Award. The Johansons reside in Berkeley.* BLAKE EDGAR *is a writer and an editor at* Pacific Discovery, *the magazine of the California Academy of Sciences in San Francisco. He studied anthropology and zoology at the University of California, Berkeley, and science communication at the University of California, Santa Cruz.*